PRAISE FOR *VAGABOND*

'*Vagabond* is classic travel writing at its finest, brimming
with history, character and the spirit of adventure.
Mark takes you on a journey through the heart of Spain
which is rich in detail and bursting with life.'

Sir Ranulph Fiennes

'A wonderful account of the kind of journey most of
us dream about but never dare to make. A vivid and
vivacious account of walking across Spain.'

Victoria Hislop

'Mark's is a proper journey, whose every step and backstep is
recounted in detail and drama. Frank and funny in parts,
Vagabond is a free-roaming love letter to Spain.'

Sarah Barrell,
National Geographic Traveller **(UK)**

'Mark's account of his epic trek is a super-rich, immensely
readable portrait of a country where modern life drips with
the ghosts of centuries past. I felt like I was with him every
step of the way – only without the agonizing blisters.'

James Manning,
Time Out

T0349109

'Like a latter-day Laurie Lee, Mark Eveleigh takes us on a compelling journey from Gibraltar to Spain's most northerly tip. Staying true to his original travels as a young man, he sleeps rough, and, in doing so, gets under the skin of the Iberian Peninsula in an engaging and delightful way. Vagabond is packed full of colourful observations and amusing characters met en route. A highly entertaining read.'

Louise Roddon,
travel writer for *The Times* and *Sunday Times*

'A pilgrimage with no particular purpose, yet that's the vagabundo way. Eveleigh takes a backpack and a sharp eye to the dusty trails of Spain. It's a drifter's delight.'

Tom Chesshyre, author and travel writer

'Vagabond is a must-read for anyone with even the barest interest in hammocks, hiking and exploring Spain on foot. With an original writer, and replete with interesting material and encounters, this book is a genuine adventure over 1,200 km, walked in the high heat of summer. What's not to like?'

Robert Twigger,
author of *Walking the Great North Line*

'Mark Eveleigh is travel writer who enjoys a natural affinity with the places he visits and the people he meets. This is particularly in evidence in Vagabond, with Mark taking us with him on a remarkable journey that is almost as memorable for the reader as it was for him.'

Ashley Gibbins,
The International Travel Writers Alliance

Vagabond

VAGABOND

An Hachette UK Company
www.hachette.co.uk

Summersdale Publishers
Part of Octopus Publishing Group Limited
Carmelite House
50 Victoria Embankment
LONDON
EC4Y 0DZ
UK

www.summersdale.com

Printed and bound by Clays Ltd, Suffolk, NR35 1ED

ISBN: 978-1-83799-427-4

This FSC® label means that materials used for the product have been responsibly sourced

MIX
Paper | Supporting responsible forestry
FSC® C104740

Substantial discounts on bulk quantities of Summersdale books are available to corporations, professional associations and other organizations. For details contact general enquiries: telephone: +44 (0) 1243 771107 or email: enquiries@summersdale.com.

MARK EVELEIGH

Vagabond

A HIKER'S HOMAGE
TO RURAL SPAIN

summersdale

For Lucía, who inherited her papá's itchy feet

CONTENTS

FOREWORD

I fell in love with Spain's wild mountains, endless plains and evocative old towns 30 years ago and spent almost two decades there, working as a reporter for international magazines and newspapers. I was so fascinated by the country and its people that I couldn't stay still and through the 1990s and 2000s I trekked – as a backpacker and a budding travel writer – through every part of the Iberian Peninsula.

Every journey soothed my yearning for adventure, but fuelled dreams of another. I explored most of the wildest parts of the Spanish mainland, camping, walking, hitchhiking and even travelling on horseback. I slept in orchards and ruined barns, under bridges and in shadowy nooks beneath the walls of Moorish fortresses.

Mostly I travelled alone but my path often coincided with itinerant labourers, migrant workers, nomadic punks (*punkis* as the Spanish call them) and some of Spain's unique *Gitano* communities. For a few memorable weeks I trekked in Aragon with three septuagenarian brothers who were the last truly nomadic migrant shepherds on the Iberian Peninsula.

During one of my early journeys, I met an unforgettable old man who described himself as a *vagabundo*. We were both almost penniless but fate had somehow contrived to provide us each with the handful of pesetas necessary to catch a train in Badajoz, near the Portuguese border. We chatted in Spanish as the train clanked past a series of dusty sidings. The old man was homeless and owned nothing but the clothes on his back. I was in a similar situation. In my case though it was purely by choice. I was between jobs and don't even recall now where I was going. Nor why, uncharacteristically, I was travelling by train rather than hitchhiking or walking.

The old man also habitually travelled on foot, he told me, around a circuit that he could complete roughly every two years. It was, he believed, the perfect pace to ensure that he was welcomed back in the villages along his route.

'*Hola señora, soy vagabundo,*' he'd yell cheerily. '*Necesito algo pa' comer*' – I'm a vagabond. I need something to eat.

In each hamlet he'd be greeted as an old friend and I gathered that his entire livelihood lay in trading laughter and tales of the road for a meal and a glass or two of vino. Then he'd move on. He almost certainly completed his last circuit long ago and has no doubt passed on to other stomping grounds by now.

He had no home, no family and no money. Yet that happy hobo lives on in my mind as the most bright-eyed, contented and fun-loving person I ever met.

Almost 30 years after meeting him, as I had just tipped over into the wrong side of 50 – about the same age that my 'old' *vagabundo* friend would have been when I met him – I set out to recapture some of that spirit. In fact I realized that I was now older than that famously crazy old Spanish gentleman Don Quixote was said to have been when he embarked on his own errant adventure. Probably I should have been old enough to know better. Was it reckless, I wondered, to be setting off on a midsummer walk that would take me 1,225 kilometres up the length of Spain? The answer, I found out later, was yes. It turned out that it was extremely reckless but I was not to know when I started my journey that I'd be walking through the hottest summer since records began in Spain over a century ago. By some estimates more than 11,000 people died from the heat in Spain that year.

In honour of my old friend, it seemed important that the trek – from Gibraltar to Estaca de Bares (the most northerly point on the Iberian Peninsula) – should be completed in true vagabond style. Wherever possible I intended to sleep in the open air, *en el santo suelo* ('on the sacred ground' as the Spanish call it). Or, preferably, suspended a metre above it in my trusty hammock. I was haunted by the feeling that I would only ever be flirting with a state of 'vagabondage'. Even as I strung my hammock across a hidden irrigation ditch on the outskirts of a village or curled up on a groundsheet on a remote hilltop, I often had the hypocritical feeling that my sense of insecurity was itself just a mild sham. Part of an act. For countless thousands of people, after all, the state of homelessness was far from romantic.

Nevertheless, I was driven by a hunger to return to my old hobo ways, sleeping rough wherever I could, bathing in streams and grabbing a meal when the opportunity arose. I wanted to sacrifice a rigid itinerary for a chance to regain the love of aimless freewheeling that had motivated my earliest travels.

Estaca de Bares

Lugo

Ponferrada
Astorga

Zamora

Salamanca

Cáceres
Mérida

Seville

Gibraltar

Asturias

Cantabria

Basque
Country

Navarre

La Rioja

Galicia

Castile and León

Catalonia

Aragon

Madrid

Valencia

Extremadura

Castilla-La Mancha

Murcia

Andalusia

Across the South

CHAPTER 1

Across
the South

Andalusia

Seville

Los Palacios y Villafranca

Las Cabezas de San Juan

Arcos de la Frontera

Algar

Jimena de la
Frontera

Gibraltar

As I peered out from among the cocooning folds of my hammock one May morning, I felt unseasonably cold droplets of dew settle on my face like a cold flannel. I was a castaway in a sea of swirling mist; my little desert island of scrubby grass and stunted olives floated in a soupy cloud.

The weather had been clear the previous evening so I hadn't bothered to string the plastic bivouac roof over my hammock. I'd felt privileged to look up at the stars, ensnared within a crooked web of gnarled branches and twigs. The lights of a distant village had glowed amber on the plain, like the clustered campfires of an entrenched army. Now, at daybreak, the hillside was draped in mist. The only noises were the distant crowing of cockerels and what sounded like the dim clanking of rattled chains approaching along the curve of the hillside.

The sound was vaguely familiar but it took a moment for my sleep-befuddled brain to realize that a herd of goats was moving along the hillside towards me. The heavy bells around the necks of the billies clattered eerily.

It was a dawn chorus that would have been familiar to the inhabitants of this hill two thousand years ago. I'd set up camp near a maze of crumbling walls, the remains of a nameless Roman city that was already considered ancient when Christ was born. The evening before I'd explored the ruins as I searched for a sheltered sleeping spot. Eventually I'd given up on the shadowy cisterns and spooky chambers and had settled on a tangle of olive trees.

I realized now that it was the sound of the approaching goats that had woken me. The males were grunting like gazelles in rut. It crossed my mind that they might well be accompanied by shepherds – and perhaps even by ferocious mastiff dogs. With this in mind, I decided that it would be wise to break camp quickly and move down the hillside before the herd surrounded me.

It had been three days since I'd walked out of Gibraltar. I'd slogged uphill for most of the first 100 kilometres and only now, on the southern flank of the Sierra de Aznar, could I begin to convince myself that I was on the downhill slope towards Seville.

* * *

Mark Twain must have seen Gibraltar on an unusually beautiful day when he described it in *The Innocents Abroad*: 'majestic Gibraltar glorified with the rich colouring of a Spanish sunset and swimming in a sea of rainbows.'

It had always struck me as fitting that the little enclave – less than 7 square kilometres – seemed to have imported its own British weather. The damp eastern wind that blows up the Strait is known as the levanter and it's over Gibraltar that it invariably delivers its cargo of rain. There are few days when The Rock isn't crowned with its own wispy grey tiara and Gibraltarians will tell you, with barely concealed pride, that the levanter cloud is often the only one visible for 50 miles across southern Spain.

'If you look closely,' they say, 'you can see "Made in England" stamped on its underside.'

But the first hint of dawn was yet to bleach the starry Mediterranean sky when I began walking from Gibraltar's southern tip.

I'd rented a room the previous night in the heart of Gibraltar's old town, savouring what I figured would be my last night in a bed for at least a month. My English landlady Marie had gone beyond the bounds of normal hospitality by suggesting she'd wake even before first light to drive me south to my starting point at Europa Point (Gibraltar's southern tip), thus saving me an added 4 kilometres on my long trek to Spain's more northerly extreme.

'Around that corner you'll find an alley that leads to the beach,' Marie reassured me as she gesticulated through the darkness beyond the salt-smeared windows of her little hatchback. 'Just walk across and you'll find a tunnel that will lead you back up onto Main Street. You can't get lost.'

It turned out that I most certainly *could*.

It took a while even to find the access to the beach in the dark, and the tunnel that I eventually stumbled into came to a dead-end after just a few metres. Much of Gibraltar is riddled, like a gigantic, fossilized rabbit warren, with man-made tunnels and caverns. I was reluctant to waste my first morning looking for a shortcut among the estimated 167 caves that honeycomb The Rock so I promptly turned back to retrace the route Marie had driven along Levanter Way. Striding past the Al-Saud Mosque, I could make out the glimmer of Ceuta (one of the two Spanish enclaves on the coast of Morocco) cutting through the haze of the Straits. Few people today recall that Gibraltar was originally named Jabal Tariq (Tariq's Mountain) after the Muslim general who landed here at the head of 7,000 Berber warriors in 711 CE.

I'd been looking forward to this predawn ramble but how could I not feel daunted by the prospect of the thousand kilometres or more that lay to the north? It struck me as a highly unpropitious beginning that I'd been lost even before my walk began. If I could get lost even with that gigantic granite slab looming above my right shoulder, what chance would I have on the relatively featureless plains of Extremadura? It was a moment of soul-searching but now at least I was underway and determined to keep resolutely heading northward.

The reflected glare of the Europa Point lighthouse threw a faint orange sheen across the rock face and I wondered if the iconic apes were even awake yet. Nobody knows for sure how the Barbary apes (Europe's only wild monkey) originally arrived on The Rock. One suggestion is they walked here along 20 kilometres of tunnels under the Straits, and a Gibraltarian myth has it that a secret monkey graveyard still lies hidden in an undiscovered cave. Some believe that the apes walked across before there was water in the Straits, or that the Moorish invaders brought them over. Most likely it was British troops who bought them from African traders as pets and then released them when they outgrew their cuteness. Whatever the reason, it has been prophesied that Gibraltar will cease to be British on the day that the apes leave. During World War Two Winston Churchill, learning of diminishing numbers, ordered that ape 'reinforcements' be brought in from their homelands in Morocco.

It took me the best part of 2 hours to walk from Europa Point through the tangled alleys and winding streets of old Gib. At this early hour the only people on the streets were dog-owners who would nod, mutter a staunchly English 'Mornin'' and clutch little bouquets of plastic poop-bags to their chests like talismans. I was now officially underway, yet there was a strange feeling of limbo in the fact that I'd not yet even entered Spain. I passed Trafalgar Cemetery and the tiny King's Chapel, so old that the '1560' chiselled by the door is said to relate only to a renovation that was made after it was damaged in a pirate raid.

Lights were flickering to life inside a café at the southern end of Main Street and I grasped at the prospect of a few minutes to sit still and collect my thoughts now that I was underway.

'Start as you mean to go on,' I muttered to myself, 'never refuse a coffee.' I didn't realize yet that this was just the first instance of the unceasing monologue that would carry me through the next 1,225 solitary kilometres.

The inside of the café was hung with old prints of ships, naval memorabilia and a lithograph of the Battle of Trafalgar. Chairs were still upturned on tables and the barman was sweeping inside so I took my double espresso out to a pavement table. A pair of early dog-walkers stopped nearby, giving me an irresistible chance to eavesdrop on the fascinating 'Spanglish' conversation that is an iconic part of Gibraltarian culture. The dog-walkers were able to switch, completely seamlessly, between English and Spanish according to whatever phrases tripped most easily off the tongue: '*Tengo que* go to a wedding *mañana*,' one of them was saying.

'*Joder*,' the other swore in sympathy. 'Whose wedding?'

'It's an old *amiga de mi hermana*.'

My coffee finished, I shouldered my pack again and walked onwards past the infamously rough-and-ready Horseshoe pub where, during my first visit to the enclave in 1987, I'd found casual work as a glass collector. It had been a favourite with the Royal Navy boys when they were in port... and a favourite with tobacco smugglers the rest of the time. The alley at the side of the building saw more than its share of brawls on nights when both sets of clienteles were simultaneously present. In my professional capacity I was sometimes called into action as a reluctant doorman and was there, trying to break up a fight one Saturday night, when a young sailor was half-blinded. It would probably have been just another good-natured punch-up between friends, except that one of the drunken brawlers forgot to drop his cigarette before he punched his crewmate in the eye.

But at this early hour on a Thursday morning The Horseshoe was peaceful. There were some shattered glasses in the alleyway to show that maybe things hadn't changed all that much.

Even today the chain of battlements, bastions and batteries lend Gibraltar the atmosphere of a besieged fortress. At the bottom of Main Street I crossed Casemates Square where a flock of pigeons took off, slapping wings applauding the coming sunrise. Then I entered the gloomy Landport Tunnel, like an image of Dickensian London, to emerge beside the sturdy stone wall of Couvreport Battery.

For more than three centuries the British bulldog has refused to slacken his tenacious grip on the foot of Europe, despite Spain's determined attempts to shake him loose. El Peñón (as The Rock was known in Spanish) was first captured by the British fleet in 1704. Then, nine years later, the Treaty of Utrecht ended the Spanish War of Succession, ceding 'ownership of the city and castle of Gibraltar, together with its port, defences and fortresses' to the British Crown. Since that time the people of Gibraltar – a mixed population of British, Portuguese, Italian and Maltese descent – have been almost unanimous in their determination to resist Spanish attempts to regain sovereignty. People still laugh about the 1967 referendum when almost the entire population (about 25,000) voted in favour of remaining British; the story goes that a grand total of 44 voted for Spain... and in the week after the ballot there were numerous accounts of tearful old ladies admitting that they'd accidentally ticked the box in favour of ceding to Spain.

I followed Winston Churchill Avenue onto the apron of the airport runway that completely bisects the neck of the peninsula. By now it was light enough to make out the pockmarked face of the sheer cliff known as The Notch. In the late 1700s besieging Spanish forces had managed to creep so close that it was impossible for the British to angle their guns down upon them. So an ambitious plan was devised to carve almost 200 metres of tunnels, galleries and gun emplacements out of the solid rock, using pickaxes, crowbars and precious measures of gunpowder. I'd seen a plaque up there in what is known as Windsor Gallery commemorating the completion, in 1783, of that monumental project by Sergeant Major Ince of the Military Artificers and one Lieutenant Eveleigh of the Corps of Engineers.

Fortunately, peace now reigns and the tricorn-hatted Guardia Civil and uniformed British 'Bobbies' around the border are mostly for show. At the northern end of the great breezy stretch of runway, motorbike-mounted commuters and countless cyclists were weaving through a traffic jam. The riders fumbled with wallets or tugged at ID cards that hung around their necks. These were the lucky ones who could traverse the border at will, since in this post-Brexit era the offices once again echoed with the hollow *thunk* of passport stamps.

At times in the past when diplomatic relations had been strained, Gibraltarians had complained that Spanish border guards had deliberately adopted a go-slow policy in processing vehicles. Some went so far as to accuse Spain of human rights violations for keeping people waiting for hours in temperatures that exceeded 40°C.

Laurie Lee had visited The Rock in 1935 and wrote about the experience three decades later in *As I Walked Out One Midsummer Morning*. The British enclave had struck him as an 'interloper'. It appeared to him as if it had been towed out from Portsmouth to be anchored under its own private shroud of English drizzle.

In Gibraltar the authorities couldn't understand why the British writer was hobo-ing around Spain and he was taken to see the Chief of Police who struck Lee as 'a worried but kindly man'.

Lee wasn't destitute exactly. But neither was he... well, entirely 'respectable'. The general consensus was that it just didn't seem to be cricket. 'It doesn't *do*, you know – if you'll forgive my saying so,' the chief complained. 'Nothing personal you understand...'

Finally Lee was allowed entry only on the condition that he agreed to sleep in the police station at night. But the restriction of sleeping in a police station was tedious and after a few days of bacon and eggs, Lee was relieved to head back into Spain.

I was leaving after just a single night and, like Lee, was anxious to get back into Spain. Although there was a jam of incoming traffic very few people were going *out* at this hour on a weekday morning. Because there was nobody to follow, I misjudged the exit route and a very brusque British border guard called me over and demanded to see my passport. His clipped moustache and equally clipped accent gave him the air of a cad from a 1920s movie, but his automatic rifle commanded a certain respect.

'Where did you arrive from?' he asked gruffly.

'I arrived in La Línea by bus yesterday,' I told him. 'I only visited Gib overnight… fancied a pie and a pint.'

My mildly matey effort to win a smile had no visible effect.

'Working in Spain?' he asked.

'No. Just on holiday.' I jerked a thumb at my backpack.

I hoped that he wouldn't push me into a direct lie by asking where I intended to stay that night. Instead he turned his nose up at my pack as if it were some particularly offensive form of roadkill.

'It doesn't *do*, you know,' I expected him to say, '– if you'll forgive my saying so.'

But a cursory nod ushered me on my way and, a minute later, I was embroiled in an almost identical conversation in Spanish with an equally unwelcoming official: 'Looking forward to getting back to some *jamón serrano*,' I told him.

He too had heard it all before. The heavy *thunk* of an entry stamp going into my passport served to remind me that, thanks to Brexit, British arrivals to Spain are often reluctantly tolerated these days rather than actively welcomed.

* * *

As I stepped into the street, I took a moment to register the fact that I'd now taken the first of roughly one and a half million Spanish steps that would be required to reach the coast of Galicia.

It was hard to imagine on this crisp, sun-blessed Andalucían morning (with the merest smudge of patriotic cloud hovering like a battle standard above The Rock) that the community I was entering has often been described as Spain's most troubled town. La Línea de la Concepción sprawls up the coast on the Spanish side of the border and my first challenge was to find a 10-kilometre path through the network of highways that riddled this hinterland, effectively barring me from the wild Andalucían landscapes that I'd been dreaming of. The people of La Línea de la Concepción have traditionally had a complex love–hate relationship with what they call the Rock Scorpions. Perhaps it was the Gibraltarians' enforced isolation during the years of the dictator Franco's siege that made the inhabitants of The Rock so gregarious. One tale that shed a brilliant light on the local character described how the entire Gibraltar community turned out at the border to watch Franco's Guardia Civil lock the frontier gates. It was 1969, John and Yoko had just got married on The Rock and the Gibraltarians were as fired up with Beatlemania as they were with patriotic fervour. As the gates banged shut 15,000 faces turned defiantly towards Spain and 15,000 voices sang out in a rousing chorus of 'we all live in a yellow submarine'.

The decade that followed – when besieged Rock Scorpions were often described as 'rocky happy' (or, more accurately, 'rock crazy') – turned smugglers into local heroes. After all, only the Gibraltarian *contrabandistas* could come and go as they wished, taking advantage of a smuggler's moon to convey their illicit cargoes of tobacco. The most famous among these outlaws became part of a uniquely Mediterranean Robin Hood myth, operating super-fast speedboats that could easily outrun the best that the Spanish coastguard could command.

In recent decades the smuggling story has turned to a darker chapter, however, and La Línea has become the frontline in the war on European drug smuggling. Calle Canarias, not far to my east and running along Sobrevela Beach, was reputedly one of the most dangerous streets in Europe thanks to the activity of various feuding cartels and street gangs.

At neighbouring La Atunara beach, smuggling had once been so blatant that Gibraltarian speedboats would pull up in broad daylight. The neighbourhood women who offloaded the boats hand-painted pedestrian crossings across the four lanes of Paseo del Mediterráneo to minimize the risk involved in the constant shuttling of waterproofed packages.

A coastguard chopper pilot whose machine had been stoned by supporters of the neighbourhood's drug clans once likened the experience to combat flying in Vietnam.

As I followed the curve of the esplanade alongside Avenida de España – with the clanking dockside cranes of Algeciras like an iron forest along the western shoreline – it occurred to me that I was caught between a rock and a *very* hard place indeed. It was not a place where I would want to spend the night on the streets and I hoped to be high in the hills by sundown.

It was all a simple accident of geography. At the time of my first visit to this area, in the late 1980s, the triangle of choppy water between Morocco, Gibraltar and Spain had been transitioning between tobacco smuggling and the running of more lucrative cargos. There were 24-foot Phantom speedboats in Gibraltar's marinas with their hulls and the casings of their six-cylinder engines camouflaged with matt-black paint. Suspicious, to say the least, but no questions were asked. All that cloak-and-dagger engineering just to run cartons of Marlboros or Winstons a kilometre up the coast? A shrug and a wink. 'Nuff said.

Rigid fibreglass hulls were prone to damage. The waterborne *contrabandistas* therefore switched to inflatable Zodiacs whose semi-rigid designs were more forgiving of the brutal sea conditions in what old sailors called 'the gut'. These so-called 'rubbers' had the added benefit that they could be hidden and transported to launching points by lorry.

A smuggler could cover the cost of such a craft several times over from a single run with a boatload of hashish harvested from Morocco's Rif Mountains. At the height of the smuggling – coinciding with the 2008 economic crisis – an estimated 2,500 tonnes of what the Spanish called *goma de la sierra* (mountain rubber) was being smuggled across the Straits each year. Small-time drug runners carried packages on the Ceuta and Tangier ferries. *Bajamos al moro*, people would say – let's go down to visit the Moor. It was street slang for a hashish run. I'd made the short voyage frequently (some would say *suspiciously* frequently) between Spain and Morocco during the 1990s as a struggling travel writer. I'd never smuggled anything more incriminating than a fake Rolex but I remembered being searched at the ferry terminals.

'Est ce que vous avez un petit quelque chose de spécial pour le weekend?' a winking customs guard had asked me once – Are you carrying a little something special for the weekend? The implication seemed to be that, if I wasn't, he might be able to set me up with a score.

The Moroccan customs officials and Gendarmerie Royale could be paid off almost as a matter of course but, even so, it was only small-time *contrabandistas* who bothered with the ferry. Bigger consignments were delivered on fishing boats, yachts or specially outfitted speedboats financed often by international cartels. The Straits of Gibraltar had become Hashish Boulevard. One thing led to another until the port of Algeciras, just across the bay, became the main entry point for cocaine from Latin America.

In April 2018, Spanish police confiscated almost 9 tonnes of cocaine in a single operation. With an estimated street value of more than €450 million, that is to say close to US$500 million, it was nothing to sneeze at. The cartels fought back, however. At one point the La Línea clans were so powerful that they were able to mount an assault with 20 gunmen on a hospital to liberate a drug boss who was under police custody there.

La Línea was sometimes called 'Little Medellin'. During one particularly dangerous period an estimated 30 gangs were said to be operating in the town. If the temptation to work for the *narcos* was often irresistible, then the risk of refusing was almost unimaginable. As one local informant told a reporter from *The Guardian* newspaper: 'The guy with a scooter and a mobile phone who keeps an eye out for the Guardia Civil will get €1,000 a day…

and the guys who drive the drug-boats can make up to €60,000 a trip.'

Unemployment is still rife in La Línea and the authorities worried that the tightening of border restrictions with Gibraltar was likely to add to the problems. The dusty streets, lined with cracked-plaster townhouses and flats with broken windows, were more reminiscent of the suburbs of northern England than of southern Spain. I hurried onwards. Scuttling away from the shadow of The Rock towards the sunlit hills of Andalucía.

* * *

Tobacco, perfumes, fake watches, hashish, cocaine. There can be few things that have not been smuggled across the Gibraltar–Spain border at one time or another.

I am able to claim a certain level of notoriety, however, for being almost certainly the only person who ever smuggled *his own head* across the international border.

The recollection came back to me halfway along La Línea's esplanade. As I passed a row of wrought-iron lamp posts I tried to recognize one with which I had briefly become intimately familiar. Some friends and I had camped on the beach here, long before the concrete esplanade had even been dreamed of. I would cross the border every evening for my shift at The Horseshoe pub. We'd often sit beside our old decommissioned British Telecom van watching hordes of rats scavenging along the rocky shoreline.

Sometimes I would wake before sunrise to jog along the waterfront. One morning I was still getting into my rhythm – staring at the cracked pavement in front of my running shoes – when, for no reason at all, Thor's hammer smashed me in the forehead. I'd run full-tilt straight into a lamp post. Presumably my arm must have collided at the same moment because my old Seiko exploded off my wrist. I heard what sounded very much like the midnight chime of a church bell as I crumpled to the ground. I was dazed but, even in that instant, I giggled at my own stupidity as I scrabbled for pieces of my now worthless watch.

The humour in the situation promptly evaporated when I felt the blood running from my forehead. I staggered back to the rat-infested beach, hoping that I wouldn't lose consciousness. The only thing that kept me on my feet was a marked reluctance to provide a meal for the resident rodents.

This was before the days of the European Union and hospitalization in Spain might end up being prohibitively expensive. If, however, I could successfully smuggle my own head into British territory we knew that I'd be able to get free medical attention. The border guards barely gave me a second glance as I staggered, with a bandage wrapped tight around my head and a cap pulled down low over my bleary eyes, into the British enclave and up the hill to the hospital.

As it turned out, hospitalization was unnecessary. In fact, my visit to the Gibraltar sawbones was surprisingly brief; I was out in less than an hour because the eight stitches were administered without anaesthetic, apparently minimizing the risk of shock related to a head-wound.

The treatment, resulting in a Harry Potter-style scar running like an exclamation mark into my hairline, was free of charge since I refrained from admitting that my injury was a souvenir of the Spanish side of the border.

* * *

It was around nine in the morning when I turned away from the coast, making a beeline for the hills above La Línea. Some of the taverns along Calle Real were opening for breakfast business. I passed 'Venta La Guita' (slang for 'money') and 'La Bodeguita de Henry' (carrying a hint of Gibraltarian Spanglish). I resisted the temptation to stop for a second coffee at 'Bar Tres Hermanos' (Three Brothers) where a couple of old men – two of the brothers perhaps – were grumbling over their morning papers.

'*¿Has visto esto?*' said one, smacking a headline with the back of his hand – Have you seen this?

'*¡Me cago en la leche!*' the other grunted, reading over his shoulder – I shit in the milk!

I wished I could have stopped to find out what exasperated them, but I had several kilometres of dual carriageway to traverse before the town of San Roque. As I scrambled along the litter-strewn rainwater gully I could only hope that this sort of terrain would not be a regular occurrence along my route.

An hour later I'd left the streams of traffic on the Autovía del Mediterráneo behind and was walking with delight into the first of many Andalucían *pueblos blancos* (white villages). A sign declared this to be the *'Muy Noble y Muy Leal Ciudad de San Roque'* (the very noble and very loyal city of San Roque). More village than city, San Roque was officially founded in 1704 by Spanish exiles from Gibraltar but its history goes back to Moorish and Roman times.

Appropriately enough, my first major landmark after leaving Gibraltar was a place that was named for the patron of pilgrims. San Roque is an unusually busy saint because he's also patron saint of those afflicted by plagues and pestilence and, more bizarrely, also the patron saint of dogs. Legend has it that he survived the plague with the help of a dog which licked his sores and brought him bread. Less fortunately San Roque was later imprisoned as a spy by his own uncle. I'd be confronted by San Roque's image frequently on churches and monuments over the coming weeks. It was impossible to mistake the stalwart figure in the windblown cloak and floppy pilgrim's hat, with his trusty dog. He's often depicted raising the hem of the cloak coquettishly to reveal a particularly manly thigh (albeit scarred with a plague bubo). It might have been a frivolous and unchristian thought, but I hoped that my own thighs might also look a little more muscular by the end of my trek.

After the urban sprawl and intimidating highways of La Línea de la Concepción, sleepy San Roque embraced me with its whitewashed houses and cobbled alleys.

I stopped for breakfast at Bar Torres, on the southern edge of Plaza de Andalucía. It was so busy that I wondered if there was a fiesta in the village, but I found a stool by the bar and propped my pack against the wall.

'¿Que hay pa' comer?' I asked the young woman behind the bar – What is there to eat?

'¿Eres inglés, verdad?' the barmaid asked over the roaring gush of the milk-frothing machine. I tried not to feel offended that she'd guessed my origins accurately despite the fact that I'd spoken precisely four words in my best Andalucían accent. Okay, so my Spanish fell somewhat short of flawless, but after having spent 16 years based in Madrid and Pamplona I'd have appreciated being mistaken for a native speaker at least once in a while.

Pleading guilty as accused, I ordered coffee, orange juice and a toasted baguette with cured ham.

'¿A 'onde va?' she asked as she passed my *tostada* over the counter – Where are you going?

'Voy andando a Galicia' – I'm walking to Galicia – I answered in an undertone. Even now that I was finally underway, I still found the question vaguely embarrassing. To answer honestly seemed ridiculously presumptuous. Boastful even. Down here, in the far south, the remote north-western region of Galicia was an impossibly distant target to aim for. I'd have to cross the sierras that separated us from the plains around Seville. Next would come the expanses of Andalucía. Only after that would I cross into the sweeping desolation of Extremadura whose mere name – implying 'extremes' – struck me as almost overwhelmingly forbidding. Then would come the province of Castilla y León and the most challenging mountain range of all as I crossed the high passes of

Galicia before descending again to the verdant coastal plains of 'Green Spain'.

'It's a mistake to disclose that you're passionate about going anywhere,' Paul Theroux once wrote, 'because everyone will give you ten reasons for not going. They want you to stay home and eat meatloaf and play with the computer. Which is what they're doing…'

Fortunately the barmaid was suddenly busy with another rush of orders and there was no need to elaborate upon my route.

Later when I was asked where I was heading, I was sometimes tempted by humility to claim that I was bound for somewhere closer. I couldn't shake a suspicion, however, that to claim a less distant goal might somehow be jinxing myself.

From San Roque my planned route for that day would head cross-country towards the hill town of Jimena de la Frontera. I hoped that I could cover those 30 kilometres in 6 hours or so. I wasn't sure what provisions I could find along the way, so I stopped at a supermarket on the edge of San Roque and bought a packet of *jamón serrano*, half a dozen peaches and enough mineral water to fill my two canteens.

I was about to learn a valuable lesson; within 10 minutes I was at the edge of San Roque where an old stone fountain jetted crystal-clear water in three spouts from a natural spring. A sign by the road advised me that Fuente de María España had been supplying fresh drinking-water to the local populace since the eighteenth century. In the old days the water had been carried in panniers on the backs of donkeys, or in pitchers on the heads of housewives and this morning a young woman was filling up gallon containers in the back of her car.

'*El agua es muy dulce y super-saludable,*' she told me – This water is sweet and super-healthy. 'There's no better water in all of Spain.'

The fact that people would take the trouble to drive here to collect drinking water convinced me to sacrifice all my purchased water in favour of the waters of this natural spring. I'd been worried about all the plastics my trek would create, figuring that I might leave as many as 200 empty bottles in my wake. The water-filter I carried would cut this to an absolute minimum, but María España fountain served as a timely reminder to ask around about the location of springs and fountains.

* * *

My last glimpse of Gibraltar was from the ridge above San Roque as I hiked upwards along a lane that was edged with waves of multicoloured blossoms. Entire hillsides were covered with camomile and the scarlet banks of poppies, interspersed sometimes with eye-catching stands of purple Mediterranean poppies. There were blushing hollyhocks and snapdragons, coyly swooning in the growing midday heat, and as I walked onwards I bent to drag my hand through clouds of sky-blue agapanthus.

I turned to look back and, with a sense of gratitude, saw that Gibraltar was already falling far behind me, diminishing in size, like a feature in a model landscape.

It was still early summer and recently arrived swallows swooped and dived overhead, scything across a cloudless sky. I remembered hearing that, across the Straits in Morocco, people traditionally believed that these tiny birds travelled as passengers, riding snuggled among the bony ribs of migrating storks: after all, they always seemed to arrive at the same time as the storks... and the diminutive swallows were clearly too small to make the long journey from Europe under their own steam.

Now I too was undertaking my own migration. Like the swallows I had no obligation beyond continuing my forward motion, eating and sleeping when opportunity allowed. But breaking free and making the decision to get moving gets harder as you get older. Like a padlock that has accumulated rust it takes more effort to turn the key, to release the latch and step out. I'd been nominally homeless at times, once for a stretch of several years, but even then I'd really only been playing at it. I'd lived in hotels, hostels, flophouses and guesthouses (in Asia, Africa and Latin America), paying the bills through a perpetual series of magazine and newspaper assignments. Now I was 54 years old, and it had been well over two decades since I'd last slept rough in Spain.

I ought to have been old enough to know better and yet here I was, embarking on what would surely be the most strenuous trek of my life. During the last 25 years working as a travel journalist, I'd led several tough expeditions. They'd involved certain risks and challenges but there had been nothing quite as physically daunting as what I was now setting out to do. I'd travelled often on luxury assignments for magazines and, while I'd enjoyed the pampered lifestyle, it had always been adventurous trips to remote wildernesses that gave me the greatest thrill. I knew that this challenge might well have been beyond even the younger, tougher me. I was sure that there would be many times when I would want to give up. Throughout the trek I would carry in my back pocket a hand-written note from my wife at home in South Africa. 'I'm so proud of you', she wrote, 'for dreaming up this journey and for having the courage to commit to it.'

Aside from that, Narina put no pressure on me whatsoever. Nevertheless, I convinced myself that my failure would disappoint her.

'Giving up is not an option!' was the name of a document on my phone that I could refer to at my moments of greatest self-doubt. It was basically a list of the people who believed in me. I'd made a note of passing comments from my daughter Lucía: 'You'll manage, Papá,' she'd said with blind confidence as we'd strolled by the river near her home in Pamplona. 'I don't think you'll slack.'

Other members of my family also featured in the list of well-wishers. Going public on social media with my plan had been another deliberate way of burning my bridges and making it harder to back down. When I hit the low points that I knew would come I wanted to ensure that it would be even harder to give up than to continue.

The material support offered by my sponsors Polartec and Jack Wolfskin had been greatly appreciated but, equally important, their investment would serve as a powerful incentive to me that I had to 'get the job done'.

The document on my phone also included random comments that people had made when they heard what I was embarking on: 'Well, Laurie Lee did it,' someone had pointed out, 'and he did it against the background of a civil war.'

I knew that the comment was not historically accurate, but the implication was that it shouldn't really be all *that* hard. Lee had finished his walk in 1936 just as the Spanish Civil War erupted and I was aware that the trek had taken its toll, both physically *and* mentally, on the 19-year-old writer.

This was evident even in his first impression of the long trek that would eventually take him from Galicia to the Mediterranean coast of Andalucía. 'That first day alone,' he'd written, 'steadily declined in excitement and vigour.'

I'd half anticipated a similar feeling as I set out on my own midsummer walk in the opposite direction but, inexplicably, a feeling of carefree jauntiness increased with each step I took into the hills. Here I was under an African sun among the *pueblos blancos* of Andalucía. I couldn't imagine anywhere I'd rather be.

'I noticed a strange feeling coming over me,' the American hobo known as Ralph 'Hood River Blackie' Gooding recalled in 1940 at the start of his 25-year journey across the United States, 'a kind of pleasant swelling sensation in my chest that I now know was freedom.' Christened Ralph Gooding, he ran away from home at the age of 14 to become famous as Hood River Blackie. He was a sort of hobo-historian who planned to write a multivolume history of the hobos' underground subculture, complete with 611 biographies of men who spent their lives on the rails. Unfortunately it was never written but by the time Blackie died at the age of 57 he'd left notes, articles and recordings detailing life on the road. His notes sometimes read like a guidebook for hobos, complete with warnings about particularly risky hobojungles (spots where the homeless could sleep rough) and the towns with overly aggressive 'bulls', as the guards who worked the rails were known.

I shared Hood River Blackie's thrill at this early sense of freedom – at this very moment, I could feel that same pleasant swelling sensation in my own chest – and it was clear that technology had made hobo-ing easier; I had no need of a guidebook because I'd been able to scout the trails north of San Roque on Google Earth. It appeared that I only needed to cross a small residential area of homesteads and allotments before I could turn off the tarmac onto a country dirt track that headed unerringly northward across the sierras. This little residential settlement (inexplicably called Los Leones – The Lions) consisted of some grand houses set within protective walls. The angry barking of a series of dogs emanated from behind these barricades as I passed along the street, like an ocean roller clattering against a seawall.

Before long I arrived at the edge of the dirt track and cheerfully set off into what I'd pictured as the wilderness section of my trek. I'd seen on the map how the trail passed a ranch house before snaking sinuously towards the Arroyo de la Madre Vieja (Valley of the Elderly Mother).

I'd sauntered only a hundred metres, however, when I came to a gate that was hung with a hand-painted sign: *Ganado Bravo*. 'Savage livestock' could mean only one thing in what was, after all, the heart of bullfighting country.

I retreated to the tarmac in search of an alternative route. As luck would have it, a Mercedes SUV was just emerging from one of the fortified driveways. Before the electric gateway obscured my view, I made out the neon sheen of a lawn and the glint of a swimming pool. Mercifully there were no savage dogs so I trotted towards the car with my pack bouncing on my back. The elegant woman in the driving seat cracked her window down just a few centimetres – whether this was in distrust or just in reluctance to waste the precious air-conditioning, I couldn't tell.

'*Buenos días,*' I smiled, 'I'm walking to Jimena de la Frontera but I've just learned that the path goes through a bull-ranch.' (I was doubly reticent to admit now that I was ultimately heading for Galicia since, for the time being, even Jimena might be out of reach.)

'You want to go to Jimena de la Frontera?' she repeated. 'Well the last thing you want to do is to start from here!'

* * *

Rather than backtrack all the way down to the highway I found a shady spot and scanned Google Earth for alternatives. A narrow trail ran along the edge of a field bordering a patchwork of allotments, but it came to an abrupt stop at the edge of a canyon. It was possible that it was blocked by a cliff but, lacking any other alternative, I decided to investigate.

I was lucky and managed to scramble down through thick bush to a stream. By jumping across sandbanks I reached the far side without even removing my boots and was soon heading up through a forest of conifers towards the other side of the valley.

It was the first of several setbacks during that first day's trek. The problem was that most of the land here was fenced for livestock – savage or otherwise. For the next 2 hours, as I walked along the boundary of a huge orange and avocado plantation, I saw nobody from whom I could ask directions. Then, on the edge of an immense electricity substation my path was blocked again. The map was marked with a trail and yet I now saw that a sagging fence had been drawn across and secured with barbed wire. A sign read *Coto Privado de Caza* (Private Hunting Reserve). I tried to subdue a feeling of panic at the thought that the entire trek might consist of constant backtracking.

With the temperature rising to 35°C I decided that it would be wise to string my hammock up and rest in the shade during the midday heat. I strapped the portable solar charger onto the top of my pack and left it charging in the sun. Then I relaxed, dipping into an e-book on the phone that would serve as library as well as navigation device (loaded with maps for offline access too), notebook, dicta-phone, camera and all-round mobile office.

I was reading *A Tramp Abroad*, an account of Mark Twain's 'trek' across Europe. Despite having been published over 140 years ago it was surprisingly light-hearted and timeless. From the outset Twain had absolutely zero intention of trekking, and endearingly – for a man who'd been a Mississippi riverboat pilot and a silver miner, among other things – he made a joke of his lack of intrepidity. In the typically crisp, ironic tone of his usual travelogues he wrote about two German women he met who walked 45 kilometres a day through the Black Forest. The fact that those women covered such distances in hobnail boots and carrying what Twain described as 'blanket-bags' qualified them for headline billing on my 'Giving up is not an option' motivational list.

I must have dozed off because I was woken about an hour later by the sound of a vehicle rattling up the track. It was a work-van from the electrical substation, so I scrambled out of my hammock and jogged over to ask about the blocked trail.

'Nobody will *shoot* you,' the driver said as if reassuring a child. Apparently, I was free to ignore the sign and continue onwards across the hunting area. He must have noticed my dubious expression: 'Mountain-bikers go that way all the time. Anyway, it's not even hunting season.'

So once I'd packed my hammock away, I took his advice and unlatched the fence. I was happy to see that, along with the tracks of deer and wild boar, there was indeed evidence of cycle-tyres running through the sandy soil. For an hour and a half I followed the tracks across the vast hunting area until they finally converged on the bank of a canal. The water was flowing fast and most of the bank was dangerously steep but eventually I found a gently sloping section where I could strip down to my boxer shorts and enjoy a cool dip.

Small herds of free-range cattle clustered here and there along the shady bank. I had to choose either to ease around the fringes or sidestep along the steep bank with my pack hooked only on one shoulder in case I slipped or had to run. These big brown bovines were clearly not *de raza brava* as the Spanish would say ('of the savage race'). They had calves to protect, however, and guessing that they were probably not accustomed to pedestrians, I felt better when I had a hefty stick in my hand as a deterrent.

By now I'd covered 30 kilometres. My legs felt heavy and blisters were starting to twinge on my heels, yet still there was no sign of re-emerging onto a main thoroughfare. Just as I was considering the distinct possibility that I might have to spend the night in the hunting reserve, the canal swung abruptly westward and I found myself beside a locked gate and a high fence. It was with immense relief that I found a gap which was just wide enough to allow me to slip through, dragging my pack after me.

'Conservation Area', said the sign in Spanish on the other side of the gate, 'Access forbidden to unauthorized personnel'. I'd made it a personal rule that at no time in the trek would I trespass and yet I'd inadvertently spent most of my first afternoon trekking illegally through a conservation area.

* * *

As much as I'd looked forward to trekking through wilderness, I was now delighted to be back on a highway. This unbroken stretch of tarmac led northward to Jimena de la Frontera and I set off again at a jaunty march, singing so raucously to myself through much of the next 3 hours that I almost lost my voice.

It was mid-afternoon and I'd finished my ham and was getting hungry again when I saw a sign up ahead that was emblazoned with the word 'Cruzcampo'. The Sevillian beer company was founded in 1904 and, in an area where it was too hot to drink red vino, icy glasses of Cruzcampo (often translated as 'Cross-country' but named after a monument called the 'Cross of the Country') would become daily highlights of hot afternoons on the Andalucían section of my trail.

The Cruzcampo billboard informed me that I'd arrived at Venta la Adelfilla. *Ventas* are basically roadside taverns, often built, like this one, at a junction between villages which once served as waystations and trading centres. I knew all that, but it took a dictionary to show me that *adelfilla* was the Spanish word for willowherb or fireweed, the leaves and roots of which were apparently brewed as tea to treat gastro-intestinal complaints, prostate problems and to serve as a laxative.

When I'd quenched my thirst with a leisurely bottle of Cruzcampo I asked what was on the lunch menu.

The barmaid looked up at the clock on the back wall: 'I'm sorry but the kitchen closed ten minutes ago.'

She had long blonde plaits that reminded me of a Hofbräuhaus waitress. Or perhaps it was just the bulk of the pint-sized tankard as she scooped foam off – Spanish style – with a wooden spatula.

'Isn't there *anything* I can eat?' I persisted. Even to my ears there was a clear note of pleading desperation in my voice.

She ran manicured fingernails along the cool aluminium counter as she peered into a glass display cabinet at the other end of the bar.

'There's some *ensaladilla rusa* left,' she said. 'And we have olives.'

So my meal that first day, sitting at a table under the awning in front of the *venta*, was a dish of 'Russian salad' (insipid tinned vegetables in mayonnaise). But the fresh, crusty bread, dipped in olive oil – Andalucía's liquid gold – made it seem like a feast as I watched a farmer trot along the road with a cart hitched to a sturdy mare.

'Spain reeks of rank olive oil,' V. S. Pritchett lamented in *Marching Spain*, the 1928 book about his hike across part of Extremadura and Castilla y León. 'The fumes of that oil, which is used by the peasants for lighting their fires, for burning their lamps, and for cooking their food, hit out from every doorway with a blow that at first sickened... the abominable stuff.'

Fortunately Spain is still pervaded by the scent of olive oil and I wouldn't have it any other way. I could have stayed there, contentedly sucking the flesh from olive stones, for the rest of the afternoon but even now I was still 10 kilometres short of Jimena de la Frontera.

'Guess I'd better get moving,' I said to myself with a sigh, '... and also maybe I ought to stop talking to myself.'

Although I was still only on day one, I'd fallen into the solitary traveller's habit of mumbling to myself. It occurred to me now that what I came to think of as perpetual 'mutterances' had been dubbed over the top of every decision I'd made since I started walking.

As Paul Theroux pointed out in *Ghost Train to the Eastern Star*, 'all writers, when they are alone, talk to themselves'.

Freelance writing is the sort of solitary job that lends itself to this mild symptom of insanity. I wondered if two months on the road travelling solo was likely to leave me with a permanent imbalance.

* * *

'I guess I'd better start looking for a place to sleep,' I muttered under my breath a few kilometres farther up the road. 'Don't want to push too hard on day one.'

Thanks to detours, I'd covered 45 kilometres since I'd left Europa Point that morning and was now limping, nursing the swollen bubble of a blister on the back of my left heel. I knew that I'd have little problem sleeping no matter where I chose to bed down for the night.

I passed some polo grounds where I called a polite *'buenos tardes'* to a dozen lanky white storks, sauntering on their evening *paseo* through the cropped grass. From nests on the top of a row of electricity pylons other storks clattered their bills as if in reply. I took their call as a summons and, although I could see nothing in the way of promising hammock trees, I passed under their nests and went to investigate an overgrown farm track that snaked up the hill.

The grass grew almost to shoulder height alongside the track, providing excellent cover. In the absence of hammock trees it would have to do. I walked straight in and then dog-legged to the side so that I'd be hidden from view even if somebody walked within a few metres of my sleeping spot.

I'd recently heard of the concept of 'stealth camping'. It had become a social media catchphrase lately and one stealth-camping website defined it as 'a thrilling experience similar to wild camping but with an element of stealth from remaining undetected'. The site explained how it could be done whether in a tent or a motorhome. I'd most often travelled with a hammock. A tent was an unnecessary luxury and invariably I did my best to fly under the radar. I'd had no idea that I'd been 'stealth camping' all over the world for decades.

A herd of black cows stared nervously from a neighbouring field, doubtlessly suspicious of the 'stealthy' human who seemed to be stalking them in the tall grass.

I lay my hammock's bivouac roof flat for a groundsheet and spread my sleeping bag out on top. I'd bought some insect repellent and rather than carry the bottle I'd simply poured it over my hammock strings, trusting that it would effectively impregnate the rest of my kit in any case. Foolishly, I'd bought repellent that contained DEET and now I saw that it had already begun to corrode the outer mesh pockets on my brand spanking new pack. I lay the impregnated hammock strings in a repellent loop around me, trusting that it would help to keep mosquitoes – and perhaps any other nocturnal visitors – at bay.

Finally, I pulled off my boots, wincing as I eased the merino wool trekking sock away from a cluster of angry blisters that seemed suddenly to sting like bees. Inflating balloons were already burgeoning through the new skin under freshly burst blisters and I was amazed that on day one I seemed to be reaping a second crop.

I threaded a needle with dental floss (which doubled as unbreakable sewing-thread) and sterilized both needle and thread by dipping them into a small bottle of iodine, which would be useful for cuts as well as for water purification in an emergency. Then I pierced carefully right through the blister, leaving the ends of the thread loose for drainage. The thread stung but I couldn't tell whether this was from the iodine or what was proclaimed as 'new minty freshness' on the label of the dental floss. I performed the same operation on a smaller blister on the ball of my right foot and then liberally dusted my feet with antiseptic powder.

Free to relax now, I lay back and gazed contentedly up just as the first stars began to speckle the Spanish dusk. A gentle breeze slid through the long, dry grass with the rhythmic rustle of waves washing up a shingle beach, wafting a warm scent that reminded me of childhood summers.

I'd downloaded an audiobook of *As I Walked Out One Midsummer Morning* onto my phone. I'd read the book many times, but I was intrigued because this version was narrated by the author himself. So, I lay now listening to Laurie Lee's soft Gloucestershire accent as he related recollections of his own trek through these hills. To me too this feeling of exhaustion had a 'voluptuous quality' and – as he put it so beautifully – my own sleep, when it came, was 'caressive and deep like oil'.

*　*　*

The dew was heavy on the grass when I woke the next morning. After the 10-hour hike of the previous day my groundsheet could have been a feather mattress. I woke from a dreamless sleep to peer blearily out at a landscape that was still watery with the cool light of dawn.

The groundsheet was big enough to double over me and, although I'd stayed dry, it was surprisingly cold. Somehow I couldn't recall ever being cold in Spain during my nights of youthful vagrancy.

My sleeping bag (bought for a Land Rover expedition across the Argentine Andes) was a good one but it was old and, perhaps having spent too long stored in a compression sack, it had lost some of its downiness.

I thought how the previous day's trek had been a sort of prelude. Only now, waking on this first morning on the trail, I felt like my trek was starting for real. It had been a long time since I'd travelled like this and waking here in the tall grass felt like a resurrection. I sat up, still wrapped like a corpse, watching patches of thin mist drift like wraiths among the grazing cows.

But I couldn't lie still for long: I was burning daylight and wanted to cover as much distance as I could while it was still cool. More importantly, I wanted to find coffee.

I changed out of the board shorts that served both for pyjamas and swimwear and pulled on my bush shorts, tightening the security belt that I'd had fitted with a hidden zip-section containing an emergency stash of funds. I grabbed a clean T-shirt and then pulled on the thin fleece jacket that had served as a pillow.

I eased the thread from the (now drained) blisters and protected them with pieces cut from a roll of zinc oxide tape before coating my feet with the powder. A fresh pair of merino socks cocooned my feet and I knocked my walking boots out to dislodge any critters before I pulled them on.

Finally I shoved everything back into my backpack. Dirty clothes went into the separate zippered section in the bottom of the 42-litre pack and my folded groundsheet joined the hammock in the elasticated front section.

I checked that both the canteens were still in the side pockets, cinched the straps tight and I was ready to get walking again. It was not yet 7 o'clock.

By the time I'd waded through the long grass back onto the farm track my shorts were soaking, but it wouldn't take long for them to dry when the sun began to make its heat felt.

I was pleasantly surprised to realize how strong my legs felt. There was no stiffness from the previous day and, once they'd been deadened by the first kilometre, the blisters barely hurt at all.

'I was at that age which feels neither strain nor friction, when the body burns magic fuels, so that it seems to glide in warm air,' Laurie Lee wrote of the early days in his walk across Spain.

But perhaps because of our 36-year age difference, I was doubtful that I'd come to share his obvious enjoyment of the discomforts of the road when the going got tough. A little later in his trek Lee was laid up by heatstroke... so perhaps he'd just been hallucinating.

The storks were out strutting again, harvesting a rich crop of dew-dampened grasshoppers and perhaps the odd chilled reptile. I had my sights set on the village of Los Ángeles – an appealing name for my first landmark of the day. This mini-LA was so close to Jimena as to almost be considered a suburb and, although it would no doubt fall far short of its Californian counterpart, I was optimistic that it would at least boast a café.

Bar Restaurant Troyano was already busy with farm workers, delivery drivers and mechanics when I walked in. I had the impression that this was a regular early morning crowd that probably convened in the Troyano every weekday at this hour to begin their day with a jolt of sweet black coffee, a shot of cheap brandy and a pungent cigarette. The Holy Trinity of rural Spain.

I called a cheery *'buenos días'* to the room in general as I propped my pack next to a slot machine. A couple of old farmers at the corner of the bar paused momentarily in their conversation to respond over the clatter of saucers and the gurgle of the coffee machine. Bar Troyano was like thousands of others that were built during the construction boom of the 1970s when the Franco regime provoked a shift to urban centres. Hams hung from the ceiling and cigarette advertisements were interspersed among bullfight posters on the walls. There was a weather report on the TV, with a map of Andalucía. As usual the entire province was strung with sun icons, like an overloaded orange tree.

Despite the early hour there were about a dozen men in the bar and, with T-shirts and baseball caps emblazoned with the name of chainsaw manufacturers and livestock supplements, they could almost have been from anywhere in the world. Among the greasy ponytails and beer bellies that peeked from under half-buttoned shirts, there were a few reminders that I was in rural Spain. One man had sleekly oiled hair and brooding *Gitano* eyes and another wore cow-hide gaiters buckled over his jeans. I might have assumed he was a working cowboy but the button-down Ralph Lauren shirt and expensive jeans reminded me that, as I'd seen, polo was a popular leisure activity in the neighbourhood.

Nobody appeared to wonder where a foreigner had sprung from at this hour… nor why his jacket and hair were more thickly bristled with hayseeds than any of their own.

I ordered a *café con leche* – served Andalucían-style in a glass – and a fresh orange juice. The standard breakfast fare was toasted baguette with olive oil and a bowl of pureed tomato. It was served with garlic cloves that could be rubbed over the toast.

There was a memorable feeling of decadence about that first leisurely Los Ángeles breakfast. It was a moment of mild rebellion. I knew that I was deliberately squandering the coolest trekking hours but lazy Andalucían mornings had featured so heavily in my fantasies about this trip that I refused to let myself be hurried.

I walked into Jimena old town along the cobbles of Calle San Francisco where geraniums and bougainvillaea glowed like neon. There would be no more villages along my route that day so at a small grocery store near Plaza de la Constitución I stopped to buy some ham, a hunk of hard Manchego cheese and some dried fruit.

The Andalucían fireball was already throwing its rays onto the bleached walls of Calle Sol (Sun Street). In southern Spain people talk often about *el sol de justicia* – the sun of justice. The implication is that decent, God-fearing people should be off the streets before the 'sun of righteousness' climbs high enough to strike down the wicked.

Not entirely sure whether I numbered among the righteous or the wicked, I stuck to the shady side of the street where the shuttered windows were barred with *celosías* (literally 'jealousies'). Some say that these slatted windows serve less for security – hardly a great threat in these sleepy villages where everybody knows everybody else – and more as a throwback to the Muslim era when it was believed that the chastity of the household women had to be protected at all costs. The narrow alleyways and gleaming white walls of the *pueblos blancos* give the impression that the original town planners wanted to barricade themselves, like a besieged camel-train, against the immensity of the Andalucían landscape.

Calle Sevilla was deserted apart from one woman who was sweeping her front step. I figured that it might be my last opportunity for a coffee that day so I asked directions to the nearest bar.

When I walked into the cave-like coolness of Bar La Cuadra, the barmaid was complaining to the only other customer. He slouched against the bar as if he was part of the furniture; his face was the colour and texture of a crumpled felt hat and his sunburned forearms were like knotted vine-stems resting on the scarred teak bar.

'Mis hermanos son verdaderos hijos de puta,' the barmaid was saying – my brothers are genuine sons of bitches.

There was no apparent irony in her expression. The old man merely nodded, giving the impression that he'd heard it all before. He took the cigarette out of his mouth and cleared his throat with a sandpaper rasp before he returned my greeting. His bulbous nose was veiny, mapped with a delta of purple vino but his black eyes were bright as berries.

I ordered a coffee and asked for my canteens to be refilled. There were two glasses on the bar in front of the old man. The larger of these was two-thirds full of coffee but I had the impression that it had long since lost the last of its steam. The other was an empty shot glass. The barmaid continued her harangue but he was clearly a man of few words. When she paused for breath he muttered her name: 'Cruz'.

When she looked up, he merely tapped the counter next to the shot glass with a deliberate finger – like a man hitting the full stop on a typewriter. With a small shrug of irritation she took a bottle down from the top shelf and poured a tot of liquid amber.

It struck me as appropriate that her name was Cruz, since apparently she got cross quite easily.

'What's that?' I asked, more in a lonely effort to join the conversation than out of any real sense of curiosity.

The old man cleared his throat and removed his cigarette unhurriedly.

'Ponche,' he replied in a hacksaw voice that rasped out of a mouth like an abandoned quarry. *'Ponche Caballero.'*

I knew the so-called Gentleman's Punch – a sort of flavoured Spanish brandy made supposedly from a 180-year-old secret recipe

– from the past but had not recognized it in the shadowy bar. It comes in a metal bottle and the joke is it would eat its way out of glass. In reality it's quite a smooth drink, although I normally avoid such beverages at breakfast time.

It's hard to imagine what there was about the old man's demeanour or appearance that convinced me that he was a worthy role model. Moreover, in light of the potentially waterless 30 kilometres that lay ahead of me, strong alcohol was not a wise idea. But there was a sense of companionship in a shared snifter and anyway I figured that a shot of *ponche* might at least take my mind off my blisters for the next few kilometres.

* * *

The shot might have helped because by late morning I'd already crossed over Las Asomadillas Pass and was making decent headway into Los Alcornocales National Park. I was striding along a mountain lane high above Rio Hozgarganta – 'Sickle-throat River'. The name probably referred simply to a deep gorge (which this certainly was) but as I turned the words around in my mind, I recalled that in mediaeval times a razor-sharp sickle was sometimes laid in the grave across the throats of suspected vampires to prevent them from rising from the dead. Researchers working in a seventeenth-century cemetery in Poland had recently unearthed a grave in which a woman was buried with a sickle (a *hoz*) laid across her throat (*garganta*). It was clear that in life she had been cursed with a single protruding tooth. Incontrovertible proof then to any mediaeval witch-hunter worth his salt that she must have been a vampire. Just to make doubly sure that she would not leave the grave to haunt them, the villagers had also placed a padlock through her toe.

The temperature – pushing the mercury up towards the 40°C mark – was more than sufficient antidote for such chilling thoughts. Only a fool tempts fate by trying to walk through the midday heat in southern Spain so I began looking for a siesta spot. A short while later I clambered down to a small meadow, like a shelf high over the valley, where a group of cork trees offered a shady location for my hammock.

As a concession to comfort I carried a double hammock, rather than a single. It was so spacious that I could even lie comfortably on my front and on cold nights (or when, like now, I wanted shade) I could wrap the extra fabric around me to form a perfect cocoon.

I'd designed this hammock many years before. Christened the 'Swingers Club' hammock, it incorporated a separate mosquito net and a roof that doubled as a rain poncho. I'd left the net behind. I preferred to avoid the clammy, claustrophobic feeling of the net in any case and, if anyone did come prowling around my camp in the night, I wouldn't have relished finding myself entangled in my own mosquito net. From a security standpoint I infinitely preferred the all-round visibility of a hammock: unless in an area where there are dangerous animals, the minimal security offered by a half-millimetre tent wall is outweighed by the fact that you have no idea what's going on when you hear footsteps around camp.

I ate lunch and then lay back to read for a couple of hours, cooled by a gentle breeze that carried down the valley. I'd downloaded some information about Los Alcornocales National Park and learned now that researchers in this huge park (at 170,000 hectares one of Andalucía's largest protected areas) had listed at least 400 plants that have traditional uses. Some are well known to modern science – like arnica (for sprains and swellings) and horsetail (*Equusetum ramosoamum*, used for haemorrhage and jaundice) – but I wondered how many medicinal plants might be slipping into obscurity as the last of the old-time *campesinos* took their secrets to the grave with them.

* * *

By two in the afternoon. I was itching to get moving again. But was it better to get moving earlier and gamble on finding water or to lie low through as much of the heat as possible to conserve supplies?

I'd left Jimena with full canteens but as I trudged along the arid hillside, I knew that there was no guarantee of a refill before I reached a distant tavern that was said to lie at the top of the valley. I could only hope that it would be open, or at least that there would be a fountain or standpipe there. Since the next village lay 15 kilometres beyond the tavern, it was possible that I might not find water until the next day and the mercury had already climbed into the mid-30s.

Only four cars had passed me on the road that morning and it was entirely possible that I might not see another person that afternoon. There wasn't a single building as far as I could see along the valley and the chasm was so steep and deep as to make the river, hidden among trees at the bottom, virtually inaccessible. It might be possible to scramble down there but the water that I'd collect would barely fuel the strenuous climb back up.

The road writhed like a tortured snake as it led along the flank of the valley towards a distant stone bridge. It was an optimistic sign but when I leaned over the parapet I could see that the riverbed below was just a jumble of dry rocks like a ruined graveyard. I tried not to let my thoughts dwell on water but I realized that things were getting more serious when I started visually analysing cowpats for residual moisture. The cows I'd seen were clearly free range but if they were up here at all then it was logical that there must be a water source of some sort nearby.

My 1.5-litre canteen was almost empty by now, but it was the smaller 0.6-litre bottle that I considered to be my lifeline. It was a clever survival device created by a company which supplied filters for humanitarian use in Africa. It incorporated a microfilter membrane and an activated carbon filter which meant that I could safely drink even from the scummiest cattle trough. Unfortunately, the only water I saw in the next 2 hours lay out of reach at the bottom of a chasm far below the arches of a second stone bridge. The risk of attempting to reach that water source would have far outweighed the benefits of refilling my canteens so I reluctantly continued on my way.

I sipped carefully from what remained and analysed the sweatband on my bush hat as an indicator of my health. I was reassured when it felt damp after drinking; it was good to know that I still had enough moisture in my body to sweat in the dry heat. But 3 hours later there were only 2 centimetres of hot liquid left in the bottom of my second bottle.

The few homesteads I passed were all abandoned and although I looked into every storm drain along the side of the road, they were invariably bone dry. My imagination started to play tricks on me: the rustle of wind in the trees was like a babbling stream and when I kicked a pebble it skittered down the road with a sound like a tinkling waterfall. At least the thirst was a distraction from my smarting blisters though.

That afternoon I only saw one other person. He was offloading slabs of cork from the saddlebags of a mule on a grassy ledge about 50 metres below the road. Just as I passed, unseen, above him on the road he opened a can of beer with a hiss that made my swollen tongue throb. I considered climbing down to ask if he had spare water in the saddlebags but my pride would not let me admit that I'd set out without sufficient water... especially to the sort of mountain man who'd had so much foresight that he had even transported *beer* into the wilderness on his mule.

My path continued along the edge of steep ravines, known locally as *canutos*. It felt like a major landmark and a cause for celebration when a sign informed me that I'd passed out of Malaga province and was now entering Cádiz province. Unfortunately, I had nothing to celebrate with and the fact that the inaccessible depths of some of those *canutos* might have held the water I dreamed of only added to my frustration.

It was five in the afternoon when I arrived in La Sauceda, a little hamlet that appeared to be comprised only of deserted holiday homes. The map showed a river – Garganta de Pasadallana – but the blue line on the map could have been a mere mirage for all the water that flowed. There was a hiking refuge a short distance off the road but I cursed to realize that all the taps had apparently been turned off at the mains. Finally I discovered a small stream that trickled past the refuge into a scummy pool. It looked thoroughly unappetizing but at least I could now safely drink the last few centimetres of tepid water that was left in my canteen. I refilled both bottles and, thanks to my filter system, now had ample supplies to last until nightfall. My Jack Wolfskin trekking shirt, made of high-tech fast-drying fabric, was designed to wick sweat from my body onto its outer surface. Running my hand over my full belly I noticed that dewy droplets had gathered instantly on the surface of the cloth and it was reassuring to see that my body had rehydrated enough to afford the luxury of sweating.

While I sucked gratefully through the filter-tube on my bottle I read the refuge's information board. Apparently the little hamlet of La Sauceda had been a bandit lair before most of the thousand-strong population had fled during a bombardment at the start of the Civil War.

It was said that some of those old-time *bandoleros* were so dangerous that when they camped up in the sierras the wolves lit bonfires to keep them away. A few were so famous that they rose to the level of folk heroes. Perhaps the most notorious was Juan José Mingolla Gallardo, more commonly known as Pasos Largos (Long Steps). He may have been a regular visitor to La Sauceda before he was killed in a shoot-out with the Guardia Civil in 1932 in a cave about a day's walk east of the village. El Tempranillo (the Early Bird) – a child prodigy among bandits who killed his first man when he was 13 – was a feared king of the sierras about a century before. 'The king might rule in Spain,' he declared, 'but I rule the sierra.' El Tempranillo apparently became so popular with the masses that King Ferdinand VII finally granted him a pardon and a pension.

La Sauceda has a less fearsome reputation these days and in recent years some inhabitants had returned to take advantage of an idyllic rural highland retreat. At this season, however, the hamlet appeared to be abandoned and the only person I saw was a distant muleteer on the far side of the valley.

A working mule is a rare sight in Spain these days although a few are still used to harvest cork from the steep hillsides of Andalucía. Now that I could focus my mind on something other than my thirst, it occurred to me that these creatures might not have been mules but extremely large donkeys. Few people realize that Andalucía is home to one of the world's largest donkey breeds. The rare Andaluz-Cordobesa donkey often reaches a height of almost 1.6 metres at the shoulder (raising it officially far beyond the realm of the pony and into the league of horses). There had been less than a hundred examples of the breed surviving when, in 1989, a man called Pascual Rovira rescued five from a Cordoba slaughterhouse.

'The Andaluz-Cordobesa is the Mercedes of the ass world,' Rovira once told me, as we stared at a stallion that was by far the biggest donkey I'd ever seen. During the days of Moorish Andalucía such a donkey might have been worth 40 slaves.

'Unfortunately the poor Spanish *campesinos* realized that little North African donkeys were better suited to the small patches of land that surrounded their homesteads and were much cheaper to run,' Rovira explained. 'In effect they made the logical choice between a battered but serviceable Suzuki Jimny and a gas-guzzling Mercedes four-by-four.'

At the end of the Civil War in 1939, an estimated 1,250,000 Spanish donkeys were transporting cork, timber, charcoal, thatch, livestock products... and contraband of every type. It's been estimated that in the 1980s over a million were slaughtered. In 2019 an estimated 4.8 million donkeys were killed worldwide to feed a bizarre demand for donkey skin in China. The skin was boiled to create a jelly-like product known as ejiao – basically glue – which is said (without any medical proof) to have anti-aging health benefits and to release menstrual cramps. After reports (similarly unsubstantiated) were circulated that it improved sexual performance, donkey skin began to fetch in excess of €350 per kilo.

Pascual Rovira – whom Spanish writer Camilo José Cela called 'the donkey's advocate' – had become one of Spain's most visionary conservationists at the time I met the self-proclaimed 'assologist' in 2005.

'I can foresee a time when the donkey will take its place alongside the dove as an icon of peace,' he'd told me. I never quite knew when Rovira was joking – he was as tireless in his enthusiasm for 'assology' as he was imaginative in his use of media exposure.

Spanish newspapers had reported that he'd donated donkeys as gifts to the Spanish royal family, to his late friend Camilo José Cela, to Fidel Castro and to Bill Clinton. It seems that, in the latter case, the donkey advocate's natural mischievousness had gotten the better of him; he'd 'inadvertently' allowed Castro's 'Revolución' to impregnate Clinton's doe-eyed mare 'Milagritos'. Word of the affair was leaked (to the delight of Spanish reporters) and Clinton never made any attempt to collect his shop-soiled gift.

* * *

Sweating healthily again I continued at a jauntier pace and eventually crossed the head of the valley to descend slowly towards the *venta* at Puerto de Galiz. I'd hiked 37 kilometres in a little over 7 hours and breathed a sigh of relief when I saw cars parked outside the low terracotta-tiled building.

I'd been formulating a plan during the last hour of walking: first I'd order an iced Coke to take the edge off my thirst; then a *jarra* of Cruzcampo to really quench it; finally an icy gin and tonic for pure pleasure. Spain is arguably home to the best gin and tonics on the planet. While English bar staff fiddle around with the regulation measuring cups, most Spanish barmen simply continue to pour gin until you say *'pará'* (stop). If you happen to be tying a lace or checking your phone the glass is likely to end up almost full.

The tavern had a large covered terrace and, given the isolation, I was surprised to see five men in dusty work clothes and overalls gathered smoking around one table. I nodded in greeting and took a table in the corner where I could discreetly loosen my bootlaces and stretch my aching legs.

The barman came out to take my order and only when I was halfway through that blissfully icy G&T did I take time to look at the food menu. I was delighted to see that Venta de Galiz was a trekker's paradise full of the sort of hearty country dishes I might have dreamed about if only I'd had enough imagination: deer in mushroom sauce; partridge with roasted peppers; rabbit stew; oxtail cooked in wine...

My mouth watered just to consider the options and finally I decided on venison chorizo and a side order of homemade *croquetas*, followed by wild boar chops. When something seems too good to be true... well, it usually is.

'Sorry,' said the barman, as he wiped a cloth across the counter, 'the kitchen closed half an hour ago.'

Something in the business-like way he was polishing his workspace made me fear for the worst: 'So, errrm – what time do you stop serving drinks?'

'In half an hour.'

'Is there *anything* I can eat?'

The kitchen was locked and there was not even any cold meat or bread. An extremely sweet pastry covered in some kind of congealed jam had to serve as my evening meal. In my frustration I took an opportunity to order a second gin and tonic before it became too late even for that.

The workmen outside had apparently overheard the conversation and sympathized because, as I stood waiting for my drink, two of them came in and introduced themselves.

Miguel, the younger of the two men, had the sort of lisp that only a *Malagueño* (a native of Malaga) can pull off with any semblance of machismo. He introduced his elderly friend as Cristobal.

'*Christopher*,' the old man corrected proudly. 'In English I'm Christopher. Like Christopher Columbus!'

From the way Miguel apologized on behalf of the establishment for the lack of food I began to wonder if he might be the owner.

'I drove past you on the road today,' he said, jerking a thumb towards the vehicles across the road. 'Where did you walk from?'

'Jimena,' I replied.

'*¡Qué cojones!*' Christopher barked – What balls!

I was slightly taken aback until I realized that the old man's expression was one of undisguised respect rather than disbelief.

'All in one day?' Miguel asked. 'That's far.'

I smacked my aching thigh: 'It's more than far enough for today,' I agreed.

Suddenly we were interrupted by the sound of squealing tyres out on the road.

'*¡Me cago en la gran puta!*' A gasped oath came from one of the men outside and the three of us crammed into the doorway to see what was going on.

'I shit on the great whore!' the man said again. 'He nearly hit my car!'

Out on the narrow lane a white van – racing at top speed from the direction of Jimena – had skidded sideways across the road. The driver had jammed the brakes on at the last minute to stop his vehicle within centimetres of one of the parked cars. I assumed that it had been an accident but the manoeuvre had apparently been deliberate because now, with a grating of gears, the van jerked backwards – then brutally forwards again. A hairy forearm appeared in the open driver's window and a bearded face leaned out: *¡Cabrones!* it yelled.

The driver shot off towards the junction only to swerve sideways, snaking violently to skid almost to right-angles across the road. There was the sound of wild laughter from the passenger side as the vehicle accelerated down the road and out of sight.

'That crazy *hijo de puta* is going to kill someone,' Miguel muttered bitterly.

'Do you know them?' I asked.

The five incredulous faces turned towards me were all the answer I needed. Presumably the van was stolen. Either that or the driver was out of his mind on drugs or booze. If he'd been laying rubber down at that rate since Jimena he must have come close to sacrificing a full set of tyres by now. More importantly, it was astounding that he'd survived the mountain road.

But the witnesses around me had other things on their minds: 'He called us *cabrones*…' The man whose car had only narrowly been spared destruction sounded genuinely hurt by the insult. Then, turning to the barman: 'Call the police, Chema.'

Chema dutifully disappeared inside and a moment later we heard him muttering into the phone.

¡Qué locura! Christopher shook his head – What craziness!

* * *

'Anyway, where do you sleep tonight?' Miguel asked once we'd fully discussed the mystery of the white van and were none the wiser.

'I'm not sure. I have a hammock. I'll find somewhere farther down the road.' It occurred to me that I'd want to be far enough off the road to be well clear in case that maniac in the white van returned.

'Then it's settled,' said Miguel imperiously.

'What's settled?'

'You shall be a guest and sleep here. *¡Estás en tu casa!*' – You are in your house!

'I'm sorry but I can't sleep inside,' I said, fearing that I was being offered a room. 'I need to camp.' I couldn't possibly give in to temptation and sleep in a bed on what was only my second evening.

'Why camp?' Christopher asked.

'A promise I made to myself,' I said vaguely. 'Part of my walk.'

'*¡Cojones!*' he said again with an incredulous shake of his head. I tried to take it as a compliment to my determination, but this time I was less sure.

'Not a bed,' Miguel reassured me. 'They have no rooms but you can sleep here, on the terrace.'

I looked around, turning the options over in my mind. At least there was a thatched roof to keep the dew off. The steel supports didn't look sturdy enough for my hammock and the concrete floor would be far less accommodating than a patch of soft mountain grass.

'Ah I see. Thank you...' I paused. 'So, you're the owner?'

'No, no. But he can stay here for the night, right, Chema?'

Chema looked up from wiping a table: 'Of course, no problem. I'll just check with the boss.'

Invitations had been flying thick and fast so I was surprised to hear now that the boss was yet to be consulted.

Chema disappeared into a room behind the bar. I could hear a muffled conversation. I wandered outside to think the offer over... and to save any embarrassment should the invitation need to be revoked for some reason or another.

There was a farm gate on the opposite side of the road and beyond it a sparse forest of cork trees that were ideally spaced for my hammock. The grass under them had been grazed flat although I could see no livestock. A sign declared that this was yet another private hunting reserve. Perhaps this was the source of all that deer, rabbit, partridge and wild boar on the menu. The gate was unlocked though and I knew I could sleep well if I could get permission to string my hammock in there.

But the owner, who introduced himself as Carlos, was as hospitable as his customers and when I explained this plan roundly rejected my suggestion.

'You're walking to Galicia? *¡Vaya hombre, qué fuerte!*'

I smiled at his enthusiasm.

'Why don't you do something like that?' said Carlos as he nudged Miguel.

'Ni harto de vino,' the other man grimaced – Not even if I was full of wine.

'You'll be our guest and sleep here,' said Carlos. 'It's decided.'

Still I hesitated. I didn't want to appear rude but this was my second night on the trail and I'd been strolling past perfect hammock trees all day. I suggested that, since the evening was clear, I could sleep just as well under the stars as under a roof but Miguel rode roughshod over my objections with determined hospitality: 'It's all arranged. You'll sleep on the terrace and Chema will serve you breakfast – my invitation – tomorrow morning when he arrives.'

How then could I turn it down? It was the sort of hospitality I'd come to see as a part of the national temperament throughout many journeys in rural Spain.

One by one, the customers left with handshakes and well-wishes for my journey. Then Carlos locked the door and Chema promised to return in the morning and have breakfast ready at eight-thirty.

Once I was alone on the terrace, I created a sort of nest on a narrow stone ledge that served as a bench in the corner. I bunched my hammock and plastic roof to form a relatively padded mattress then I found an outdoor tap where I could bathe. The blister on my heel had split to form an oozing crater half the size of a beer coaster and I smothered my feet with antiseptic powder. The pain, bearable when I hiked, paradoxically increased when I removed my boots. I knew that I would have to look after my feet; an infection could mean the end of my trek.

Although there were still about 4 hours of daylight left I was grateful that there was no need to push on farther. Tired as I was, I knew that I wouldn't be able to sleep until dark. I lay for a while reading the last chapters of *A Tramp Abroad*. My phone's small screen made for tiring reading and, much as I enjoy the dry humour of Mark Twain's travelogues, I was already regretting my harsh decision to refrain from carrying a real paperback.

As I read, I kept one ear cocked for the sound of a van tearing back up the hill. It crossed my mind that maybe Carlos was happy to have someone on security duty that night. From what little I'd seen of the van driver he was a big guy and he was highly aggressive. There was little doubt about that. I wouldn't have appreciated a scuffle with him at the best of times. Throw the unpredictability of drugs into the mix and I really wouldn't have fancied my chances. And there were two of them. I hoped that to Carlos's way of thinking I wasn't honour-bound to repay my night's lodging by defending his *venta* like a lonely little Rorke's Drift.

On the opposite side of the road there was a huge free-standing boulder. When I'd investigated earlier I'd seen that the front of it was protected with a picket fence and decorated with a small garden gate. It was just turning to dusk when I shuffled across in my flip-flops to investigate the little shrine that was decorated with wreaths and bunches of wild flowers and garish bouquets of plastic roses. A statue of Nuestra Señora de los Milagros (Our Lady of Miracles), in her customary blue robe, stood in the centre of the shrine.

I certainly don't consider myself religious and the motivation for my trek was far from spiritual. Nevertheless, here I was at the start of an intimidating challenge. In a moment of weakness I apologized for my hypocrisy in having the effrontery to make a request despite an almost lifelong silence: 'Would it be possible,' I asked, 'just this once if you keep the rain off my head for as long as possible?'

It was probably an unusual petition for her to hear. Doubtless, in this farming country the request would usually be for *more* rain rather than *less*. It occurred to me that maybe she'd grant it for the sheer novelty of the thing. I was less worried about the midsummer heat of the plains than about having to camp in highland storms and to endure soggy walks with my kit weighed down with water.

As I walked back across the gravel car park, my flip-flops scuffling over the deep skid-marks of the van, I wondered if maybe I should also have asked the Virgin to keep any drug-addled crazies at bay. Normally I feel entirely at ease sleeping in the wilderness. Had I been ensconced in my hammock among the cork trees I need not have feared any number of drug-addled crazies in white vans.

As I lay on my stone shelf turning the situation over in my mind it occurred to me that maybe he had a grudge against the establishment. Why drive all this way, otherwise?

I tried to recall if there had been a note of particular venom in his parting cry.

¡Cabrones! echoed in my head as I fell asleep.

* * *

My ideal strategy was to get walking by 7 o'clock, before the heat began to build. Day three started with an enforced lie-in, however. I felt that I should be patient and await the late breakfast that had so generously been promised.

Fortunately, I had some sachets of 3-in-1 (an instant coffee, sugar and milk powder combination) in my pack along with a small folding cup that concertina-ed into itself. There would be many times ahead on the trail when I'd wish I could have taken a small camping cooker. I habitually hiked with a tiny tin snap-open cooker (the kind favoured by the SAS) which was fuelled with smokeless fuel tablets. One tablet – smaller than an overcoat button – could boil a cup of water. But in midsummer much of the landscape I'd be crossing was a tinderbox just waiting for this sort of unguarded flame. At the last moment I'd reluctantly made the decision to leave my cooker behind and so now needed to subsist on lukewarm 3-in-1 shaken up into a sorry sort of frappuccino in my concertina-cup. So much of Spain is incinerated each summer in bushfires that campfires are strictly prohibited in most wilderness areas.

Had I started walking I could have covered most of the 15 kilometres to the next village by the time the tavern opened. Miguel had been incredibly hospitable in his insistence that I should want for nothing, however, and I couldn't bring myself to shun his kind invitation to breakfast.

It was Saturday morning and the little terrace was bustling with Lycra-clad cyclists and leather-clad bikers by the time my breakfast was served. I was amazed that it was so busy but its location, set among the spectacular valleys of Los Alcornocales Park, had apparently turned the tavern into a destination in its own right. It might also have had something to do with the hearty breakfasts that were served: coffee, fresh orange juice and several huge hunks of toasted bread were served with three types of homemade *manteca*, like a type of lard, flavoured with chorizo, loin and crackling. There were already about 15 cyclists and five motorcyclists by the time I shook hands with Chema and Carlos and hauled my pack onto my back.

'*Que le vaya bien,*' one of the cyclists called – Go well.

* * *

I'd only been walking for half an hour when I narrowly missed stepping on a viper. I'm not particularly nervous about snakes but the bite of a viper is said to be extremely painful as well as potently venomous. It would have been highly unlikely to kill me, but it would certainly have brought my trek to a premature end.

The snake was over a metre long, lying unconcernedly at the edge of the road. It surprised me with its reluctance to move even when I stepped within a few centimetres of its curled tail. I don't consider myself superstitious but it crossed my mind that early wayfarers might have considered it an ominous sign; a warning maybe from Our Lady of Miracles that I was about to be punished for my presumption in requesting her protection.

Less than a minute after I cautiously side-stepped the serpent, a hoopoe darted across my path in a shimmer of gold and black. The sweeping crest that lay flat in flight sprung up on landing, as if the bird was surprised to touch down safely on the uppermost branch of an oak. To my untrained eyes these Eurasian hoopoes were identical to the ones I'd seen so often when I'd been training for this trek in South Africa – jogging through the nature reserve near our house, with small herds of zebras and wildebeest cantering ahead. Hoopoes are relatively rare in Europe but I'd see these birds from time to time as I trekked through Andalucía and Extremadura. Although they gave me a jolt of homesickness, I began to think of them as good omens. A sighting invariably lent me an added burst of energy when I needed it.

I was now making good headway and was moving steadily downhill for the first time since I left Gibraltar. Although the blisters hurt more going downhill, I was surprised that stiffness had still not crept into the muscles of my legs.

The road was shimmering in a heat-haze that I associated more with Africa. When I crossed the strangely named Viaducto del Sapo (Viaduct of the Toad) a midday sun that felt more African than European chased me into the shade of a road-tunnel, like a mouse dashing into its burrow under the shadow of a hawk. I paused in the echoing coolness to drop my pack on the ground and to savour the first hint of a breeze I'd felt since I started walking that morning. The tunnel also reminded me of Africa with its profusion of mud-wasp nests, antlion burrows, and fat semi-transparent geckos – none of which I would expect to see later on in northern Spain.

As I poured one of my sachets of energy-enhancing rehydration powder into my water bottle a delivery van squealed to a halt and reversed back to me.

'Where are you going?' the driver shouted. 'Need a lift?'

I could almost feel the breeze of the van's aircon tempting me.

'No thanks,' I called back. 'I'm happy walking.' Only as I said it did I realize how completely true it was. The offer of hospitality and support was appreciated but I suddenly realized that I was entirely happy to be doing what I'd set out to do. Despite the burgeoning heat and twinging blisters, I was *exactly* where I wanted to be. Even the feeling of homesickness seemed like something to be savoured.

I stepped out of the northern side of the tunnel back into the blinding glare and onto another viaduct overlooking the wide, arid plains surrounding the rapidly shrinking Guadalcacín Reservoir.

The view here too struck me as powerfully reminiscent of Africa. A herd of black cattle trudged like buffalo along the muddy water while the slopes were covered with acacia and prickly pear (sometimes known as Barbary fig). Vultures threw wheeling shadows across the cracked earth as they rode the thermals.

Algar sprawled across two hills, the lower slopes of which were blanketed with rows of olives that formed a patchwork of silver-green corduroy under the snowy-white cap of the hilltop settlement.

I hurried on across the first hill which appeared to be purely residential and devoid of bars or shops. In the saddle below I stopped at a petrol station where I pushed through the flyscreen door to find the drinks cooler I'd been dreaming of for the last 2 hours. I sat on the curb, while a man at the petrol pump tried to avoid making eye contact with the aged guttersnipe with the can of Pepsi pressed to his forehead.

There was nothing to eat, however, and the cashier told me that I'd need to climb to the plaza at the top of the next hill to find a meal. It would be worth the detour since I planned to pass the mid-afternoon hours here anyway.

As I dragged myself onwards up the whitewashed street towards the centre of Algar, a three-wheel Vespa car blurted past me, hauling a cloud of hot dust. Other than this the village seemed deserted. Shuttered windows were clenched like heavy eyelids. I imagined that the villagers were in their darkened rooms, shooing away the fat flies that bothered their siestas.

I found a table on the shady side of Plaza de la Constitution and ordered the largest glass of beer available. In Spain beer is usually served in small glasses which is very logical in a climate where your drink is likely to lose its chill before you can finish it. The English side of my character was unable to resist the feeling of well-being that was inherent in the solid heft of a pint glass. In Spain the largest beer glass is usually a *jarra* (literally a jug, but better described as a tankard). It falls just a little short of an English pint and I was certain in any case that I'd finish it long before it lost its chill.

Whenever I imagined the trek, I'd pictured myself sipping *vino tinto* and tucking into hearty three-course *menús del día*. During midsummer in this hottest part of the country I was finding that a frosty glass of Cruzcampo was more appealing than tepid red wine.

I'd joked to my wife that my daydreams of the trek centred completely on a countrywide chain of pretty little plazas and endless glasses of wine. I was dimly aware, of course, that there would have to be some hours of actual *walking* between those plazas. I just chose not to think about them.

There was already proving to be ample walking. I'd already covered 110 kilometres, after all, in the first three days of walking.

As far as those culinary fantasies were concerned, however, things weren't working out quite as planned. Half a week had passed since my last proper meal – a steak-and-ale pie paired with a pint of Kilkenny at a Gibraltar pub the night before I started walking. My plan to fuel my journey with great plates of hearty midday sustenance was falling sadly flat... and once again the kitchen was inexplicably closed.

The best that I could find in Algar's Plaza de la Constitution was a plate of octopus salad and some olives and bread.

Fortunately, Algar's little plaza lived up to expectations in other ways. It would be too hot to start walking for several hours yet and this would be an ideal place to soak up the peace of a Saturday afternoon.

Hundreds of swallows shot like darts across the square of blue sky overhead and a pair of storks clattered their bills on the church roof with a sound like falling tiles. While they preened atop their gigantic nest, the swallows swooped tirelessly into gaps among the sticks. Was there a squatter-community of swallows living in there I wondered, or were they merely harvesting bugs?

Other swallows had set up home in their little inverted mud igloos under the eaves of surrounding houses and the town hall on the opposite side of the plaza.

Once I'd finished my lunch, I wandered across the square to read a signboard outside the church. Apparently, the village's name came from *Al-gar* (Arabic for 'the cave') after nearby cave settlements that were occupied as early as Neolithic times. The village itself was founded in 1773 by Domingo López de Carvajal, a Spanish traveller who narrowly survived a shipwreck and built Algar in honour of his saviour the Virgin of Guadalupe.

The church door creaked with a tormented lament, like the deck planks of a foundering galleon, and I stepped into the cavern-like chill of the Church of Santa Maria de Guadalupe. There was a silence in here – like the echoing stillness of an underground cavern

– that was so profound that I could hear the wax sputtering on a candle beside a silver cross in front of the Baroque altar.

I was reminded of V. S. Pritchett's response to such places, which had a characteristic bitterness that I always found curious in a writer who clearly loved this country. 'There is nothing more sinister and terrifying than the mounted, lance-like silver cross,' he pointed out. 'The Spaniard likes Jesus because he was gashed and bled. For the same reason he likes bulls.'

By the time I got back to my table a family of four had arrived on the terrace. The two small boys, twins in Real Madrid football jerseys, ran off to kick their ball across the paved expanse of the plaza. The adults and a teenage daughter all wore green bandanas around their necks and the smallest child (perhaps five years old) was resplendent in a primrose flamenco dress and bright yellow dancing shoes. A silver plastic *peineta*, like a crown adorned with yellow roses, completed the look but, despite the ostentatious air of adulthood, she rarely removed the dummy from her mouth.

'The village fiesta starts today.' Papá was obviously surprised when I complimented the dress and asked the reason for the bandanas. Why else would I be here after all? *'Fiesta de la Virgen de Guadalupe,'* he added as if it would jog my memory.

It was still early, he told me, but later in the afternoon the whole town would be busy. I realized then that the kitchen was probably closed because the staff were preparing for the afternoon rush. At four in the afternoon *vacas bravas* (fighting cows) would be released into the streets to get the fiesta underway in typical Andaluz style.

When Papá ordered a round of drinks, Mamá took the opportunity to ask for a cigarette lighter from the waiter.

'Are you running with the *vacas*?' I asked Papá. I could guess from the look of his sporty Nikes what the answer was likely to be.

'He *always* runs,' his wife confirmed with obvious pride. 'Never misses a year.'

'I don't like bullfights,' the man told me. 'But I love running.'

'Tiene cicatrices,' his wife interrupted – He has scars.

With simulated annoyance the man sighed and pulled up his shirtsleeve to show the marks of stitches across his shoulder: 'Not from here,' he said. 'From another village.'

When the waiter had offloaded the tray, the woman took the borrowed lighter, walked briskly across the plaza to the chapel. I guessed that she'd be lighting a candle beside that 'sinister' silver cross – petitioning the Virgin to protect her husband from a new batch of scars that afternoon.

The little flamenco dancer sucked noisily on the froth at the bottom of her milkshake glass while her big sister stared into her phone.

'Are you going to run?' Papá asked me now. He cast a dubious glance at my hiking boots.

'I lived in Pamplona for ten years,' I told him, '... but I stopped when I realized that each year the bulls got faster.'

It was a standard joke but he had the decency to chuckle. It was partly true in any case: I ran with the bulls in the narrow streets of Pamplona more than 40 times but the last time I'd been hit squarely. The bull had picked me up between his horns and carried me 10 metres down the road without even slowing. I'd narrowly missed being crushed when he tripped and fell over the top of me. I was lucky to escape with a score of cuts and bruises and just a slice of scalp that I'd left on the cobbles.

In truth my taste for the *encierro* (the 'bull run') had long waned before that incident. I couldn't support the bullfight and had felt increasingly uncomfortable about the undeniable connection of the bull run with the so-called art of bullfighting. (The old bull-runner's excuse that it was 'a chance for the bulls to even the score' had never really rung true in my mind.)

I didn't want to get into a discussion about all this and, in any case, by now Mamá had returned from the church. She too was clearly happy when her husband assured her that the street was not going to be cluttered up by a clumsy tourist in hiking boots. I'd be content merely to watch from the sidelines.

Grateful not to have to suffer the (once familiar) feeling of increasing nerves at an impending stampede in a narrow, cobbled street, I sat contentedly as the shadow of the church steeple probed across the plaza like an accusing finger.

The little princess in the yellow flamenco outfit removed her dummy once in a while to make desultory gurgling sucks at her milkshake. Her older sister, around 12 years old, was clearly at that age of uncertainty as she approached adolescence. Unsure whether she was supposed to act as an adult or a child, she checked her hair in her phone and practised pouting selfie poses. Bored with that – but even more so with the conversation of her parents – she turned to clap patronizingly at the antics of the two small soccer players. There was an air of supercilious patience about her cheerleading that went unnoticed by the twins and, flattered by the attention of their big sister, they dashed evermore frantically across the baking paving stones.

* * *

It was mid-afternoon when I paid my bill and shouldered my pack to walk down to watch the stampede of the cows through Algar. Ideally I still needed to kill an hour or two for the heat of the sun to diminish but I was already beginning to get an inkling that this trek was going to be as much a test of patience as of endurance.

The lanes behind the church were lined with citrus trees, and oranges were so plentiful that they were simply left to be trodden into the cobbles. Finally I discovered where everyone was on this strangely deserted day of fiestas. White sheets had been pulled across from balcony to balcony to shade much of the length of Calle Real and tables had been laid out, like loosely linked cabooses, along the length of this tunnel.

Neighbours and families sat noisily tucking into dishes that (despite my octopus salad) made my mouth water. I tried not to stare at the banquet that was laid across the tables or at the women who paraded with swaying hips sheathed in polka-dot flamenco dresses.

'The running takes place along Calle del Llano up to the Plaza de Toros,' an old man informed me between puffs on his cigar. 'Should be around four o'clock, *más o menos*.'

I decided to wait around to witness whatever drama would take place between the heavy timber barriers that had been set up along Calle del Llano. Four o'clock came and went. Then 5 o'clock and I was still sitting on these barricades chatting with the villagers and waiting for the cows to be delivered. There were no bulls and I was happy to hear that, though the cows would run into the bullring, there'd be no death in the afternoon that day in Algar.

Although the animals running would not be real *toros*, I knew enough to have a lot of respect for the females of the fighting bull species. Ancient tradition has it that a fighting bull gets his courage primarily from the cow that bore him, while his strength comes from the bull that sired him. At the ranches where they're raised, it is the cows that are tested for bravery in an often brutal trial known as the *tentadero*. Only the females that continue to brave the fearsome lances of the picadors are deemed suitable for breeding. The cows that make the rounds of village festivals are often fearless professionals, travelling from village to village, like angry gladiators.

'Only a fool underestimates the cows,' an aficionado had once warned me. 'Unlike the *toros* which will almost never have had contact with a man on foot, the *vacas* know all the tricks necessary to run you down.'

Finally, around five-thirty, a truck arrived and the clatter of hooves and horns from within confirmed that this was the bovine consignment. Now it appeared that the mayor had to call a veterinarian to sign the necessary permits.

The runners waiting in the street took full advantage of the delay for an extended opportunity to posture and stretch in front of the girls in their flamenco dresses. The man I'd chatted to while he was having lunch with his family in Plaza de la Constitution was doing flamboyant leg stretches and lecturing a group of young women who were draped over the barricades.

'Don't lean through *la barrera*,' he told them. 'That space must be kept clear for runners.'

'*¿Qué más da?*' one replied, as if she'd heard it all before – What's the difference?

'*¿Qué más da?*' he mimicked. 'Well, I'll tell you. If I jump up on that fence to get away and you get kicked in the head you'll say it was my fault...'

I figured he was just passing the time with a little drama. After all, when the cows shot out of that truck and started galloping up the hill he wouldn't be caught hanging around this far down the route.

But when I finally saw the first cow shooting into view, like a furious four-legged black cannonball, I was extremely grateful that my blisters and aching legs – and perhaps a little simple common-sense – had conspired to keep me out of the street. My boots were hardly suited to running in any case and to risk injury so early in my trek would be insanely foolhardy. But in my heart I knew that these were just excuses. As the saying goes, you shouldn't let anything stop you but fear.

This was not like the usual *encierros* where six bulls typically run in a herd. The natural herd mentality means that most runs tend to be relatively *limpio* (clean) with the animals running in a tight group. *Limpio* is a relative term in the world of bull-running since, in the famous runs at Pamplona for example, the situation would invariably be one of blind panic and even in a run that could be described as 'very clean', 30 or 40 people might be treated for injuries. Only maybe once in every ten or

20 runs would you see the moments of intense life-and-death drama when a single bull would be separated from the herd, sometimes even turning back down the street, goring anything that moves.

I'd imagined that the cows would also run as a herd until I saw the first jet-black demon shoot out alone, to go ricocheting up the street, sweeping men up on her horns. It all happened so quickly that there was very little time for a runner to get out of her way. She barrelled into the doorway directly across the street from me, narrowly missing a young man who instinctively pirouetted out of harm's way. Then, in less time than it took to blink, she'd hammered into the barrier by my feet, almost knocking me off balance. It's been said that a fighting bull can accelerate quicker than a racehorse and can turn tighter than a polo pony. The cow had zigzagged along the six blocks to the bullring in less than a minute to leave the street looking like a warzone.

'*Muy limpio,*' an aficionado next to me nodded knowledgeably as a few young men helped their wounded friends out of the street. It had been a very 'clean' run.

* * *

I'd only covered 16 kilometres that day and wanted to cover a lot more ground before nightfall so I couldn't wait around to see the five other cows.

Walking back out of town, I was surprised to see that the twins were – with the obsessiveness and endless energy of the young – still kicking their football around on the Plaza de la Constitution. The rest of the family were nowhere to be seen but an olive-skinned older boy was now out-classing them in their kick-around. He called out to the twins – words that I couldn't make out – as their little triangle struggled to keep the ball in the air. I wondered what a game of 'keepy-uppies' was called in Spanish.

The older boy wore a red soccer shirt with a green star across the chest and I guessed that he was one of Spain's large Moroccan population. Official estimates say that there are around 800,000 Moroccans settled legally in Spain.

Just the month before I set off on my trek, 43 would-be immigrants, from Morocco and sub-Saharan Africa, had died when their boat sank during the voyage to the Spanish Canary Islands. According to the Spanish interior ministry an average of over a thousand immigrants had arrived by sea each day during 2021 and an organization called Caminando Fronteras (which tracks data from boats in distress in the Straits) estimated that more than 4,000 immigrants were killed or disappeared during the same year trying to make their way to Spain illegally by boat.

It was not a new thing. Such tragedies had been taking place for decades. Back in 2001, I'd travelled to Tangier on assignment for *CNN Traveller* magazine and had met with sub-Saharan immigrants waiting for an opportunity to make illegal (and potentially fatal) crossings. Later that same year I headed down to the Andalucían beaches to report from the European shore on the heart-breaking story of the mafia-run 'Death Boats'.

I'd driven my old Jeep down from my home in Madrid and arrived in the port town of Tarifa on the morning of a particularly large landing. A contact at the Spanish coastguards told me that a fleet of 20 Zodiac inflatables had taken advantage of a smuggler's moon to motor out from the Moroccan coast the night before. They'd carried no lights that could betray them to coastal patrols and in each boat 60 or 70 shrouded figures had strained their eyes for the looming bulk of a tanker or the sweeping spotlights of a Spanish launch.

Soon after the unmistakable silhouette of The Rock rose out of the eastern horizon, they would have made out the first pale strands of European beaches. At more or less the same moment, the fleet was picked up on radar monitors in Tarifa and border-patrol speedboats and Guardia Civil Land Cruisers began to close in. Almost 300 immigrants (and boat crew) were caught in the noose. Best case scenario was that a thousand-strong landing party had evaded capture and made a difficult night-time landing on the wave-smashed beaches to fan out across the desolate hills near Europe's southernmost point. But this was an optimistic estimate that took no account for body-counts because nobody would ever know how many had drowned.

'Last night eleven boats simply disappeared from the radar screens,' a spokesman at the Association of Moroccan Immigrants and Workers in Spain had told me. 'Official estimates are that no less than a thousand people have drowned already this year but many more might have simply been swept out into the Atlantic without our knowledge.'

Twenty years later it was still happening almost on a daily basis.

'People have to realize that there's a war going on here,' the spokesman had told me. The enemy in that war were the mafia organizations who profited from the trafficking in which immigrants paid as much as US$3,000 for a seat on an open boat. Often this was financed on an extorted promise that the payment would be made from future earnings. You don't renege on that sort of agreement when the mafia knows exactly where to find your loved ones.

The mafia originally used traditional and often dangerously un-seaworthy wooden fishing boats. Known as *pateras*, they were bulky and slow. Worse than that, from the mafia's point of view, they were traceable through their registration numbers and so it was necessary to bribe Moroccan officials. Then inflatable Zodiacs began to show up. They needn't be registered and could be transported in the back of a truck. Once on a remote beach, they could be inflated and fitted with a motor within minutes. They were much faster than the *pateras* but, loaded with a full complement of 60 or so immigrants, they sometimes only rode a few centimetres above the choppy waves. It was an incredibly risky way to cross one of the world's busiest shipping lanes and boats were often lost with everyone aboard. With profits of US$80,000 per voyage it was a risk that the mafia bosses were willing to take.

Drownings had become so common that some Andalucían councils had to request emergency budgets to finance the burial of the unidentified bodies that were regularly washed up on their beaches.

The best that these fugitives could hope for would be to arrive, cold and wet, among the dark dunes that rise along Spain's so-called Costa de la Luz (Coast of Light). They must then cross a hostile cactus-covered hinterland, where they must avoid not only the police but also criminal gangs – frequently their own countrymen – who would sometimes kidnap them in the hope of ransoming them to their families. It was not only men who risked the crossing but countless women too. A shocking number would be seven or eight months pregnant, deliberately timing their arrival so that their babies could be born on European soil. Many women were tricked or coerced into prostitution by the same mafia drivers who'd been paid to assist their passage towards the north.

'You have to bear in mind,' a police officer in Tarifa told me, 'that these people arrive disorientated and very scared, desperate for someone – anyone – to help them get them away from the beach. It's enough merely to open the car door and they'll jump in.'

I'd sometimes be struck during the weeks of my Spanish trek by a feeling of guilt; while I was merely playing at being a vagabond I was aware that out on those same plains there might be hundreds of real fugitives, desperately trying to get away from this frontier country in the hope of finding a better life.

* * *

I walked steadily onwards for an hour and a half among rolling hills covered with olive groves and cactus and it was hard to resist a sundowner stop when a bar in the village of La Perdiz enticed me with the promise of a gin and tonic. The inhabitants of La Perdiz (The Partridge) were celebrating the season's crop of First Communions. Little princesses in lacy white dresses and sequined shoes trotted around, mascara and crimson lipstick at odds with chubby nine-year-old faces. Helicopter moms – dressed to kill in hip-hugging skirts or skin-tight jeggings – hovered over them on towering stilettos. I felt woefully underdressed in dusty bush shorts and grubby T-shirt as I sipped my drink and waited for dusk to settle on the village. I wanted to kill time until there was just sufficient light to climb the hill undetected.

During a recce of the area on Google Earth I'd come across a Roman ruin on the hillside just north of La Perdiz. It would mean a detour of several kilometres but there was something irresistibly enticing about the thought of camping among the spooky ruins of a Roman garrison.

The setting sun was throwing its last rays through the gnarled olive trees and onto the arches of an ancient cistern when I reached the top of the hill a kilometre and a half north of La Perdiz. I'd crept past an old farmhouse and scrambled hurriedly up the hill, praying that any farm dogs would be comfortably settled for the evening, leaving the hillside to the feral creatures of the night – myself included. I wasn't sure of the legality of camping here. I prided myself in leaving any sleeping spot so it would be hard for anyone to tell that I'd even been there. Nevertheless, my nerves were set on edge more by the thought of being run out of town as a 'fugitive' than by any thought of ghosts.

'A homeless man has no time to be superstitious,' the legendary hobo W. H. Davies wrote in *The Autobiography of a Super-Tramp*, 'he fears the living, and not the dead.' The Welsh writer had tramped far and wide across the United States in the late 1800s. Spurning regular work, he'd lived mostly from begging and slept wherever he could in hobo-jungles, graveyards and, not infrequently, in jails.

I'd read that the Romans had established their garrison on this hillside around 200 BCE and had occupied the spot for the next 600 years. Then the Almohads (Berbers from North Africa) became the landlords for the following two centuries. The site – rarely visited, and uninhabited for 1,400 years – is still known locally as Cerro del Moro (the Peak of the Moor).

Three days had passed since I left Gibraltar but, as I wandered among the ruins, it was easy to imagine that I'd walked back a thousand years. The hilltop must have been an important strategic point, commanding views across the Guadalete valley on one side and the Majaceite valley on the other. Most importantly, in an area where permanent water was a valuable commodity, the site was blessed with a spring that was capable of filling the 2-million-litre cistern. This *castellum aquae* (water castle) had been fenced off at some time in the past but the fence had fallen inward. I explored the arching tunnels that led into the cistern but – despite a surprisingly chilly wind that was cutting across the hilltop – I was reluctant to claim one of these nooks for the night. My reluctance was due as much to the fact that such alcoves looked like ideal habitats for snakes as to respect for the site. I explored other sheltered spots at the foot of the 3-metre-tall garrison walls. Masonry that had survived two millennia could surely be expected to survive one more blustery night but I knew that if the wind picked up, those several tonnes of balanced boulders would, metaphorically speaking, weigh heavily on my mind.

The entire hillside was so jumbled with rocks, tumbled walls and clambering roots that it would have been impossible to pitch a tent. The leeward slope – which would have been far too steep for a tent in any case – was covered with ancient olive trees that had great potential for a hammock. In Spain such trees frequently live over a thousand years. (A Spanish database lists more than 4,400 millennia-old olive trees and the oldest in the country, a national treasure, was believed to have been planted 1,700 years ago.)

I strung my hammock between the gnarled trunks of two relative youngsters which had probably been standing side by side for a mere two or three centuries.

The hammock's side pocket contained my toiletries: deodorant, a block of soap (which served also as shampoo and detergent for clothes) and a small tube of toothpaste. There was also a bamboo toothbrush that I'd sawn in half. This was partly as a light-hearted reminder of trans-Atlantic racing yachts where the skippers forced their crews to go to such weight-saving extremes... and partly to serve as a timely reminder each morning to keep my own weight to an absolute minimum.

I cleaned my teeth and treated the day's crop of blisters then lay back blissfully to enjoy the view over the distant lights of La Perdiz and across the plains towards the Guadalacín Reservoir.

My boots hung by their laces from the hammock near my feet and I used a carabiner to clip my backpack to the end near my head. I tend to sleep extremely soundly in a hammock but even so it was unlikely that anyone could have removed either without waking me.

Spain is basically a very safe country but Spanish bandits have traditionally been portrayed as almost diabolically cunning. There's a delightful incident in *Don Quixote* when a befuddled Sancho Panza awakes on the ground with just his saddle and four long stakes strewn around him; a bandit had carefully propped Sancho's saddle up on four stilts while he slept... and then quietly walked his beloved donkey out from underneath. Apparently Sancho also slept soundly because it was only when he awoke in the morning and stretched that he tumbled to the ground.

I was only woken once during the night by a brisk wind that flapped at my hammock. Even through the moonless blackness I could sense tendrils of mist dashing across the hillside around me, like a silent army in skirmishing order.

* * *

I was surprised in the murky light of dawn by the clang of what sounded like chains being dragged over the fallen masonry of the Roman city. Perhaps I'd been dreaming because my first thought was of a slave caravan and it took several moments before I recognized the sound as the hollow tolling of goat bells.

The animals were as yet unseen beyond the soup-like mist that was draped across the slope. I unzipped my sleeping bag and hurriedly broke camp, bundling my sleeping bag into its stuff-sack, unclipping the hammock and shoving it into the big mesh pocket on the outside of my pack. I peered into the mist, scanning for a first glimpse of movement on the hillside, as I hurriedly laced my boots. I wondered if the animals would be accompanied by goatherds or perhaps by the mastiff dogs that even today sometimes sport vicious spiked collars as defence for fighting wolves. I walked briskly down the hill, scanning the ground for a hefty stick. My route zigzagged between trees that were large enough to clamber up at the first hint of angry barking. The farm dogs I'd seen so far didn't look like the sort of creatures that you could make bargains with and I knew from past experience that, in a land where wolves and bandits were once common, the huge mastiffs have an inbred tendency to be over-protective of their charges.

As I neared the farmhouse at the bottom of the hill two smaller dogs sprinted barking from the yard. When I pulled a stick out of the tangled verge they backed off. I hurried on my way, keeping my protective stick with me all the way back into La Perdiz village.

It was an unsettling thought that I was starting this new day – as I'd ended the last – feeling like a fugitive.

The bars would not be firing up their coffee machines for at least another hour so I sat in a patch of sunlight against the whitewashed wall of the Chapel of Nuestra Señora del Carmen and prepared cold coffee in my collapsible cup. It was still only 7 o'clock by the time I'd taped and powdered my feet and set off to cover the 15 kilometres that lay between me and Arcos de la Frontera.

I promptly descended into a valley where what seemed to be an entire plain of sunflowers were turned towards me as if staring in curiosity. The blue Andalucían sky and crisp freshness of the morning made me feel grateful for the early wake-up call and I was cheerful and strong. All along the verge of the road, columbine, morning glory and sweet sultan shimmered as their petals caught the dawn breeze. Lavender and gladioli strived to reach the sunlight through a haze of white daisies and the swaying scarlet disks of poppies that reached towards a forget-me-not sky. It was like walking through the sort of Hallmark card that you might pick for a dowager aunt.

Sometimes there's a price to pay for such beauty though. With my eyes fixed on these colours I almost failed to notice a small, perfectly camouflaged viper that basked at the edge of the road. I noticed it at the last moment and danced hurriedly aside. For the second time in 24 hours, I made a mental note to try to be more observant in future. It was only a small specimen, but I remembered a herpetologist in Africa telling me that young snakes are often more dangerous than adults since they haven't yet learned to conserve their precious venom. Apparently a young snake will sometimes inject a full dose, which might be life-threatening, when an experienced adult would inflict only a warning bite.

An hour later and I'd already left that florid valley for hills that had been bleached the colour of a lion's hide. The crumbling strip of tarmac I was walking along now looked more like a lava field. Fissures ran in sinuous lines as if the entire road might simply melt and slip down the hillside in a syrupy black blob.

The heat continued to increase through the morning and I stopped more frequently to sit in the shade. It was almost midday when the town of Arcos de la Frontera finally appeared up ahead, sprawled like the dusty remnants of a glacier across the crest of a steep hill.

My walk down to the valley floor was slowed by a shepherd driving his flock of scraggy sheep onto the grazing land along the banks of the Rio Guadalete. I stopped to familiarize myself with the skyline using the map on my phone: dominating the hilltop was the Basílica de Santa María de la Asunción and next to it I could make out the spot that was marked as Mirador del Coño. I knew that *coño*, the Spanish 'C-word' for the female genitalia, was used so commonly as an expletive as to have lost its sexual meaning almost entirely but it was bizarre that one of Arco's major landmarks should have been christened with such apparent vulgarity.

A near vertical climb – steep enough to shove my blisters painfully back against the heel of my boots – led me on a tortuous path towards a row of squat houses that lined the ledge like fat pigeons roosting on a telephone wire. Only in Spain could a road with several centuries of history be known as Calle Nueva (New Street) but Arcos – Colonia Arcensis to the Romans – was already ancient when the Muslims established the city they knew as Medina Arkosch here.

The stroll through the whitewashed streets was soothing after the glaring heat of the hills and I was grateful for the overhanging balconies, like swallows' nests on a cave wall, that threw their shade into the alleyways.

At a small general store I bought some chorizo and bread and then sat on a nearby bench, next to a bronze bust commemorating the local poet Julio Mariscal Montes, to savour a bag of plums and a can of Coke. A Sunday-morning street-sweeper nodded as he worked his way past me, the soft swish of his broom purging the town of the evidence of any minor Saturday-night sins.

Feeling revitalized, I gave myself the luxury of temporarily lessening the weight on my back by pouring out the last of my warm water, figuring I would get more before I moved onwards from the shelter of the town. It was a mistake and a timely reminder never to take water for granted. In less than half an hour I'd descended to the outskirts of Arcos and was walking through a quarter that seemed to be deserted. There were no more shops or bars and the only fountain, in the centre of a little plaza that was baked like old bones, had long since dried up. In this residential ghost-town every house appeared to be either permanently deserted or at least shuttered securely against the heat.

Just as I was close to giving up hope – seething with frustration and considering the hike back up to town – I spotted two figures. An old man was talking across the wrought-iron railings to a woman who held a dripping watering-can among the few terracotta pots of geraniums that decorated the tiled patio.

The old man was in full rant and the woman, in housecoat and slippers, appeared to be anxious for an opportunity to get back to the shade of her open doorway.

So I opted for the old man: 'With your permission *señor*…'

'What do you want?'

'I was hoping to find some water in the fountain back there. Perhaps you can tell me where I could fill my canteens.'

I knew that in this region it would be almost taboo to refuse a request of water to a traveller. It was just my luck, however, that I'd struck upon one of those old gentlemen who pride themselves on being 'something of a character'. What's more, I'd struck upon him on a particularly quiet Sunday morning when he had little to do but to impress that character more fully upon the lady next door.

'There's no fountain here,' he replied shortly.

'Nowhere to find water…?' I stalled. 'So I'd need to walk back into town…'

I didn't want to give the idea that I was on the scrounge: 'I could pay for a bottle if there is somewhere I can buy some.'

'The bars are closed. *Es domingo*.' In case I hadn't noticed.

I took a deep breath: *'No quiero molestarle...'* – I don't want to 'molest you' – I used the formal Spanish term to emphasize politeness, 'but could I ask you to fill my bottles?'

'You don't want to molest me,' he said, with a sidelong smile at the neighbour who'd been staring silently from face to face since this interaction began. 'But you *are* molesting me. I don't have a garden tap.'

'Okay then,' I mustered my heartiest smile as I started to turn back towards the town centre. *'No pasa nada. Muchas gracias.'*

'Give me!' he called.

'I'm sorry?'

'¡Dame las botellas, joder!' – Gimme the bottles, for fuck's sake.

Gratefully taking my bottles back through the wrought-iron fence I asked what I owed him.

'Estamos en paz,' he shrugged – We're quits, or more literally, we're at peace.

With my canteens finally filled and a smiling *'buen viaje'* ('safe travels') from the old man I went on my way.

Time-consuming as the whole saga had been, I had to admit that the old fella was indeed 'something of a character' and, despite myself, I decided that I liked him. In some ways he reminded me of a grumpier, more obstreperous version of my grandfather.

For the next 3 hours I walked across a plateau of swaying corn between distant hillsides that were blanketed in the polka-dots of olive trees. I stopped beside a huge stone barn to eat some chorizo, which I shoved with my thumb into torn hunks of crusty campesino bread. The warm, cloying scent of olives impregnated the gnarled timber of the barn's heavy doors, seeming to add flavour to my simple lunch. Swallows dived in through holes in the walls to nests that must have been seasonal homes for countless generations of winged African migrants.

Perhaps it was the image of swooping swallows that provoked a sudden recollection that I'd slept rough on a hillside near Arcos de la Frontera once, many years before. I couldn't remember where I'd come from or where I'd been going but I vividly recalled the sense of solitude I'd felt lying in my sleeping bag at dusk when suddenly I heard a train whistle. The AVE bullet train rocketed out of a tunnel below, like a silver dart from a blowpipe, to slice an arc across the plain below me.

'Never has man produced a more lonely sound than the whistle of a steam locomotive,' the hobo-writer Hood River Blackie once wrote. 'Follow me all the days of your life,' the locomotive whistle called to the old hobos of the American West, 'and as you lay down to die, you'll pray with your last breath to follow me once again.'

The sound had certainly brought a sense of loneliness to me on that hillside. It had been easy to imagine the passengers comfortably sipping vino and thinking about their imminent arrival in Seville. In less than an hour in their air-conditioned cocoon they'd cover a distance that it would take me a solid week to walk.

I packed the remnants of my chorizo and bread away and tried to force any thoughts of loneliness from my mind. It seemed that, as I'd feared, the coming weeks might involve an unhealthy amount of time in my own head. Dwelling on mistakes I'd made and regrets that were too old to amend. Before I began the trek my daughter Lucía had told me – with a level of insight that was far beyond her 18 years – 'You're going to have a *lot* of time to reflect... Many people wouldn't want that.'

'Some people might come back very changed,' Lucía's mum had pointed out.

* * *

I finished the last of the plums and reluctantly spat the stone as I continued along the highway.

I'd only covered about a kilometre, however, when my attention was grabbed by what looked like a stone shrine. Scrambling through the thorny roadside scrub, I saw that this alcove loomed at the end of a long concrete trough which contained a few centimetres of water.

There was unmistakable reverence in the way that the arched vault had been built and I thought that perhaps it dated back to the time of the Moors when water was considered sacrosanct in this arid landscape. I drank my fill and then replenished my water bottles from the cool, clear liquid in the alcove. The overflow ran off into the trough where a bed of waving green algae was flourishing, nourished by the sunlight and perhaps by the slobber of livestock.

The inside of the vault was wide enough to have made a blissful bathing spot. I fantasized about soaking in there, hidden from the road and sheltered from the sun, for an hour or so. It was probably just a trough for cows but I couldn't shake the feeling that there was something unmistakably sacred about the spot. As far as I was aware there were no houses or homesteads within several kilometres but, from the way the source was protected from animals, there was a good chance that it might sometimes serve as a water supply for humans too.

Finally, and with great reluctance, I walked down to the farthest end of the trough – where my bathing needn't contaminate the water even for drinking goats – and, clad only in boxer shorts, grabbed a quick bath.

It was fortunate that I made that decision because I'd only just dried myself with the oversized sarong that served also as a sheet and was pulling my boots on when a Land Rover pulled onto the gravel track. I greeted the driver, who introduced himself as José, and complimented him on the beauty of the spot.

'We have water at the farm,' he told me, as he dragged two plastic drums out of the vehicle. 'But this is the cleanest and freshest water in the whole area. Better still, it never dries up.'

I was immensely relieved now that there were no tell-tale soap suds floating in the vault, testifying to my sacrilegious behaviour.

José was heading to Las Cabezas de San Juan but I refused his kind offer of a lift in the Landy.

'It's about ten kilometres from here to Gibalbín,' he pointed out dubiously, 'and about twenty more from there to Las Cabezas. And it's going to be hot…'

'I know,' I smiled. 'But I have plenty of water now and I'll take it slowly.'

Unusually, José had heard vaguely of Estaca de Bares: 'Perhaps from school…' he mused. 'I think it's the most northern point of the country. It's a long walk – and you're doing it at the hottest time of the year.'

'You've heard what they say about mad dogs and Englishmen?' I laughed. 'I'm English and I'm more nervous of facing the cold in the mountains than I am of the heat on the plains.'

* * *

Perhaps they were frivolous words because that afternoon was to become my Andalucían rite of passage and a baptism of fire rolled into one.

For the next 2 hours I traipsed across a lowland basin that concentrated the heat. I was close to the area that is known as *la sartén de España*, the frying pan of Spain. The previous summer the town of Montoro (not far to my north-east) had broken the national record when it reached a high of 47.4°C.

Laurie Lee once summed up the feeling of Andalucían hiking in an article for *Mademoiselle* magazine: 'Half the country is mountain and wilderness,' he wrote. 'It knows a savage climate, vast aching skies, interminable landscapes of distance and silence. But within the bright walls of its towns and villages it has developed a gregarious and extrovert ritual of life in which there are few outsiders and little loneliness.'

Far from this picturesque image of Andalucía's delightful *pueblos blancos*, Gibalbín turned out to be just two parallel rows of bleached buildings facing each other across the road, like a Mexican stand-off.

It was mid-afternoon when I walked into town. I was hugely relieved to find that one of the two eateries shown on my map was open for business and, in fact, La Choza (The Shack) surpassed all expectations by supplying the first real meal I'd had since leaving Gibraltar. My eyes and brain already felt pummelled by the heat so I shunned the roadside tables and chose instead to hide from the afternoon glare in the dark timber bar. While I sipped my *jarra* of Cruzcampo I perused the menu. Surprisingly the owners had taken the trouble to translate it into an English of sorts: while something called 'tack to the chopped garlic' was cryptic in the extreme, 'oxtail of yearling calf' seemed, if anything, unnecessarily descriptive. Despite the fact that I was so far from the ocean I was tempted more by 'Galician ostopus' than by 'Iberia ass oriment' (presumably 'assortment'). Finally I ordered a glass of refreshing gazpacho followed by 'wild boar in salsa'.

I spent the next hour hiding from the sun and watching a Sunday afternoon kids' movie called *Pápa Piquillo*. The slapstick plot revolved around a scruffy but good-natured *Gitano* patriarch who lived with a pet ape and a whole gaggle of guttersnipe flamenco-dancing grandchildren. It's possible that my brain was frazzled by the heat (or maybe by the subsequent Cruzcampos) but *Pápa Piquillo* was an illuminating window into Spain as I'd first known it.

The movie was extremely dated. Barbary apes being hawked around the Mediterranean beaches as photographic props was already becoming a rare sight by the late 1990s when the movie was filmed. Even by modern standards, however, it struck me that some of the script was a little edgy for Sunday afternoon viewing.

'If you're not a junky,' a detective asked Pápa Piquillo at one point, 'what the fuck were you doing in that heroin-filled shack?'

'There are moments, señor inspector,' the old man responded with unexpected philosophy, 'when life gets so tight, that one has no choice but getting into hell itself in search of help.'

Wondering if I was being overly prudish, I started to count the number of times when someone swore; that ubiquitous *'coño'* exclamation was presumably more disturbing to an English prude in the 2020s than it had been for the Spanish board of television censors in the 1990s because I lost count.

As the movie was drawing to a close I ordered a caffeine jolt in the form of a *cortado*, with just enough milk to cloud a double espresso. The barman kindly refilled my bottles and clued me in on the condition of the northbound road. I was surprised to learn that there was a lake about 5 kilometres away. I'd seen no such patch of blue marked on the map but, even so, was already picturing an idyllic lakeside campsite when the barman spoke again: 'You might not notice any actual water... but you'll know it's there from the stands of cane growing around the edge.'

* * *

The road out of Gibalbín passed through a ramshackle little settlement of homesteads. Sagging shanties, cobbled together with car bonnets and fridge doors, seemed to be in the process of melting in the heat. Most were inhabited by a few skinny goats that lived, apparently in reluctant harmony, with the mastiffs that lurched at their chains, barking furiously as I passed. One threw itself ravenously against the wire fencing, making the links clank against the aluminium uprights. I was close enough to see the saliva frothing in its jaws and stepped back hurriedly when I saw the cracked concrete upright shuddering under its weight. The slavering dogs seemed to serve as an ominous warning as to what I might find in the uninhabited hills ahead.

I'd decided to sleep somewhere on the uninhabited hillsides and then make an early start for the hike into Las Cabezas de San Juan the next morning.

I never did see that 'lake' but there was a low-lying sump shrouded with long grass and I guessed that a little water *might* actually gather there from time to time. After a particularly wet winter.

In this wild frontier landscape, it was wise to plan my trip almost like a sailor navigating between the shelter of a string of islands. The paradox in this scenario was that in my case the 20 or 30 kilometres that lay between towns and villages might be entirely waterless. During long stretches I could carry 3 litres of water, but there were times when that would barely be sufficient. I tried to keep enough water in my bottles at the end of the day so that I need not go to sleep thirsty or set off thirsty in the morning.

Although the hills north of Gibalbín appeared to be uninhabited this was clearly private land. There were fences along much of the road and occasionally I passed statuesque gateways, secured with rusty padlocks and so overgrown that I wondered how long it had been since anyone visited. I imagined that maybe they were owned by wealthy absentee landlords who never quite had time to make the hour-long drive down from Seville to saddle the semi-wild white horses I saw in some of the fields or to peruse the (far wilder) black bulls that rested in the shade of the scraggy oaks.

'Coto Privado de Caza' read a sign on one fence post – Private Hunting Reserve – but apparently this area was rarely visited even by hunters because in the hills north of Gibalbín I saw more rabbits than I'd ever seen anywhere in Spain.

Three hours remained until sunset and even now the sun still felt like a golden gong swinging over my head. I trudged desperately onwards with my eyes set on the next pool of shade into which I could dive for a brief moment's refreshment. I was struck with the illusion that the pitiless sun would reach any shady patch the very instant that I arrived and that it would be just as hot there as anywhere else. It was easier simply to keep moving than to crawl into the dusty patch of darkness under a scraggy roadside bush.

Shortly after I left Cádiz Province and crossed into Seville, I climbed a small hill which offered a strategic vantage point along the road both to the north and south. The trees here were too spindly to hold a hammock so I simply laid my bivouac roof down as a groundsheet and removed my boots for my ritual evening foot inspection. The balls of both my feet were bulbous with semi-transparent balloons that threatened to burst and the back of my left heel was entirely covered with a gruesome wound. The second set of blisters had drained but the skin had broken and new ones were ballooning through the tender, pink skin underneath. The wounds stung painfully when the scabbed blood came away with my sock. I'd realized by now that the rash enthusiasm of that first day's 45-kilometre hike from Gibraltar had reaped a batch of blisters that I would nurse for the next few weeks. I'd continue to operate and tend them each evening before sleeping, only to rouse them into fury the next morning when I started walking. Fortunately, a kilometre or so of early-morning limping invariably brought numbness that tended to last until a particularly rough or uneven section of trail agitated them.

I covered the split blisters with antiseptic powder, in the hope that they would dry somewhat overnight, and treated the newly erupting crop. When I lay back to relax, my eyes rested on those of a large rat that was scuttling across the branches just above my head. He looked like an adept climber and I doubted that he'd fall on me.

That rat continued to scuttle busily back and forth across the darkening lavender sky until I finally lost sight of it against a backdrop of deep violet that was clotted with stars.

* * *

Figuring that I had sufficient water for a 2-hour hike I set my alarm for a predawn departure. I woke once during the night – as always happy to find myself surrounded by nature (but apparently abandoned by the rat) – and lay awake for a while watching clouds scudding across the spangled stars.

I'd broken camp by four-thirty and walked down the hill through the tall grass by the light of my headtorch. I stumbled across the thorn-tangled ditch and onto the black ribbon of tarmac.

It was logical to try to reach Las Cabezas de San Juan before the full heat of the sun kicked in. Now, however, in almost complete pitch darkness, I realized how difficult it was to follow the white stitching of the centre-markers, like a drunk walking the line. The headtorch only disrupted what little night-vision I could muster so I switched it on only when I needed to reassure myself that I wasn't about to fall into a pothole or trip over a rabbit. I knew realistically that the most dangerous animal I might encounter here would be a wild boar but it was a struggle to keep my mind off wolves. I knew that real wolves had recently been declared extinct in Andalucía but feral mastiffs (of the sort that I'd seen in Gibalbín) would surely have found extremely lucrative hunting territories on these hills that were plagued with rabbits.

An aeroplane passed high overhead, its lights seeming intrusively bright even at altitude. I guessed that it had probably taken off from Madrid and was on a bearing that would most likely take it to South America. As far as I was aware the nearest human habitation was about 10 kilometres away so those trans-Atlantic passengers, jammed elbow-to-elbow into their seats, were almost certainly my closest neighbours at that moment. I wondered if anyone was looking down and wondering what the solitary little light in the darkness signified.

I'd been walking for an hour when the merest cuticle of moon finally rose, a silver scythe slicing weakly through the darkness to illuminate the tarmac like a dim ribbon of mercury. An old Spanish belief had it that the dying moon, shaped like a C, was a reminder of *Cristo* on the cross. When the moon was growing towards fullness it resembled the D of *Dios*. An eclipse, so they said, happened when God and Christ put their heads together, crying for the sadness on Earth.

The soap-sud of stars was already slipping down to the western horizon when the first car of the morning shot past me. I climbed onto the verge and switched my headtorch to its red warning bulb so as not to glare the driver. Others followed and they too hurried on their way, perhaps wondering nervously what sort of lunatic or ne'er-do-well would be walking across these isolated hills at this hour. Only one lorry driver slowed perceptibly – clearly ready to offer assistance until my smile and thumbs-up sign reassured him that this particular lunatic was at least doing this out of choice. With a happy toot of his horn, he passed out of sight.

Just as the sun began the first barrage of its daily attack, I reached a junction where a signpost pointed towards a town with the intriguing name of Espera (Wait). I took this as 'the sign I'd been waiting for' and sacrificed some of my precious water on a cup of cold coffee.

My bottles were long since empty and the sun was high when, 2 hours later, I arrived on the outskirts of Las Cabezas de San Juan. If my last impression of Gibalbín had been of scraggy goats and mastiffs, then my first impression of Las Cabezas was of mules, turkeys and even more mastiffs. A particularly huge white dog woke as I shuffled past and charged viciously, hate in its icy blue eyes, until its heavy chain brought it up just short of the flimsy chicken-wire fence.

I made a beeline for the first café I saw and the tiled subterranean gloom was like stepping blissfully into a swimming pool. I ordered *café con leche*, fresh orange juice and toast with *jamón*. Then I called my wife in South Africa for a chat over a second coffee. I reassured her that Las Cabezas would be an opportunity to get laundry done and, with luck, to find a swimming pool where I could get a shower. Even during the planning of the trip Narina had seemed anxious about the level of personal hygiene I could expect to maintain.

I'd been too busy fantasizing about babbling brooks and chilled mountain springs to take her worries seriously. I had to admit now that it had been an embarrassing rookie error for someone who'd trekked through southern Spain so frequently in the past. There had been few streams in the hills I'd passed through so prospects didn't look great now that I was approaching the flat, open plains.

'It will probably do you good to soak your legs in a pool,' Narina said now, 'but maybe try to keep your feet dry so that it doesn't soften the blisters.'

When I pointed out that it would be hard to soak my legs without getting my feet wet, she suggested that perhaps there would be a kids' paddling pool. I pictured myself leopard-crawling into the pool to lie with my feet up in the air.

It might have been an ideal way to bag a night's accommodation in Cabezas de San Juan police station.

* * *

The only laundry in town was still closed when I eventually found the address. I telephoned the number on the door and an hour or so later two women arrived. I gratefully left my bundle of clothes on the assurance that I could collect them after lunch.

With time to kill I went in search of the municipal swimming pool. I had hopes of finding the sort of outdoor pool that was surrounded with sun-loungers and perhaps with a small cocktail bar serving drinks with mini-parasols. It was too much to hope for but – near the appropriately named Calle Virgen de la Consolación – I found a big ugly concrete block that was permeated with the telltale odour of chlorine. Still, this might be my only chance for a hot shower for some time and I could only hope that it wasn't reserved for members only.

'I walked into town this morning,' I explained to the young man at the entrance desk. 'Is it possible to leave my pack with you and can I pay admission for a swim?'

'Where did you walk from?'

'From Gibraltar.'

'And where are you going?'

'Galicia.'

'*¡No me digas!*' he laughed, slapping his hand on the table – Don't tell me.

'*Si,*' I smiled. '*Paso a paso.*' Step by step.

'*¡No me digas!*' This time shaking his head by way of variation.

'Yes. So… ermm. Is it possible? Do I pay here?'

'*Si si. Es posible.* But I won't accept your money.'

'*¿Y porque no?*'

'I will invite you!'

'No, no, it's okay. I can pay.'

But the young man – who now introduced himself with a handshake as Jesús – was determined to be my saviour. 'It will be my pleasure,' he said grandly.

In a cubicle in the changing rooms I soaped myself under the blissful flow of hot water. Then I rinsed. Then soaped, and did it all over again. Finally I pulled on a pair of board shorts and headed to the pool. It was half-price for pensioners that morning and the pool was so busy that I had to share a lane with an old man who weaved helplessly from port to starboard in a spectacularly unseaworthy fashion. It didn't matter to me, however, because I was happy merely to soak my overworked calf muscles and was certainly not in need of any supplementary exercise.

By the time I'd finally retrieved my pack from beside Jesús's desk, a school group was lined up along the street. Healthy country kids, waiting to go into the swimming pool and bursting with the excitement of their thirteenth summer.

'Jesús told us about you,' the teacher said, as he reached out to shake my hand. '*¡Chapeau!*' He tapped his forehead with his thumb and forefinger, as if doffing a non-existent hat.

I thanked him and as I shouldered my pack to set off down the street, he told the kids to give me three cheers. Their enthusiasm was even more rejuvenating than the hot showers had been.

Las Cabezas de San Juan would perhaps have been an all-time highpoint of my walk if I could only have found a square meal. In every bar and restaurant I enquired at, the kitchens would not open for another 2 hours. So, finally I had to settle for a *tortilla* baguette, washed down with a beer. Connoisseurs will tell you that a real *tortilla española* must contain nothing but eggs, potatoes and onions. Despite the simplicity of the recipe, a good *tortilla* is almost impossible to find in a bar. Only with homemade *tortilla* do you find the perfect level of moistness running through the middle. By the time I'd struggled through the crusty bread and washed the dry *tortilla* down with Cruzcampo it was time to collect my laundry and bid *adiós* to Las Cabezas de San Juan.

* * *

For the last four days the compass that was clipped to the shoulder strap of my backpack had shown that I'd been edging consistently in a north-westerly direction. I was certainly drifting heavily to port off my northbound course but knew that I ought to be happy as long as the forward momentum continued.

I was happy too that, for once, I knew *exactly* where I wanted to spend the night. I'd been intrigued when I first started researching my route to see a place called El Fantasma (The Ghost) marked on the map. It appeared to be nothing more than a highway service station but the name was irresistible, and I was determined to camp in the little patch of supposedly haunted woodland that surrounded El Fantasma. I was almost certain that this would be feasible since I'd had an unexpected opportunity to reconnoitre this potential campsite the previous week as the bus flashed past on the Autovía del Sur bound from Seville to Gibraltar. Barring any ghosts, the little copse of eucalyptus trees had looked like an ideal hammock spot.

It had taken a total of 19 hours to travel by bus from my daughter's home in Pamplona through Vitoria, Bilbao, Burgos and Cordoba to Seville. In Seville I'd caught another bus for the 4-hour journey through Vejer de la Frontera, Tarifa and Algeciras to arrive finally in La Línea de la Concepción, a few blocks from the Gibraltar border. The 1,400-kilometre road trip was made more enjoyable by the fact that I knew I'd have ample chance to reverse the bad karma of zipping through such beauty at a relentless 60 kilometres per hour.

For much of the journey I stared out of the window and tried to hone my innate talent for spotting hammock trees. I scanned the landscapes obsessively, scouting for perfectly spaced trees in secluded locations. Ideally they would be near flowing streams but far enough away from marshy mosquito habitats. Malaria was officially eradicated in Spain in 1964 so I was happy to remove my hammock's mosquito net before leaving home. I'd first contracted the recurring form of malaria on an expedition in Borneo, then again in Madagascar (in the form of what was once called 'Malagasy fever'). I carried it for upwards of six months each time and counted myself lucky, finally, to shake it at all. Then I contracted cerebral malaria in Ghana – the region that was once known, for reasons that became frighteningly obvious to me, as 'the white man's grave'.

Just three months before I began my trek through Spain, The National Library of Medicine reported the country's first locally contracted case of malaria in almost six decades. A patient had contracted the potentially fatal cerebral form of the disease in a hospital in Campo de Gibraltar.

Even so, there was no reason to be particularly worried about the possibility of Spanish malaria but – given my previous track record – it was something I pondered during the long bus journey south. The bus had taken me through Jaén province just after sunrise and rank upon rank of equidistant olive trees had been revealed against the pale sky. There are an estimated 60 million cultivated olive trees in that province alone. To a hammock addict they're all inconveniently widely spaced and as I gazed out of the bus window, I came to the conclusion that there probably wasn't a suitable pair of hammock trees in the entire province.

I knew that on the desolate plains of Extremadura the situation would be worse still.

Racing past El Fantasma service station, however, I'd seen that it was flanked by a delightful little eucalyptus woodland, stretching up the bank on either side of the highway. It would have been too steep and rutted for a tent but for a hammock it looked ideal. These thirsty Australian invaders are perhaps not the most environmentally friendly trees, but they are strong, sturdy and straight. And they tend to create an unfavourable habitat for flies and bugs.

I'd seen on Google Earth that the service station boasted a truck stop and a restaurant so I was looking forward to an evening meal and chance to relax at a table over a bottle of vino and bring my notes up to date. I'd covered less than 20 kilometres since daybreak but with clean clothes, a clean body, a nutritious meal under my belt and updated notebooks I'd certainly be able to convince myself that I'd had a productive day.

Unfortunately, once again, the restaurant was closed and the best I could manage was a sandwich, a Coke, a packet of crisps and a chocolate bar.

Apparently it had never occurred to the cashier that 'The Ghost' might be an unusual name for a service station. She wasn't from this neighbourhood, she said, and was unable to tell me where the name came from. I did some research as I sat on the curb beside the truck stop and learned that inexplicable apparitions had been witnessed on a surprisingly regular basis in this neighbourhood. A news report from the *ABC de Sevilla* newspaper told how three drivers in this area had reported to the local police that a woman 'with long hair and strange clothes' kept appearing and disappearing on the road ahead of them. Then, in November 2020, a whole group of Cabezas de San Juan residents had witnessed an apparition of the Virgin Maria among the trees near the service station. I wondered if my friend Jesús from the swimming pool had been among them but apparently the editor of *El Cabezeño* newspaper was on hand: 'At night we went to the place and the first image struck us,' he reported in an interview. 'An image of a Virgin, with a kind of cloak, no crown could be seen, just a headdress.'

The apparition became known as 'La Virgin del Tronco' – the Virgin of the Trunk. Even two thousand years after the birth of her son, the Virgin has a habit of popping up in obscure parts of rural Spain. There have even been reports of plastic figurines of the Virgin shedding 'real' tears. While there's Nuestra Señora de Alcantarilla (which some have translated, slightly sacrilegiously, as 'Our Lady of the Sewers'), these visitations most often tend to appear in forests. There are Virgins associated with many types of trees: the Virgin of the ash tree; Virgin of the thorn tree; Virgin of the almond tree; Virgin of the carob tree; Virgin of the oak…

Over the centuries religious statues, discovered in caves and in hollows in ancient trees all over the country, have almost routinely been accepted as miracles. The mystery is not so hard to explain though. Through the course of seven centuries of Muslim control many towns were conquered, lost and re-conquered and it wouldn't be surprising if precious statues were hidden from potential plunderers by the faithful who – for one reason or another – were later denied an opportunity to reclaim them.

To my knowledge there has never been a Virgin of the Eucalyptus (the seeds of which were apparently imported from Australia by a Galician monk in the nineteenth century) but perhaps there will be before long since several apparitions have taken place in different sections of the little eucalyptus woodland around El Fantasma.

Astoundingly these sightings had been witnessed by entire crowds of people. These thoughts were forefront in my mind as I slipped furtively into the 'haunted woods' beyond the truck stop.

Right in the middle of the little forest I found two perfectly spaced trees, out of sight both from the service station and the road. It was still early so I lay listening to the soft Gloucestershire burr of Laurie Lee's narration until the aroma of warm eucalyptus oil and the gentle rocking of my hammock lured me to sleep.

I woke only once during the night and lay for a while listening to the rumble of traffic. There was something reassuringly sociable about the flickering headlights cutting between the silvery trunks and I was happy to be spared any more dramatic visitations.

* * *

I was up and out of the hammock at first light and surprised the night staff at the service station by my sudden appearance and request for a coffee.

My route crossed the *autovía* and then set out unwaveringly across a plain that, even from the bus, had appeared almost endless. Now nothing lay between me and the outskirts of Seville but this vast landscape of crop fields, networked with concrete *acequias* (the irrigation channels that are still known after the *al-sāqiyas* of Moorish engineers).

I kept myself busy with a challenging half-hour racing a floating stick that was being washed along a roadside irrigation channel. The stick was resolutely northward-bound and, like me, it was heading towards the mighty Guadalquivir River. I could keep pace with it in a straight race but I knew that in the long run it would beat me on pure stamina. I figured that it would be halfway to the Atlantic about the time I unhitched my hammock the next morning.

White cattle egrets foraged on a ploughed field near the road. I couldn't decide whether this was a positive omen or simply a reminder that I was still much closer to Africa than to Central Europe. Then a phalanx of glossy ibises flew overhead – about 40 birds in a V-formation that stretched across the sky. They'd probably come from the great wetland wilderness of Coto de Doñana National Park which lay just an hour's flight away and was home also to thousands of flamingos.

Eventually the village of El Trobal appeared ahead, like a cartload of salt-blocks tipped randomly on the plain. I steered straight towards a bleached belltower, rising like a spade-handle from the centre of those flat-topped blocks. I hoped that it would mark the location not just of a church but also of a bar or café.

In the centre of this bone-white cluster of buildings I had ordered breakfast at a bar with a terrace overlooking the bleached plaza. It was already mid-morning and the heat was growing. It would be about 2 hours before I reached Los Palacios y Villafranca so I ate quickly and headed on my way.

Back out on the road there was little in the way of shelter from the sun, but I wet my bush-hat from one of the irrigation channels and strode onwards. In these farmlands water could only be found either in run-off from agricultural land (perhaps contaminated with pesticides and chemicals) or in mud-holes where it was churned by hooves and colonized by the algae that feasted on manure. A bath would have been appreciated but the prospect of soaking the open wounds of my blisters in such fluids was not appealing.

But I was grateful that there was ample water here and that, thanks to my filter bottle, I had no reason to go thirsty. After 5 kilometres or so I sat by the road, under the shade of a scraggy bush, lazily pitching pebbles into a stream. After about 20 minutes I figured that the stream was now full enough for my liking and reluctantly set off once again up the road.

The land was so flat – and my pace so slow in the growing heat – that, like a sailor on a doldrum sea, I raised the skyline of Los

Palacios y Villafranca about an hour before I finally scuttled into the shade of its streets.

A wide area of sunken grassland stretched along the banks of the canal, appearing almost as a moat around the south-western edge of the town. On the far side of this 'moat' a flock of sheep were raising a cloud of dust into the stagnant air. A horseman on a majestic black steed cantered along the skyline, below the terracotta steeple of the church. If not for the obvious nobility of the horse it could have been Don Quixote going to do battle on the scraggy Rocinante. A row of poplars and a single soaring palm tree rose above the buildings, making the scene almost achingly romantic. It was the sort of image that I had dreamed about since I started planning this trip.

The Spanish word for horseman (*caballero*) could be applied equally to a knight or a gentleman. The traditional implication was that a gentleman rode while a peasant walked. In the old days it was only *hidalgos* (literally *hijos de algo*, sons of substance) who rode. Sancho Panza, Don Quixote's page, said that there were 'but two families in the world: the haves and the have-nots'. Things hadn't changed all that much and I still felt like a peasant as I shuffled into town on dusty boots, with hayseeds in my hair.

Vagabundo though I was, I spent my afternoon in Los Palacios y Villafranca doing a passable imitation of a gentleman of leisure. A supermarket façade wobbled in the heat haze, as if bludgeoned by a non-existent wind and inside I bought a picnic brunch – bread, pâté, yoghurt and a punnet of cherries. I sat under the palms in a deserted plaza lazily enjoying the luxury of the warm, dry air on my blisters.

It was more than just laziness that kept me drifting around Los Palacios y Villafranca in my flip-flops for the next few hours. Seville now lay less than 30 kilometres to the north; while I'd always enjoyed visiting Spain's fourth biggest city, I'd be reluctant to sleep rough in the suburbs of any big city. Instead, I planned to sneak up on it under cover of the evening and be in a position to catch it by surprise on a dawn raid the next day.

I wandered slowly through Los Palacios y Villafranca until a blackboard on the pavement of Avenida de Cádiz lured me into Restaurante Casa Joaquín. I ordered a Cruzcampo and finished reading Twain's *A Tramp Abroad* before I even put in an order for lunch. I wasn't particularly hungry after my picnic but the last week had taught me that it was unwise to overlook an opportunity for a square meal.

I feasted on chilled *salmorejo* (a more substantial version of gazpacho) with ham and boiled egg on top, followed by succulent pork loin in whisky sauce. It was served with a carafe of wine and some *Casera* soda so that I could mix a refreshing *tinto de verano* (summer wine). For dessert I had crème caramel and a *cortado* (espresso with milk) for a caffeine jolt. At ten euros, the entire meal cost less than the junk food I'd bought at the service station the evening before.

By 5 o'clock I figured it was a reasonable time to get back on the trail. I'd spent more time scouting this section of my route on Google Earth than any other part of my journey. The bus ride out of Seville had confirmed my opinion that the only way I could effectively reach that city from the south would be via the town of Dos Hermanas (Two Sisters). Unfortunately the A-4 highway was the only viable walking route into what was effectively an industrial town on the outskirts of the city so for most of that evening I walked along a garbage-strewn service road that ran parallel to the dual carriageway. Even though I'd anticipated that this urban hinterland might be the most unpleasant part of my journey, it was hard to maintain high spirits as my boots scuffed among empty Coke cans and cigarette packets.

I stopped to explore a ruined bar beside the highway. Cracked ceramic tiles – the traditional blue-and-white tiles that are known as *azulejos* – made me wish I could have seen the place in better times. I pondered the wisdom of staying the night but in a back room I found a stack of cardboard and the ashes of an old cooking fire. Unmistakable signs that the place was familiar to other vagrants.

Towards sunset a breeze blew up but instead of cooling me it just raised chaff, twigs and dust. It felt like I was being pelted with handfuls of hot rice and the plastic bags that blew against my legs felt like a personal insult.

There'd been an element of undeniable romance in playing at being a vagabond in the wilderness but dossing on the outskirts of Seville was a very different matter. I'd been nervous since I first planned the hike about the necessity of 'stealth camping' in what was by far the biggest city I'd walk through.

As a backpacker in the old days I used to sleep rough in cities from time to time (including many nights on the plazas and parks of Pamplona) and it invariably felt riskier than sleeping in the countryside. In the country I would always try to get as far off the beaten track as possible but, if it was unavoidable that I sleep in a city, the vicinity of a relatively busy road was preferable to the sort of isolated urban wasteland that might be the haunt of addicts or hoodlums.

I'd expected to have to negotiate a high flyover, crossing the Autovía del Sur, on my path into Dos Hermanas but the insurmountable 2-metre fence and six lanes of frantic traffic came as a shock. It would be foolishly reckless to attempt that dash with a 12-kilo pack. Even if I was successful, I doubted that I'd get over without attracting the notice of traffic police. I weighed that prospect – unappealing on so many levels – against a retreat to Los Palacios y Villafranca and an attempt on Seville via another route.

I'd always wanted to walk the route that Laurie Lee had described so beautifully in *As I Walked Out One Midsummer Morning*. But the Spain he'd known in 1936 had become almost unrecognizable even by the time he finally wrote his memoir three decades later:

'It was not, after all, so very long ago, but no one could make that journey today', he wrote. 'Most of the old roads have gone, and the motor car, since then, has begun to cut the landscape to pieces, through which the hunched-up traveller races... seeing less than a dog in a ditch.'

In the nine decades since Lee's walk, Spain has been shackled under 15,000 kilometres of railway line and sliced with 700,000 kilometres of roads. This was only the first of several cities I'd have to cross and I was beginning to wonder if my romantic idea of a trans-Iberian country stroll had become an impossibility.

Then a beacon of hope emerged on the horizon – in the form of a Shell service station sign.

The pump attendant explained that my best option was a small gravel road that veered westward from the highway a few hundred metres farther on. It looked like a private access, he said, but it was open to the public and would lead me eventually to the back side of Dos Hermanas town.

This tradesman's entrance led through an olive grove which I explored with an eye to finding hammock trees. I was put off by the fact that the base of each trunk was rigged with the plastic tubing of an irrigation system. I had no idea how often the sprayers would be activated but it seemed logical that it would be in the evening when the evaporating power of the sun was at its weakest. Not relishing the thought of a midnight soaking I kept moving.

This was my sixth day on the road and it was reassuring to see for once that, despite all the indecision, the needle on my compass had pointed unwaveringly northward for almost the entire day.

An hour later the warehouses on the outskirts of Dos Hermanas emerged, standing sentinel beyond the last fields on the far side of the *autovía*. Beside the bridge the highway embankment was forested with small but sturdy trees and a short walk away from the road I found two ideal hammock trees that were completely hidden from the highway by the dense thicket. Spanish law permits free camping in areas that are not privately owned and not classified as protected areas, as long as you are not in a group and only stay for a single night. Nevertheless, it seemed likely that the local cops would be particularly vigilant for 'vagabonds' along the southern outskirts of such a big city and it would make sense to stay 'under the radar' if I hoped to have an uninterrupted night. After all, Seville would be a primary target for many illegal immigrants who could be making their way up from the southern beaches at that moment. In this area 'stealth camping' was a matter of life and death for hundreds of unfortunate people. While my main priority was to stay out of sight of any police patrols, I was aware that the more secretive I tried to be the more suspicious I'd appear to any of the townsfolk who spotted me.

The only weak point in my defences was a rutted gravel track that ran along the edge of a ploughed field where tufts of yellow hay made the clods of earth look like severed heads. It was very unlikely that anyone would pass that way so late in the evening and even if someone did, I'd be completely hidden unless they happened to glance to the side right at the point when they passed my hammock. I tied my hammock up and wrapped the camouflaged green nylon over my lurid red sleeping bag.

All I asked for was an uninterrupted night's sleep. I hoped that I wouldn't have to face any more guttersnipe hikes along the litter-strewn highway and that tomorrow evening would see me safely beyond Seville's northern suburbs.

As luck would have it, the only car to pass along the gravel track in the entire evening stopped *exactly* in the only spot from which my camp could be seen. I was certain that I'd been spotted and breathed a sigh of relief when I realized that it was just a man taking his dog for a walk.

It was almost dark and I'd nearly dozed off when I heard his feet crunching back along the gravel. His busy little Jack Russell was sniffing frantically along the hedgerow. Surely it couldn't help but notice me. Then it would bark and I knew that the game would be up. But no, head down and snuffling fervently for rabbits or rats, it didn't even catch my scent when it passed within 2 metres of me.

As the man unlocked the car he called to the dog: *¡Venga!'* – Come!

Then a second time more emphatically: *'¡Venga chico! ¡Hostias!'*

He held the door open while the dog hopped in.

I breathed a sigh of relief.

But instead of getting in the car himself the man now came around to the back of the vehicle. He stood fumbling with the front of his jeans and I lay frozen as he started to irrigate the undergrowth, a bare 5 metres from the spot where I lay hidden with all but one eye covered by the green nylon. It wasn't a sight I wanted to focus on and I covered my face until the sound of splashing had finished.

But when I peered again he was leaning over the fence, staring hard in my direction. He was trying to focus into the shadows where my hammock must have looked like a gargantuan green cocoon. Clearly, he was unsure what it was, or whether it could be occupied because now he looked around and, finding a stick, he aimed it right at me!

When I heard it strike the dry grass next to me I sat up and yelled as if in surprise: 'Woh!'

'¡Me cago en la hostia!' The man jumped back in fright – I shit on the host!

I laughed – hoping that I sounded harmless, rather than maniacal.

'Jesus! You scared me!'

Fortunately, he laughed too.

'Are you going to sleep here?' he asked when he'd recovered.

'Yes. I hope it doesn't bother anyone. Just camping for the night. I'm on a pilgrimage and heading to Santiago de Compostela.'

It was the perfect alibi and he seemed to accept it without question. With a nod and a hearty *'buen camino'* he was on his way.

* * *

Despite my evasive tactics I knew I was still only really *playing* at being a vagrant. I had my passport, business cards and credentials as a journalist and I knew that in reality it wouldn't take much to talk my way out of police trouble with just a slap on the wrist. I had the hypocritical feeling that my sense of insecurity was itself just a mild sham. Part of an act. For so many others in this region the state of homelessness was something far more serious.

It is estimated that there are about 35,000 people currently living on the streets in Spain. The economic traumas of the COVID-19 pandemic had boosted the figure but it was said that immigrants made up the majority of homeless people. The figure is believed to be almost eight times greater for England. The hopelessly outdated British Vagrancy Act defines rogues and vagabonds as 'every person wandering abroad and lodging in any barn or outhouse, or in any deserted or unoccupied building, or in the open air... or in any cart or wagon...' I'd be doing all of those things many times over the coming weeks. Established in 1744, the act further defines homeless people as 'beggars, idles, vagabonds and rogues'. Repeat offenders are categorized as 'incorrigible rogues'.

Fortunately, I'd only ever flirted with vagrancy as an antidote to routine and a means to adventure. Regarding the charge of periodic idleness and vagabondage, however, I stood guilty as charged.

Clearly in the eyes of the law I was an 'incorrigible rogue'.

* * *

Although less than a kilometre from Dos Hermanas, I struggled desperately to find a way into the town centre. An immense industrial park – heavily pervaded with the smell of olive oil and protected all around by electric fences – blocked every access route I tried.

After an hour of twisting and turning, like a rat in a cage, I scrambled over a section of well-trampled fence and my trail finally converged with a road that was lined with ugly factories and warehouses.

I feared that the perilous labyrinth of highways (barricaded with 2-metre-tall chain-link) was only going to get increasingly impenetrable the nearer I got to Seville. In a Dos Hermanas café two anxious old ladies convinced me of the folly of risking arrest – 'more likely death,' one said – by attempting to walk through the web of highways and railway tracks that enclosed the city.

I'd only been on the road a week and was frustrated at the thought of having to catch a bus. It was little consolation that the 10-kilometre ride was more than compensated for by the extra distance I'd covered through back-tracking and detours on my first day out of Gibraltar.

At the otherwise deserted bus stop I asked a schoolgirl if the bus driver would accept cash.

'Where are you walking to?' she asked, nodding at my backpack.

She was one of the few people I'd met who'd heard of Estaca de Bares and she immediately said that she'd pay for my bus ticket.

'Thank you but I can pay.' I laughed uncomfortably. 'I have cash.'

Wondering if maybe I was entering too effectively into a state of vagabondage, I resolved to take a look in a mirror the next time I came across one. She clearly saw the doubt in my expression because now she explained that she'd walked with friends 150 kilometres through the Sierra Morena the previous summer.

'It's very expensive when you pay with cash on a bus,' she clarified, 'but it's almost free with my travel card. And besides, it will be my pleasure.'

It was one of several unexpected moments of spontaneous generosity that I encountered during the trek and that schoolgirl gave me a renewed sense of optimism for the day on the trail.

She was continuing farther into Seville city centre so I thanked her and bid *adiós* when I left the bus at the first opportunity.

I walked up Avenida de la Palmera past the monasterial bulk of Hospital Fátima where a couple of green-uniformed Civil Guards stood at the door. The poet Federico García Lorca had described them as 'those patent-leather men with their patent-leather souls'. They eyed me suspiciously and I kept my own eyes guiltily averted, trying not to recall the fact that their shiny tricorn hats always made me think of patent-leather dog-bowls.

Established as a paramilitary peace-keeping force in 1844, with 5,501 officers, the Guardia Civil was so successful that it had quadrupled in size and boasted over 2,000 bases by the end of that century. They were officially known as *La Benemérita Guardia Civil* (The Praiseworthy Civil Guard) but there were certainly times, even in their recent history, when they'd proven to be anything other than praiseworthy. After word first leaked of the military rebellion that sparked the Civil War, the hated Guardia Civil were among the first victims of retribution in Spanish villages. They retaliated violently with summary executions and Federico García Lorca was one of their early victims. According to some reports Lorca – reputed to be a socialist, a freemason and a homosexual – was shot twice in the rectum before the coup-de-grace from those patent-leather men put a final bullet in his brain.

As recently as 1998 the director general of the Guardia Civil became a fugitive after he was found guilty of fraud, embezzlement and tax evasion. He was finally caught in Bangkok, repatriated to Spain and served 15 years in prison. After he died in Zaragoza in March 2022 it was reported that the bulk of his €10-million fortune was still missing.

I looked back once to see if the *Guardias* were still watching me and tripped on a loose manhole cover… no doubt convincing them that I was not only down-and-out but probably drunk too.

It was the proximity of my nose to the cast-iron surface of that manhole cover that first brought Seville's unusual slogan to my notice: the cryptic 'NO8DO' was embossed in heavy letters. As a provincial bumper sticker you'd think that this strange piece of code leaves a lot to be desired and many *Sevillanos* are themselves unaware of its rather convoluted meaning. *'No me ha dejado'* (she has not abandoned me) was how Alfonso the Wise expressed his sentiments when he heard that Seville would stand by him in the war against his rebellious son Sancho. Confusingly the figure 8 in 'NO8DO' is not a numeral; instead it represents the skein of wool that is known in these parts as a *madeja*. Hence 'NO-*madeja*-DO'.

* * *

I strode onwards, sidestepping commuters on bicycles and electric scooters, as I skirted the gardens of Jardines de las Delicias and Parque Palomas (the Park of Doves). I made a short detour through the leafy walkways and plazas of Parque de Maria Luisa and negotiated the six lanes of traffic that circled Glorieta de los Marineros (Roundabout of the Sailors) to arrive on the bank of the river that once saw the caravels of Columbus and Magellan.

I knew the eastern bank well from previous assignments so resisted the temptation now to veer towards the monumental Gothic cathedral and the 91-metre Giralda minaret which was built by Mansur the Victorious (sworn enemy of Richard the Lionheart). Even at this time of the morning the plaza near the cathedral would be ebbing and flowing with tides of sightseers, shoppers and *buscavidas* (hustlers). But it was the much more mysterious and rarely visited western bank that I wanted to walk through now. It is only in the old Gypsy quarter of Triana where you can still get a sense of what Laurie Lee described as 'a creamy crustation of flower-banked houses fanning out from each bank of the river'.

I'd been worried about the southern approach to this city and with my major challenge behind me, I was delighted to spend some time exploring the shady streets of Triana where the air felt cool as the running water in the Rio Guadalquivir. As I turned into a narrow street that was named for the Virgin of the Valley, a jolt of excitement quickened my heartbeat as I caught the guttural strains of flamenco wafting down from an apartment window: *'Vamonos pa' casa ...'* Camarón de la Isla was bellowing – Let's go home.

I recalled Gypsy flamenco bars I used to frequent during my years in Madrid. At two or three in the morning I'd sometimes go with friends to knock at a sliding spyhole on an unmarked door in Calle Cava Baja. A tattooed doorman would – if he judged us sober enough – let us go down to the basement of this Spanish speakeasy where we'd order vino and listen to melancholy flamenco guitars and the sort of wailing laments that harkened back to purely tribal times. In Calle de Echegaray the owner of Los Gabrieles (now also long gone) once took me down to the cellar to show me the private flamenco hangout that was designed to mimic a miniature bullring. I would sometimes haunt a threadbare nightclub called Cardamomo, parting the curtain at the back of the joint with a sense of trepidation to drink with *Gitano* gang members who referred to everybody as *primo* (cousin).

It was fair to say that during my younger years in Spain the allure of haughty, dark-eyed *Gitanas* may have been part of the attraction but then it was also possibly the tribal atmosphere and the inherent risk that was exciting. To offend one 'cousin' would be to fall foul of the entire community. Fortunately, I never caused offence and had always – after a period of understandable suspicion – been accepted and greeted as a friend.

I regretted bitterly seeing how, on subsequent trips to the capital, all those places slipped into the mainstream and were converted into French-style bistros or generic Irish bars.

I left Camarón de la Isla's tortured wails behind me and the next sound I caught was a shrill whistle piercing through the sinuous alleys. This simplest of melodies, played on a penny whistle, was once heard daily in almost every village and town in Spain yet I figured that it had been well over a decade since I'd last heard it. After a brief pause it echoed again and I decided to follow it. After all, as long as I kept the shady side of the street on my right shoulder I knew that I'd eventually emerge from this labyrinth on the northern edge of Seville.

The whistle (from a simple instrument known locally as a *pifia*) led me to a tiny plaza where I found a roving *afilador*. Like a knife-wielding Pied Piper, his whistle and the traditional summons – '*El afilaooo, el afilaooo...*' – lured housewives out of their homes brandishing carving knives to be sharpened on the spinning grindstone that was mounted on the luggage rack of his moped. For three euros I got the blade on my Swiss Army knife honed to razor-sharpness.

'*Vaya con Dios,*' the *afilador* said – Go with God.

Moving on, I turned the corner beside a leather workshop where tough cowboy boots were stitched for bull-herding *vaqueros* and passed a butcher who specialized in horseflesh and *rabo de toro* (oxtail) from fighting bulls. There was a ceramics workshop, still producing the iconic blue-and-white *azulejo* tiles that were fashionable a thousand years ago when this was a Moorish settlement.

A delivery man, like a convict in his orange overalls, rumbled heavy gas canisters over the cobbles, calling out to shop owners and dispensing the day's gossip as he made his rounds. In small stores along Calle Pureza ('Purity Street') craftsmen made Spanish guitars and seamstresses prepared flamenco dresses for fiestas and the April Fair. Two old ladies, arm in arm and dressed all in black, turned into Capilla de los Marineros (Chapel of Sailors), perhaps to make offerings to the golden effigy of Christ which emerges once a year to reflect the glare of the Andalucían sun during the Easter processions.

I stopped for breakfast (bread with oil) at Casa Remesal bar where workmen sipped Osborne brandy against a wall covered in a collage of bullfighters, flamenco singers, teary Madonnas and tortured Christs. Hot-blooded Seville is often considered the epitome of Spain. 'A city of traditional *alegría*,' Laurie Lee called it, 'where gaiety was almost a civic duty, something which rich and poor wore with arrogant finesse simply because the rest of Spain expected it.' While a modern traveller might notice that this 'gaiety' is still present, on the surface at least it, the stark reality of poverty in this city of 700,000 is likely to be less than picturesque.

To an outsider today, Triana in particular is a neighbourhood with spectacularly bi-polar tendencies. The locals appear to see nothing strange in a soundtrack that shifts haphazardly from raucous flamenco to funereal Semana Santa marches. Passing the headquarters of Esperanza de Triana Hermandad I thought about the many brotherhoods that parade the streets during the Easter celebrations – often barefoot and bleeding, with whips and chains tearing their backs – and recalled that this 'city of *alegría*' also has an unexpectedly morbid side to its personality. I only had to peer into the windows of the religious shops where statues and effigies were sold to see icons of Jesus (invariably in agony or clutching a bleeding heart), his mother weeping tears of blood or a whole variety of saints undergoing gruesome tortures.

The Spanish have a saint for pretty much everything; Saint Elmo is the patron saint of people with stomach disorders and Saint Blaise was beatified after he saved someone from choking on a fishbone. (Predictably, it didn't end well for either man: Elmo was disembowelled with red-hot hooks and Blaise was torn apart with wool combers' irons.)

A cursory perusal of the honours list of Catholic martyrs can make for disturbing reading: there was 12-year-old Saint Faith who was roasted on a red-hot brazier; poor Saint Agatha who had her breasts cut off; Saint Agnes who was dragged naked to a brothel to be raped...

I stopped in front of a religious store featuring a printed backdrop of Jesus preaching the epistles to the apostles. There was a cluttered display of rosaries and reliquaries, cowls, chalices and ciboria. In the old days the particularly pious (and sufficiently wealthy) could buy a special ceremonial syringe filled with holy water (supposedly from the River Jordan) to baptize an unborn child but I didn't see such an implement for sale here. Instead, there were warlike statues of San Miguel impaling a cringing dragon and a horseback Santiago trampling fallen Moors. San Roque was there too, revealing his muscular pilgrim's thigh as he stood beside his trusty dog.

I certainly don't consider myself religious, but every traveller is susceptible to a little superstition. We're perpetually on the lookout for omens. At one window I scanned the crowds of effigies until I spotted Nuestra Señora de los Milagros (Our Lady of Miracles) and gave her a self-conscious nod of recognition. I hoped that it wouldn't be considered hypocritical of me to remind her once again that I'd *really* appreciate it if she could keep the rain off my head with some sort of cosmic umbrella.

It might seem somewhat presumptuous to name a baby girl Miracles but it was a safe bet that Milagros would be a common name in this traditional, pious, if feisty, neighbourhood. Camino (Path) was more common among girls in northern Spain but all over the country babies are still named for places where, through one miracle or another, the Virgin was believed to have appeared: Montserrat, Leyre, Begoña, Guadalupe, Lourdes, Roncesvalles, Fatima...

Every year hundreds of Spanish girls are christened with names that might in another culture sound more like a curse. The happy playgrounds of Seville echo with names like Dolores (Pain), Angustias (Anguish), Soledad (Loneliness) and Crucifixión. If they're fortunate they might get away with Remedios (Remedies)... but they might also get lumbered with Consuela (Consolation) or even Circuncisión (Circumcision). To an outsider it might seem unthinkable to call a son Jesús let alone to name a daughter

Inmaculada Concepción (Immaculate Conception) but any large family in Seville is likely to have a little Jesús, Inma or Conchita on the roll call.

I spent a peaceful hour sitting on a terrace on the shady side of Plaza Santa Ana. I was torn between a reluctance to leave what had long been one of my favourite cities and an urge to be gone before evening found me stranded, like some human flotsam on the banks of the Rio Guadalquivir.

* * *

I followed the riverbank northward and was surprised to see a traditional caravel moored next to the *plaza de toros*. The historic bullring was the grandly named Plaza de Toros de la Real Maestranza de Caballería de Sevilla and the replica timber sailing ship bore a name plate that said *Nao Victoria*. She was a faithfully constructed replica of the only survivor of the so-called Fleet of the Spices which left Seville in 1519 under the command of Ferdinand Magellan. Of the 245 men under Magellan's command, only 18 returned. By the time the Basque captain Juan Sebastián Elcano finally sailed the *Nao Victoria* back to Spain in 1522 he'd completed the first circumnavigation of the globe. Magellan had been killed in the Philippines and 227 others in his command had lost their lives.

Even the nails and spikes for this replica *Nao Victoria* (built for the 1992 Expo) had to be custom-made and the timbers were sourced from across the country. In 2006 the ship had successfully replicated Elcano's voyage… this time, fortunately, without loss of life.

Farther up the riverbank I paused to look at the bronze statue to legendary Seville-born matador Juan Belmonte. In his non-fiction homage to bullfighting, *Death in the Afternoon,* Ernest Hemingway had famously said that Belmonte 'would wind a bull around him like a belt' and there's a strange story that when Belmonte heard that 'don Ernesto' had taken his own life the bullfighter simply said 'well done'.

All too soon I was leaving the last of Seville's red-roofed buildings behind. On the northern fringes of the city I passed more ramshackle dwellings, cobbled together under a highway flyover and then a last *Gitano* settlement complete with snarling dogs and leggy fighting cocks.

I was keen to put as much distance as possible between myself and the city as I could before sunset. As I slid down the gravel-strewn hill towards the bank of the Guadalquivir I passed an old man who was walking his dog: *¡Buen camino, chico!'* he called.

While I'd been worried about accessing the city on foot from the south, I'd harboured no such fears about departing via the northern suburbs.

This salutation heralded the beginning of a new era in my trail. I hoped that navigation would no longer be a constant preoccupation since for the next few weeks I'd be walking the Via de la Plata. The 1,000 kilometre 'Route of Silver' had been trodden by countless nomads, traders, wayfarers and pilgrims since Roman times.

How hard could it be?

CHAPTER 2

Up the Middle

La Bañeza

Benavente

Granja de Moreruela

Zamora

El Cubo de Tierra del Vino

Salamanca

Morille

La Calzada de Béjar

Baños de Montemayor

Cañaveral

Cáceres

Mérida

Villafranca de los Barros

Zafra

Calzadilla de los Barros

Monesterio

Almadén de la Plata

Seville

Castile and León

Extremadura

Andalusia

'No need to run and hide, it's a wonderful, wonderful life.' An earworm was echoing in my head. It summed up what I hoped would be a relatively hassle-free period on my trek. Although I'd continue to sleep rough rather than stay in the pilgrim's hostels known as *albergues*, I hoped that I'd naturally be accepted as a 'pilgrim' now rather than as a hobo.

I was now following in a time-honoured tradition after all. For over a thousand years the Catholic faithful have walked the Via de la Plata on a pilgrimage to the tomb of Saint James in Santiago de Compostela. These days the Via de la Plata is a well-known alternative to the crowded Camino Francés (French Way) which crosses northern Spain.

Among connoisseurs of the several recognized Camino routes that lead to the tomb of Santiago (as Saint James is known in Spanish) the Via de la Plata is notorious as the toughest. I'd already covered over 200 kilometres to reach Seville (the usual starting point). It was a daunting thought that once I came to the end of the Via de la Plata (700 kilometres away in the city of Astorga) I'd still have almost 300 kilometres to reach my goal on the coast.

Some linguists claim that the name Via de la Plata came from *lapidata* (Latin for 'stone road'), others that it evolved from *balatta* (Arabic for road). Those of a more spiritual bent prefer the story that these mediaeval pedestrians navigated following the silvery path of the Milky Way.

One of the apostles of Jesus, Santiago was beheaded by King Herod. Legend has it that when his body was disinterred (around 44 CE) the head had mysteriously reconnected with the body. The corpse was transported to the coast of Galicia, in a 'ship of stone' –

if the stories are to be believed. Legend has it that the pagan queen Lupa directed this unlikely funeral procession into the mountains where she believed they'd surely be killed by wild bulls. At the sign of the cross, however, the beasts were not only converted into meek oxen but actually submitted to being harnessed so that they could help transport the body. Lupa too was similarly converted and gave the saint's followers a palace that could be converted into a church to house the body. Nevertheless, all knowledge of the saint's whereabouts was again lost and he lay forgotten for almost eight centuries until – during the height of the *reconquista* (when Christian armies were struggling to oust the Moors) – a hermit was guided to the spot by what were described as dancing lights in the sky. It might have been more than coincidence that Santiago's body happened to turn up in that particular spot at the particular time it was most needed. 'I think it neither ungenerous nor unlikely,' wrote historian and Pulitzer Prize-winning novelist James A. Michener (in *Iberia*, his 900-page homage to Spain), 'to suggest that the body of Santiago was found not by a hermit following a star but by hard-pressed soldiers who needed a rallying point.'

In the period that followed his rediscovery, the figure of Saint James – by now often referred to as Santiago Matamoros (Saint James the Moor-slayer) – was frequently spotted on the battlefield swinging his sword from the saddle of a white horse. It is said that the saint appeared at Simancas during the battle against caliph Abd al-Rahman in 939. In 997 the Yemenite general al-Mansur – who had become so incredibly powerful that he'd take the caliph's mother (a Basque concubine) as his mistress – sacked Santiago de Compostela, carrying off the cathedral doors and taking the bells as prizes for the Great Mosque in Cordoba. It's said that five years later Santiago himself brought sudden death to al-Mansur as a punishment for sacking the cathedral.

Compostela means 'field of the stars' and – even while the saint's spirit was busy riding roughshod over Moorish infidels

– a small chapel was built to house his earthly relics. The vast number of pilgrims who came to pay homage grew over the years so that a series of bigger edifices had to be built until finally the 8,300-square-metre Catedral Basilica de Santiago de Compostela was started in 1075.

Passing through Triana I'd pondered the ethics of buying a scallop shell, the traditional icon of all pilgrims bound for the tomb of Santiago. If I had been a bona-fide pilgrim I would also have acquired the so-called *Credencial* – the 'pilgrim's passport' that has been issued by the Church as a sort of safe-conduct pass since the Middle Ages.

I'd have felt like an imposter to claim true 'pilgrimship' though, since I had no intention of ending my walk at the city of Santiago – Holy Grail of true pilgrims. On the other hand, cloaking myself (metaphorically speaking) in the guise of a pilgrim saved me from feeling like a fugitive.

I'd imagined that this would be a more sociable section of the trail but I overestimated the 'crowds'; out of every hundred pilgrims who arrive in Santiago de Compostela only three do so by completing the Via de la Plata. In the three weeks that it took to march to Astorga I would only meet 20 other hikers.

For the next 700 kilometres I could expect navigation to be considerably easier; I should be able to follow the Via de la Plata's scallop shell waymarkers and painted yellow arrows from here to Astorga, in the distant province of León. There was even an app that I could download with an interactive map. With the pressure of navigation thus relieved I almost felt that I was starting a holiday.

I would now be free to concentrate on the actual walking.

* * *

In my determination to put distance between myself and the city I hurried through the little town of Santiponce. I reluctantly ignored the Roman ruins of Italica where a signpost on the road informed me that the amphitheatre had once featured as the dragon pit in the *Game of Thrones* series.

More than 2,200 years ago, a military stronghold of retired legionaries was established here as a sort of peace-keeping force in an area that at that time was supplying well over 2 tonnes of gold and over 100 tonnes of silver to Rome annually. Two centuries later, peace had been won in what the Romans called Hispaniae, and Italica had even produced a very successful emperor. Hadrian, born in Italica in 76 CE, was ruler of an empire of 57 million people at the time of his death at the ripe old age of 62… which was not a bad innings since the life expectancy of an average inhabitant of the Roman Empire at that time was under 25 years of age.

Even before it became a pilgrim trail, the Via de la Plata had long since been established as a major Roman military road and trade route. It ran from Hispalis (Seville) through Augusta Emerita (Mérida) and Salmantica (Salamanca) to the highland city of Asturica Augusta (Astorga).

But Santiponce was, for me, a bitter disappointment. Just as I began to think about lunch, I saw a sign up ahead: 'Meson de Caipirinha – Carnes a la Brasa'. In the 35°C heat the thought of an icy caipirinha was utterly irresistible.

It may as well have been a mirage because the place was padlocked and had clearly not functioned in months. Italica and Santiponce seemed utterly devoid of their past glories and after this disappointment I registered little beyond graffiti on concrete walls: 'La policia asesina y tortura' (the police kill and torture). Santiponce now was just a place of torn election posters – ragged strips of grinning faces clinging to crumbling brickwork – and skinny cats that skulked through the dust. It was very hard to imagine that this had once been the birthplace of an emperor.

I knew better by now than to anticipate that the dream of caipirinhas and barbecues would ever be realized but, later that afternoon, a bar in the village of Guillena at least offered some consolation in the form of a beer and a *bocadillo* (baguette). Most pilgrims who start walking from Seville tend to spend their first night at the *albergue* (pilgrim's hostel) in Guillena. I was only 22 kilometres from the city, however, and hoped that I might be able to double that distance by nightfall.

* * *

It was close to sunset, about 35 kilometres north of Seville, when I was captivated by the sight of a ruined fortress that rose above the cornfields and scrubby oak-forested hills. Behind the crumbling outbuildings there was a crenellated watchtower with windows that stared past sagging shutters like dark, heavy-lidded eyes.

It was the sort of romantically haunting sight that Don Quixote would have found irresistible, and I too was suddenly desperate to explore the possibilities of sleeping there for the night. Unfortunately the castle stood in the middle of a carefully tended corn field. There was no path from my side of the valley and I was reluctant to damage the crops by crossing.

Half an hour later I came across a signpost, hand-painted unexpectedly in four languages: 'Agua, Eau, Wasser, Water'. Some rural signwriter had taken a lot of trouble to publicize this spring so I figured I should take the opportunity to reprovision. I had a suspicion that I'd regret my rashness before long if I ignored the invitation.

I wondered uncharitably if the same artist might have been behind the caipirinha/barbecue adverts since when I finally clambered down to it, the well was bone dry and the pump had clearly been out of action for some time. The detour was not wasted, however, because just across the meadow stood a perfect cluster of hammock trees.

The upturned earth under the trees showed the fresh marks where wild boar had snuffled for acorns. It was after nine in the evening and I was ready to turn in so I simply strung the hammock higher than usual, hoping that it might be more or less out of reach if any big pigs came visiting in the night.

By now I'd established a bedtime ritual. My mobile phone, passport, wallet, solar charger and knife went into the hammock's big central pocket which I would drape securely over my hip as I slept. My headtorch stayed close to hand in the smaller pocket near my right ear. The other small pocket (near my right knee) contained the lightweight guy ropes that would be used on nights when I wanted to secure the hammock roof.

The sky was perfectly clear so the canopy of the oaks was all I would need for a roof tonight. Between the sparse leaves the sky was dusted with stars. I wrapped the hammock around me, like a giant green burrito, and slept soundly until morning.

* * *

An hour after sunrise the next morning I was sipping cold instant coffee out of my collapsible cup as I sat with my back against another hand-painted signpost.

'Santiago de Compostela 927 km,' it read. And underneath: '¡ANIMO! – CHEER UP!'

It had obviously been erected, I realized ruefully, by the same multilingual signwriter who'd promised me water the day before. But I bore him no ill will. I'd already been feeling cheerful and – although my blisters were still smarting – my legs felt strong and I was confident that I was slipping fully into the rhythm of the trek.

This was fortunate because I'd be climbing steadily in altitude for most of the next 800 kilometres. Few people realize that, with an average altitude of 660 metres, Spain is the second highest country in Europe (after Switzerland). Spain might be known to tourists primarily for its coastline but pretty much wherever you are on the Mediterranean *costas* you'll almost always have steep hills at your back… and rather than descend on the other side, the top of those hills tend to lead straight onto the high *meseta*.

From the lowland plains around Seville the rise in elevation is an unusually slow one though. Seville itself is barely 7 metres above sea level and by mid-morning I'd only climbed 300 metres to the pretty town of Castilblanco de los Arroyos. I stopped for a leisurely breakfast on a sunlit patio among pots of blood-red geraniums. I knew that it would be a good idea to recoup some stamina because the trail would now start to climb more steeply towards Sierra Norte Natural Park and I'd face a challenging 29-kilometre hike through uninhabited country before I reached the other side of that mountain range.

This would be my last opportunity for provisions and my hunt for a grocery store brought me to the conclusion that Castilblanco de los Arroyos could qualify as perhaps Spain's most literary town. I strolled up Calle Federico García Lorca and cut past the end of Calle don Quixote de la Mancha. I stopped to read a ceramic sign which informed me that Miguel de Cervantes had mentioned this particular spot in 1616 in *Las Dos Doncellas*.

As I turned to walk onwards, a young woman passed with her infant daughter.

'Who's that man?' the little girl asked in a voice that her mother probably considered way too loud.

'A foreigner,' the woman answered quietly. 'He's going to a place called Santiago de Compostela.'

It struck me as bizarre that the mere sight of a backpack should lead this woman to the conclusion that I must surely be walking to a distant tomb that lay almost a thousand kilometres away. I realized that it would be like seeing a hiker walking through Bristol and assume that he *must* surely be heading for John o' Groats.

I walked onwards and realized that Castilblanco de los Arroyos was not only literary but also artistic: I detoured to Calle Goya then cut past Calle Velázquez to emerge, via Calle Miguel de Cervantes, on Calle Antonio Machado (named after the Sevillian poet). I walked past a tiny plaza decorated with more geraniums and with another ceramic sign – *'Bésame en este rincon de Castilblanco'* it said (Kiss me in this corner of Castilblanco).

Finally I found a grocery store and bought enough *jamón serrano* to last me until I crossed the mountains. Weight for weight I'd learned that serrano ham was the best thing to carry for emergency food. Salami and salchichón were delicious but the saltiness made me thirsty. I reluctantly abandoned chorizo after orange-coloured paprika oil leaked into my pack. *Jamón* was lightweight, nourishing and even more delicious once it had sweated in my pack so that it was sleek with acorn oil. Spanish bread – my favourite was the crusty *campesino* loaf – was bulky but it was filling and relatively lightweight. Bread also made me thirsty, so I avoided it in places where water was a precious commodity. Serrano ham could always be counted on to get the saliva flowing.

On the way out of town I was tempted by a bar with a terrace overlooking the grey-paved expanse of the inexplicably named Plaza Amarilla ('Yellow Square'). There was no way of knowing where my next sit-down meal would turn up.

True to form, the kitchen was closed.

* * *

By dusk I was already in the heart of Sierra Norte Natural Park.

The first 3 hours of walking had been a hot, mindless slog along a dusty highway that offered very little shade. Then walking conditions had improved markedly when the arrows pointed westward along a dirt track that headed off on a tangent into classic *dehesa*, one of the wonderfully diverse wilderness areas of sparsely forested cork and oak landscapes that provide habitats for wildlife as well as free-ranging Iberian pigs... and occasionally (although always with fair warning) for fighting bulls. Sierra Norte Natural

Park boasted populations of wild boar, foxes, otters, deer, genets and mongooses. In 2010 there were still believed to be six to eight wolfpacks, comprising around 50 individuals. They were officially a protected species in the region but during the last decade habitat loss and illegal killings (specifically by livestock farmers) had resulted in the shameful admission that wolves were now believed to be extinct in Andalucía.

I scuffed my boots through the cinnamon dust as I revelled in an evening breeze that ruffled the tops of the cork trees. The feeling of well-being was almost like a hallucination after the glare of the tarmac.

V. S. Pritchett had waxed lyrical over similar sensations: 'In Spain, when the brassy day has pounded out,' he wrote, 'flows in the scented music of the dusk, the long anointing coolness after the heat.'

I'd expected this region to be entirely uninhabited so I was surprised, a few kilometres farther on, to spot a wide sprawl of terracotta roofs through the trees. The extensive complex of abandoned buildings was painted in Andalucían style with the lower third of the whitewashed walls tinted an ochre that seemed to absorb the gold of the sunset. The buildings stood around a cobblestone courtyard and on one wall I found a small shrine with an image of Our Lady of El Rocío. I guessed that this complex accommodated travellers and wayfarers during the pilgrimage known as the Romería de El Rocío. Pilgrimages of this sort are known as *romerías* from a word that dates back to mediaeval times when Catholic faithful set out for Rome. Legend has it that, many centuries ago, a statue of the Virgin Mary was found in a hollow tree trunk on the marshes of the Rio Guadalquivir. The fame of El Rocío grew steadily, attracting pilgrims by the hundreds... until today the little village (population 1,500) lures hundreds of thousands. Unlike the pilgrimage to Santiago, *romerías* tend to incorporate the outward journey, the stay itself *and* the return home and many people travel for days, or even weeks, on horseback or seated on bullock carts, camping in the forests and on plains as they go.

I'd always wanted to experience the El Rocío fiesta (which takes place each year around Pentecost among the marshland west of Seville). Driving near Seville one May afternoon in the mid-1990s I'd detoured to investigate the cause of a huge dust cloud that hovered over the western plains. I'd eased my Jeep to the side of the track and climbed onto the roof to photograph an unforgettable procession of ox carts that trundled past, loaded with pilgrims, camping kit and wine barrels. There were women on horseback clad in flamenco dresses and riding boots. Some of the *caballeros* – in bolero jackets and *Cordobés* hats – were so drunk that I was sure they must fall off their horses. They must have been born in the saddle, however, because even the most inebriated was capable of cantering one-handed without sloshing the booze out of his glass. I was committed to an assignment elsewhere and had no time to detour. I was bitterly disappointed not to have the freedom to follow the raucous cavalry procession to the village where they would spend the next three days celebrating.

Years later I met an old farmer called Pedro who maintained an oxen cart – in the same way that other men might keep a classic car – which he used purely to transport his family on a three-week round-trip holiday each year to the fiesta of El Rocío. In Pedro's case (as in many others, let's be honest) the *romería* was completed far more in the spirit of adventure than out of any religious zeal. He had a face that was deeply scoured – like the erosion gullies in his Extremadura farm. Plenty of lines on the dial, as the saying goes. Pedro's party trick was to squirt a jet from a wineskin directly at the centre of his forehead so that he could channel the rivulets infallibly to the corners of his mouth via the network of ravines that lined his face. My friend had invited me to join him on the trip the following year and I'd always regretted the fact that I'd not found the time. He tempted me with tales of how they would, at various times during the *romería*, cook a whole sheep in a metal beer keg, seasoning it with an entire bucket of garlic and herbs. I wondered if Pedro and his little Spanish *voortrekker* convoy had ever camped in this spot, stewing mutton and performing raucous party tricks over shared wineskins.

The place was deserted now, however, and I counted myself fortunate to find a functioning fountain where I could refill my canteens. Then, in a covered section of the courtyard that apparently served as a stable I found a tap and a hosepipe. Tying the pipe to a low roof-beam I jury-rigged a shower and even took the opportunity to do some laundry.

* * *

It would be dark very soon and I doubted that anyone would pass by at this late hour. It seemed best to find somewhere more secretive so I decided to move on and look for a hammock spot in the forest on the opposite side of the valley.

As I followed the rutted trail across a small stone bridge, I heard the crackling of branches and turned in time to watch a small herd of deer scramble up the hillside just a stone's throw away. Among the deepening shadows under the conifer trees, I could make out freshly churned earth, betraying the snuffling muzzles and raking tusks of countless wild boars. I rejected the first good hammock spot I found because I could see from the roughened bark that this was a regular scratching post and some particularly huge porker had even left long, stiff bristles embedded in the bark.

The Sierra Norte is part of the 400-kilometre Sierra Morena range. Many years before I'd spent a week hiking in the central part of the range. Late one evening, just as I was looking for a place to bed down, a rustling sound on the hillside just above me alerted me to a truly gigantic wild boar that was snuffling busily down the narrow trail. It was by far the biggest I'd ever seen and it was coming directly towards me. There was no room to scramble aside and I stopped, stupidly frozen in indecision. It was only about 5 metres away when I finally came to my senses and let out a warning yell. Wild boar are notorious for being bad-tempered, short-sighted and instinctively aggressive but fortunately the huge beast spun around and took off back up the hill.

The incident brought on a cold sweat when I recalled that being gored by a wild boar frequently results in bleeding to death. In this case I was pretty sure that the huge snout would have been around groin level and I tried not to imagine the horror of a night-time scramble back down the mountain with a stab wound from those wicked tusks.

In a country where hunting is popular, wild boars are naturally elusive but I'd recently read that Barcelona had been suffering from invasive and unusually aggressive boars. The problem went viral in 2021 when pop superstar Shakira was attacked by two wild boars when she was walking in a Barcelona park with her eight-year-old son. Apparently, the boars snatched her bag.

'They were taking my bag to the woods with my mobile phone in it,' the singer said afterwards. 'They've destroyed everything.'

City authorities had reacted in various ways – the least successful of these reactions being an incident where a police officer tried to shoot a wild boar with his service revolver but missed and injured his partner.

With such thoughts to dwell on as I dozed off, I could only count myself lucky that I was safely ensconced in the wilds of Sierra Norte and not in a park in Barcelona.

* * *

I convinced myself that I was feeling a little stronger with each day that passed and the next morning I was enthusiastic to get back on the trail. My calf muscles felt a little stiff for the first half-hour and the blisters soon numbed as they settled into position in my boots.

I'd been walking for barely an hour when I came across a poignant reminder that, at my ripe old age, I ought to be wary of over-confidence. Halfway up the steep, rocky slope leading to a peak called Cerro del Calvario I came across a marble plinth etched with the red cross of Santiago: *'In Memoriam del peregrino Michel Laurent'* it read. Apparently, the Belgian pilgrim was fatally struck by heatstroke on this spot in 2016. Another pilgrim (a German) had died on the same hill the previous year. In mediaeval times it was believed that any person who died while on a pilgrimage would bypass purgatory and go straight to heaven. Likewise, time spent on a pilgrimage was directly subtracted from allotted time in purgatory – the logic being that you'd effectively elected to undergo purgatory on Earth.

The trail through the Sierra Norte had a reputation as one of the toughest sections on the Via de la Plata. After leaving Castilblanco de los Arroyos, pilgrims could not expect any shelter until they reached Almadén de la Plata. To do this they were forced to scramble up the Cerro del Calvario ridge (overlooking Almadén) right at the end of an arduous 29-kilometre hike.

I'd covered 32 kilometres the previous day but the freedom to camp meant that I was able to sleep south of Cerro del Calvario ridge and so could face the steep climb in the morning while I was still fresh.

On the summit of Cerro del Calvario I stopped to enjoy the view down to the terracotta roofs of Almadén de la Plata and a vermillion clock-tower that looked more like a minaret than a church spire. The meandering track down was so steep that I imagined that if I gave my pack a hefty enough kick it would probably land in the village plaza.

The sound of courting storks, clattering their bills on the top of the tower, echoed up the valley. In the bright morning light it was hard to imagine anything farther removed from an 'earthly purgatory'.

* * *

Almadén de la Plata was known to the Roman conquerors as Pagus Marmorarius (from the Latin for 'village of marbles') because of the marble quarry here. The marble supply has long been exhausted and Almadén is now famous primarily for its serrano ham. In a café on the corner of Plaza del Reloj I ordered a plate of the best Iberian *pata negra* (black-hoof).

'You're very late,' the barmaid commented as she passed the second glass of vitamin-packed orange juice across the counter to me.

'Who me?'

'Yes, you're very late.'

I wondered vaguely if she thought she recognized me. Or perhaps whether a few marbles had gone missing in Almadén recently.

'It's just turned eight o'clock.' I pointed at the clock over the bar. Perhaps this undeniable fact might help to restart the conversation on a more logical basis, I thought.

An old man who was the café's only other customer now turned a curious eye on me: 'But why haven't you started walking already?' he asked.

Finally we got to the root of this good-natured but confusing inquisition and I realized that they were simply surprised to see a pilgrim still in Almadén at breakfast time. Apparently any hiker sticking to the recommended schedule invariably abandoned the village *albergue* at first light. Even by the standards of the Via de la Plata, Almadén was particularly remote. Having hiked 29 uninhabited kilometres to get here, pilgrims were faced with a 3- or 4-hour hike before the nearest neighbours to the north.

I pointed out that I had no reason to hurry since I'd already put 10 kilometres behind me since dawn and was free simply to sleep wherever tiredness caught up with me. It was the second time that morning that I'd felt privileged not to be restricted to a timetable, with obligatory overnight stops that were dictated by a pan-Iberian series of *albergues*. The familiar yellow arrows directed me out of the village along a farm track and then through a farm gate into what appeared to be private land. Passing the front of a majestic ochre-painted finca, a pair of huge mastiffs ran out of the yard with bellowing barks that made my hair stand on end. Before I'd even had a chance to look around for a stick or a stone their cheerfully flapping jowls were already nuzzling at my hand. I breathed a sigh of relief and spent the next few minutes tickling them behind floppy ears the size of oven mittens.

A kilometre to my east, less than 100 metres from a quarry where the Romans had chiselled their marble, archaeologists had discovered a cave with Bronze Age artefacts and almost 200 examples of cave art dating back to Neolithic times.

I followed the signs onwards through a gate marked 'Private Hunting Reserve'. Somebody had scrawled across the words with a vicious black marker: *¡Asesinos! ¡Borrachos!'* – Killers! Drunks!

I'm no hunter myself but I wondered if the vandal who wrote with such psychotic hatred had considered the fact that Spanish hunting reserves of this sort go a long way towards protecting vast expanses of wilderness. Almost 30 per cent of what is often said to be Europe's most biodiverse country is protected land and many of these reserves (totalling over 3,700 sites) are private hunting reserves which play a huge part in conservation.

I continued along a farm track leading through meadows where black Iberian pigs foraged for acorns and rare black storks strutted after grasshoppers. The grassland was dotted with the white disks of rockrose and my boots scuffed up a heady scent of mysterious wild herbs. The trail shrunk to a strip of scuffed dirt that barely resembled a goat-track – so narrow that, as a Spaniard might say, a cow and a Christian could not walk abreast. It was hard to imagine that this goat-track had been a thoroughfare during several millennia for pilgrims, traders and sundry vagabonds. I might have been tempted to backtrack had it not been for the fact that, even here, somebody had taken the time to paint yellow arrows on occasional boulders.

* * *

It was almost midday when I hobbled up to a bench in El Real de la Jara's plaza and peeled my boots off to find that a huge blister, almost like a supplementary toe, had developed on the back of my left heel. I decided not to operate and hoped that, by the time the heat of the afternoon had waned and I started walking again, this bulbous appendage would have shrunk of its own accord.

I dropped my boots and my pack in the doorway and limped into Café Bar El Chati in my flip-flops. The barman advised me that this little village (population about 1,500) boasted a municipal *albergue* and no less than three guesthouses that were dedicated to pilgrims.

I ordered a calamari sandwich and a Cruzcampo and sat at the bar while Miguel the barman told me with obvious pride how business was booming these days in El Real de la Jara.

'It gets very busy sometimes,' Miguel emphasized in response to my comment that I'd yet to meet a single pilgrim since I joined the Via de la Plata in Seville. 'Last week we had *three* hikers in this bar at the same time!'

I needed to kill time while the sun's power diminished so after shooting the breeze with Miguel for a while, I moved a few hundred metres down the road for coffee at Bar Casa del Pueblo. I sat at a pavement table and forced myself to wait until the sun's rays had crept across the road to touch my feet. In this way an idle hour slipped away, wholly immersed in watching village life revolve around me, until the sun touching my toes convinced me that it was time to bid farewell to El Real de la Jara.

By this time my supplementary toe had shrunk to a manageable size and I was ready to get moving towards the great glowing walls of the fourteenth-century castle at the edge of the village. Legend has it that a female deer (which appears even today on the village's coat of arms) led the castle's architects to the ideal spot. The doe turned out to be a military strategist of note because the hilltop commanded a view over the town, and the majestic square towers provided defence from the attacking Moors and protected pilgrims from the bandits who plundered this frontier country.

A few minutes later I crossed the Arroyo de la Víbora (Ravine of the Viper) and took my first step into Extremadura.

* * *

I'd been walking by now for nine days and had covered a little under 300 kilometres (about a quarter of my total distance). I figured that it would take me ten days at least to cross the 350 kilometres of shimmering Extremadura plains that now lay to the north.

The first building I passed in this new province was another ruined fortress, this time protected by circular turrets which were designed to be more resistant to 'sapping' (undermining) and better at deflecting projectiles from siege weapons. Throughout the Middle Ages, Spain was largely policed by competing orders of warrior-monks: the Orders of Calatrava and Santiago and, of course, the legendary Knights Templar.

While these orders (and many others) were technically allies, they invariably had their own battle axes to grind and these two citadels appeared almost like chess pieces, facing each other across the Ravine of the Viper.

The Knights Templar had been founded in Jerusalem around 1118 under the rather verbose title of 'The Poor Fellow-Soldiers of Christ and the Temple of Solomon'. Their mandate was to protect pilgrims from bandits in the Holy Land but, with the endorsement of the Pope, they became incredibly powerful, with property and castles throughout Spain and, in fact, throughout Christendom. When, in 1147, the Templars were unable to defend the castle of Calatrava against the Moors a group of Cistercian warriors came to the rescue and, a decade later, they set up the rival Order of Calatrava.

The bandits, fortunately, are long gone but even today this region still feels like frontier land. For the next hour there was barely a patch of shade and the landscape concentrated the power of the sun like a skillet.

I did my best to preserve water and traipsed onwards, intent on reaching a fountain or standpipe before my thirst kicked in. Three hours after stepping into Extremadura I arrived at San Isidro Hermitage, but the campsite that was marked on my map had long since been abandoned. The hermitage itself was a bizarre square structure with space-age 'stabilizer' struts protruding from the corners, making it look like the launch pad from which some heaven-bound rocket had already departed.

The entire complex was deserted but I undertook a futile exploration of the bathroom in the hope that I might find a functioning tap or even, wonder of wonders, a shower. The water was disconnected and, with diminishing supplies, I decided to continue to the spot where the dusty pilgrim trail crossed the A-66 highway before setting off, once again, across country. According to a review I read on a Via de la Plata guide, El Culebrin's 24-hour truck stop was 'a great place to get some snacks, use the toilets, get water, rest a while and watch hordes of Chinese tourists and Spanish motorbike riders mingle'.

After the peace of the trail, however, the riotous restaurant and shoving crowds in the service station dining area struck me as intimidating. Nine days of almost perpetual solitude had no doubt made me antisocial but the crew-cut Russians with their blonde mobster wives and noisy kids with tramline hairstyles freaked me out. The sight of homeward-bound Moroccan families with roof-racks overloaded with baggage and bedding piled on backseats provoked feelings of homesickness. It felt like it had been a very long time since I'd seen so many people crammed into such a small space. Hungry as I was, I couldn't face the queues where people lined up six-deep to order French fries and oily burgers. The clatter of trays and cutlery and the clouds of greasy steam wafting out of the kitchen were overwhelming. The shop too seemed to vibrate with noise and I scuttled for the door.

Three hundred metres away, across the opposite side of the sweltering car park, there was a fuel station and a distant sign shouted 'Laundry!'

I walked across the baking tarmac, past a man who knelt on a prayer mat next to an old Mercedes with French licence plates. I wondered how often the five-times-daily obligation of prayer might literally become a lifesaver as a necessary interruption to the long, drowsy drive home from France.

In comparison with the restaurant, the almost-empty shop at the fuel station was blissfully peaceful. The little laundry kiosk was clearly geared towards (relatively wealthy) truckers and the check-out girl showed how to load my seven euros into the washing machine.

Once again I missed the opportunity for a square meal and snacked instead on soggy, plastic-wrapped sandwiches and a can of beer in the little air-conditioned kiosk while I recharged my phone. The solar power-bank that travelled on the top of my pack had proved a godsend but the 90-minute washing-cycle was an ideal opportunity for a booster charge.

It was very close to nightfall by the time my laundry had dried. Since I'd crossed into Extremadura I'd seen very few hammock trees and, as I hurried across the pretzel-shaped interchange of the

A-66 highway, I was already scouting for a sheltered spot in which to lay my groundsheet.

I detoured to investigate the dingy interior of another, much older, hermitage, standing within earshot of the traffic on the highway. This one, with its turreted roof and arched door, was more evocative of a Muslim marabout than a Christian shrine. Although I had the feeling that I wouldn't be the first vagabond to have taken shelter here, the dampness and musty smell made it an unappealing place to sleep.

I was still contemplating this prospect when a hoopoe (my personal omen bird) swooped along the trail, as if leading the way. Just a half kilometre farther in I came across a little belt of eucalyptus trees that was ideal for a hammock.

* * *

The town of Monesterio was founded by the brotherhood of the Knights Templar but these days it's yet another town that is primarily famous for the production of *jamón serrano*. Even at eight in the morning the aroma of acorn-scented ham pervaded the whole town.

The route out of Monesterio was not well marked and I was already striding confidently along the main road, sated with coffee, bread and *jamón*, when a man who was walking his dog called me back.

¡Oye chico! He was yelling and pointing down a narrow trail that I'd overlooked.

My momentary embarrassment at my slack navigating skills was assuaged by his, very complimentary, use of the word 'boy'. I was yet to meet a single pilgrim so, once again, it was strange to assume that anyone walking out of Monesterio with a backpack must naturally be following the Via de la Plata. It was clear though that the town must occasionally get busy because I'd read that the local *albergue* boasts 50 beds.

I couldn't imagine where all those guests could come from and I was already well clear of the town when a large multi-lingual sign beside the track gave me a clue. The sign bid me farewell from Monesterio: *'hasta pronto'* it said, and 'See you soon'. Then it echoed the same sentiments in five other languages. Along with the expected German, Dutch, French and Italian, the sign-writers had inexplicably thought to include the Bahasa Indonesian phrase *'sampai jumpa lagi'*. I knew that this literally meant 'until we meet again' since I'd spent a lot of time based in Indonesia and spoke the language fairly well. While Indonesia is famous for being the world's biggest Muslim country, I was well aware that it also has a huge Christian population (of about 23 million people). Even so, it seemed extremely unlikely that many Indonesian hikers would ever have converged on Monesterio.

I was still puzzling over this when a cyclist came wobbling up the track behind me. Carlos, the very first pilgrim I'd met, was also unexpected in that his home was in Santiago de Compostela. Thus he was undertaking a pilgrimage and homeward-bound at the same time. He told me that he was covering an average of around 75 kilometres per day and expected to be back with his family within two weeks. I watched him cycle away with mixed feelings of envy at the ground he could cover and gratitude that my 5 kilometres-an-hour pace allowed me to take in every tiny detail of the terrain I crossed.

It was mid-morning and I was resting with my back against the trunk of a stunted oak by the side of the trail when a hiker appeared over the crest of the hill. Fran, a Basque from Vitoria, had spent the night at the *albergue* in Monesterio. He'd hiked other sections of the Via de la Plata at various times during holidays from work.

'One of these days I'll complete the entire route,' he shrugged, 'but there's no rush.'

I admired his relaxed outlook, which was so much healthier than my obsessive tallying of kilometres and days.

'I try to average no more than about twenty kilometres per day,' he said. 'This way I can stay fresh and am always enthusiastic to start hiking the next morning. I'm not really a pilgrim so I'm not obsessed about ending up in Santiago. I'll just walk until my holiday time is over and then catch a bus back home.'

Fran had met Carlos in Monesterio the previous evening and they'd cooked dinner together in the otherwise deserted *albergue*. Pure coincidence had brought us three, very different, travellers into contact on the same morning on this remote trail. Fran expected to cover the 20 kilometres to the *albergue* in Fuente de Cantos that day. I hoped to make double that distance and – unless things went badly awry – to pass through Calzadilla de los Barros before dusk. Carlos meanwhile would already have pedalled into the (to us) impossibly distant city of Zafra by lunchtime... and would be immeasurably far out of both of our lives by nightfall.

Fran and I fell into step for an hour or so. I wasn't disappointed when he stopped for a rest because I'd seen on the map that the valley ahead was marked with a river and I was optimistic about a bathing opportunity. When the track descended into the shallow valley it was immediately apparent, however, that the Arroyo del Bodión Chico held nothing more than a few stagnant pools of tepid water.

Nevertheless, it would be foolhardy to pass up what might be my only opportunity for a wash. The track was deserted as far as I could see in both directions so I quickly stripped down to my boxers and, doing my best to keep my blisters out of the mud, hurriedly splashed water over myself. It was not the luxurious soak that I'd anticipated but it left me feeling much fresher.

I was just zipping my shorts when I became aware of the tinkling of bells and a horse-drawn cart came rattling over the hill. The farmer at the reins tipped his hat with a smile and wished me a *'buen camino'* as hooves and cartwheels splashed through my bathroom.

An hour later I passed a dead viper on the trail. A cartwheel had rolled across its neck.

* * *

That afternoon was spent crossing a series of low, scrubby hills in a landscape that struck me as metallic. My boots scuffed among iron-coloured rock, kicking up dust as sharp as steel filings. Clumps of wiry grass rustled in a hot breeze that might have come from a blacksmith's bellows. Ruts in the trail – rare signs that once in a while there might actually be water here – were the colour, texture and durability of rusted railway lines and the entire landscape seemed to have been forged by the sun.

I was crossing a plateau of sprawling corn fields when the silhouette of a bull appeared on the northern horizon. It shimmered in the heat haze, as if seen through a waterfall. While it could have been a mirage, it gradually intensified over the next hour, growing in size until it loomed high, dominating the field.

There are said to be 94 of these national icons – known familiarly to the Spanish as *los Osbornes* – along the highways of Spain. The bull's horns are poised 14 metres above the ground and their pendulous *cojones* hover far above head height.

The wooden silhouettes were only 4 metres high when, in 1956, the producers of Osborne Brandy commissioned Andalucían artist Manolo Prieto to create an instantly recognizable advertisement for their Veterano brand. As a series of laws were passed to keep billboards increasingly distant from the roadsides (20 metres in 1962, then 50 metres in 1974), the bulls grew to 7 and then the current 14 metres tall so that the red-stencilled words 'Veterano Osborne' could still be made out.

By the time another law was passed in 1988 prohibiting *all* advertising on the highways the bulls had become such a beloved feature of Spanish roads that there was a public outcry. The supreme court was forced to make an exception and, while the bulls themselves remained, only the writing was blacked out.

This particular Osborne was designed to be visible to motorists on the N-630 driving between Seville and Mérida. It was still too early to camp but I considered having an early night and shunning my hammock purely so that I could spend the night under this Spanish icon.

Unfortunately, when I finally got as close as I could I found that it was fenced off and in private land. Reluctantly I had to continue onwards.

An hour later I arrived in the little plaza of Calzadilla de los Barros. Many of the town's population had gathered at seats that had been set up in front of a large screen in a small marquee.

When I went into Bar Dioni on the corner of the plaza, I saw that almost all the Saturday afternoon patrons were clad in Real Madrid soccer shirts. The kitchen was not serving meals because, as the barmaid explained, the chef was a big *hincha del Madrid* (Madrid fan) and he'd taken the afternoon off because his team was playing Liverpool in the finals of the European UEFA Champions League that evening. Seeing my look of disappointment the barmaid very kindly offered to make me a sandwich.

I sat on the bar's little terrace sipping my Cruzcampo while she prepared one of my favourites; a pork-loin baguette with green peppers and cheese. On the opposite side of the road a drunk – dressed, like everybody else, in the white and blue of a *Madridista* – was already staggering, as if leaning into a sidewind. I wondered if it was the chef.

A young blonde woman sat down at a neighbouring table. She didn't need a pilgrim's passport – one glance at the bandaged feet in her sandals was proof enough of her credentials.

Heidi was from Germany and she was walking from Seville to Salamanca. She'd walked to Santiago along the Portuguese Camino the previous year and had clearly delighted in the sociability of shared evenings at *albergues* that were bursting at the seams with pilgrims from all over the world. By comparison the Via de la Plata was 'a very lonely experience' she said.

She was the only person staying at the local *albergue*: 'It's spooky,' she said with a little shiver. 'I had to ask for the key and let myself in. I have this huge house and nobody to share it with. It's more fun to have company.'

Some of the drinkers at another table asked if we were going to watch the match. I was disappointed to tell them that I had to move on. I'm no soccer fan but I would have enjoyed the festive atmosphere. I admitted that I was English and they cheered when I pointed out that after six years living in the Spanish capital, I felt far greater ties to Real Madrid than I did to Liverpool Football Club.

A second Cruzcampo did its best to convince me that it would have been so much more pleasant to stay in the village than it would be to heft my pack onto my back and get moving again. I'd already walked 30 kilometres since dawn but there were still 2 hours until the match started. If I stayed to watch the soccer and then I stuck with my self-imposed 'stealth camping' rule I'd end up trying to find a place to doss down after dark on the edge of a town which – regardless of the outcome of the match – was likely to have more than its share of rambling inebriates.

Heidi already had the key to the *albergue* and it was a highly tempting prospect simply to pay for my bunk and move in. She would clearly have preferred not to stay alone in the 'spooky' *albergue* and a little devil on my shoulder tried to convince me that checking into the *albergue* would be the gentlemanly thing to do…

It was almost an unfair test and with effort I shouldered my pack, wished both Heidi and the Real Madrid crowd the best of luck and tried to muster some northbound momentum.

Two Guardia Civil officers were standing near the town hall, probably grumpy at having drawn the short straw for a shift on match night. I nodded briefly in their direction as I marched by, shoulders hunched. I hoped that they wouldn't try to redirect me to the *albergue*. After all, it was now almost eight in the evening and they'd be well aware that I couldn't cover the 15 kilometres to the next village by nightfall. Just as I felt sure that they were going to call out to me, their attention was distracted by a teenager who was navigating the little plaza like a schooner, heeled over at a windblown angle. I'd done nothing wrong but despite myself I felt like an outlaw as I scuttled furtively out of town.

In the eyes of the local *guardia* it would surely appear highly suspicious that someone with cash in his pocket would actively choose to sleep in a ditch rather than join Heidi in the *albergue*.

As luck would have it, I failed to find hammock trees that evening. Instead I had to settle for a meadow overlooking the Arroyo Artaja. I'd just laid out my groundsheet among the daisies when I noticed that a skylark was fluttering and chirping frantically above my head.

'I'm sorry little fella,' I told him. 'If you'd only spoken up when I first got here I'd have gladly moved along. Now you'll just have to put up with my company until morning.'

I was woken a little later by what I thought was the crackling sound of automatic rifle fire. It took a few moments to realize that it was fireworks. Real Madrid were the new UEFA champions.

* * *

A sure sign that the solitude of the trail might be taking its toll came the next morning when it dawned on me that I was actually talking out loud to my own feet.

It was fair to say that they were taking the brunt of the strain. They needed reassurance so I was doing my best to broker a deal with them: 'Look, I'm sorry,' I told them. 'I know you didn't sign up for this and it's asking a lot of you. You've always been good to me and have carried me a long way without complaint. Just bear with me for a few more weeks and I promise I won't ask this of you again, okay?'

I suppose that both feet must have been content to take me at my word because the three of us shared a wonderfully carefree morning walking through a rolling landscape of stunted vines. Little whirlwinds blew among the vines and every signpost was iced with the crystalized white paste of buzzard droppings.

To take my mind off my feet – and, perhaps, their minds off *me* – I listened to music, wailing out Dylan's 'Like a Rolling Stone' at the top of my voice until my throat was raw.

Narina had set up an inspirational 'Vagabond' playlist on Spotify with suggested songs from family and friends. Among the classics – 'I Walk the Line', 'On the Road Again', 'Born to Run', 'King of the Road'… – there were a few that never failed to bring a wry smile to my face: 'Despacito' (Luis Fonsi and Daddy Yankee), Chuck Berry's 'No Particular Place to Go' and especially 'Sit Down' by James.

I turned off the music and ceased my howling well before I was within earshot of the little town of Puebla de Sancho Pérez. Near the town centre I stopped to read a noticeboard. The bullring in Ronda (which opened in 1784) is widely said to be the oldest in Spain so I was surprised to read that, according to Extremadura Tourism, Puebla de Sancho Pérez's *plaza de toros* was considerably older, having been in use for over 500 years.

Unusually, it is a square plaza – unlike the relatively 'modern' circular one in Ronda – and the *zorros* (or foxes), as the people of Puebla de Sancho Pérez are inexplicably nicknamed, seemed to be as inordinately proud of it as they were of the local vino.

'*El buen vino, resucita el peregrino*', ran the slogan at the top of the noticeboard – Good wine resuscitates the pilgrim.

It was barely nine in the morning so I resisted temptation. Instead I settled for a quick *cortado* caffeine shot and decided to push on for another hour before a leisurely Sunday breakfast in Zafra city.

* * *

From the moment I entered the suburbs of Zafra I was continually greeted by people wishing me *'buen camino'*. Perhaps it was something to do with the communal atmosphere of Sunday morning in a relatively small city. I was charmed from the outset with the palpable sense of hospitality of the *Segedanos* (as the people of Zafra are called).

I walked past the Mudéjar convent of Santa Clara where Jane Dormer, lady-in-waiting to Mary I of England, lies buried. The convent has been a haven for cloistered nuns for most of the last 500 years although these days only very few take the traditional vows of chastity, poverty, piety and obedience to live, entirely removed from the world, behind the heavy oak doors and high walls. There are still 15 cloistered monasteries and nunneries in Seville alone but many of these establishments have had to move with the times. The nuns at Zafra's Convento de Santa Clara, for example, had opened a small museum and a shop selling pastries.

Back in 2009 the Catholic News Agency had reported that 'the Jesuits had just 20 novices in all of Spain, the Franciscans, five, and the Vincentians, two.' Nuns were apparently being recruited from India, Kenya and Paraguay to augment convents inhabited only by elderly nuns. Almost a decade before this revelation I'd researched a story for *Spain* magazine on how convents and monasteries were trying to find innovative ways to raise revenue. Immense convent kitchens, built to feed hundreds, had been turned into commercial bakeries for products with names like nun's sighs, angel hair, pieces-of-heaven and bishop's hearts. Traditionally, such produce could only be bought at the *torno* (the revolving door that was the only access to a cloistered nunnery and concealed a view of the interior) but some modern convents had established websites for online orders. San Leandro's Augustine nuns in Seville had been so successful that they struggled to fill all their orders for bakery products and the Dominican sisters of the Imperial Monastery in Toledo had set up a website for the international distribution of their marzipans. A cooperative of 30 Spanish monasteries and convents had established a Christmas market but it had to close early since they ran out of stock.

On a terrace in the shady Plaza de España I ordered an 'angel-hair' pastry slice (known as a *bayonesa*) and a *café con leche* and sat contentedly as the vitamins from a large glass of fresh orange juice filtered through my system. I revelled in the relaxed Sunday-morning ambience of Zafra and promised myself that I'd return sometime to stay for longer and to get better acquainted.

It was disturbing to think that much of the historic grandeur of this little city, so obvious even today, had been acquired during a very dark period in history. During the fifteenth and sixteenth centuries, Zafra was an important market town where trade concentrated primarily on the sale of African slaves who were transported overland from Lisbon.

Vast wealth was brought into Zafra too from the New World when sons of the city (most notably Hernando de Soto) set sail as conquistadors. Historical records show that more than 200 townsmen joined de Soto's voyage of exploration to North America in 1539. Some historians believe that some African slaves and mixed-race *extremeños* would have been among that number (making them potentially the first Africans ever to reach the New World).

The Tower of San Francisco is all that remains of the convent that was built during the height of Zafra's slave-trading era. I was passing the crumbling old tower on my way out of town when I was surprised by a wagon-train of a sort that could almost have dated from the same era. Each of the four heavily loaded carts was drawn by sleek, healthy horses. Two also had haltered horses trotting behind. I was in the habit of snapping photos (as memory joggers rather than for any artistic reason) but just as I raised my phone to snap a shot, an elderly *Gitana* in the last cart covered her eyes with her hands. I hurriedly lowered my phone and lamely waved an apologetic hand.

It was probable that she was simply reluctant to appear in a photo but it occurred to me that there was a time – not so long ago – when Spain's *Gitano* communities retained a genuine fear of the evil eye. The most common English translation of *Gitano* is Gypsy or, these days, Romani. The word *Gitano* comes with none of the pejorative connotations that the word 'Gypsy' is sometimes loaded with and Spanish *Gitanos* – invariably sedentary and speaking a unique language called Caló – have very little in common with Romani people from other regions.

'Gitanos believe that their Gitano names and rituals lose their magical effectiveness if they are revealed to the non-Gitano world,' wrote Javier Fuentes Cañizares, author and acclaimed expert on Caló. This protective sentiment extends to the image as well. Even, in some cases, to odours. A nurse at a hospital in northern Spain once told me of a quarrel on the ward because an elderly *Gitano* accused the nurses of bathing his wife without his permission: he claimed that they had 'stolen her scent'.

I guessed that the little *Gitano* band was heading to a horse market. I would have given anything to be invited to join them. Wherever my path was destined to take me that afternoon I doubted that it would be as fascinating. I would happily have done an about-turn, regardless of the fact that they were heading in entirely the opposite direction.

I felt bad that I'd acted disrespectfully by photographing the little procession and regretted that the old lady probably considered me to be just another entitled tourist.

* * *

An hour later I'd already hiked across the grandly named (but actually diminutive) Sierra de los Olivos and down to the town of Los Santos de Maimona. The plaza was packed with people in their Sunday best, making me feel even more like a hobo in my bush shorts and grubby T-shirt.

Judging from the number of little girls in flouncy white dresses I guessed that it had been a busy day for First Communions. The young mothers too had emerged in sequined heels and ball gowns, many with carefully coutured open backs that were clearly designed to reveal a surprising number of elegant tattoos.

It was not quite lunchtime when I found an empty table at one of the bars on the plaza, but tables had been reserved for meals and the best I could get was a tapas of cold chicken, pork or tripe. Mahou (the beer of central Spain) seemed to predominate here so I celebrated this promising sign of northbound progress with an ice-cold *jarra*.

Little Los Santos de Maimona inexplicably lacked the open friendliness that I'd felt in much bigger Zafra. The plaza on a Sunday lunchtime was a good place for people-watching though so I curbed my impatience while I waited for the midday sun to lose some of its heat.

Whole processions of people arrived on the plaza, greeting friends and family with interminable rounds of hugs. I'd read recently that the hug had been proven to provoke production of a neurochemical called oxytocin which apparently has a warming and healing effect on the human body. It occurred to me that Spain must be more infused with this valuable oxytocin than, say, England. And southern Spain more so than the North. The plaza was so saturated with oxytocin that the inhabitants of Los Santos de Maimona could export it.

'Your true traveller finds boredom rather agreeable than painful,' Aldous Huxley once wrote. 'It is the symbol of his liberty – his excessive freedom. He accepts his boredom, when it comes, not merely philosophically, but almost with pleasure.'

Now, approaching midsummer on the plains of Extremadura, it was increasingly important that I force myself to sit out as much of the hot afternoons as possible. The days were long so it was sensible to confine my hiking to 7 or 8 hours divided between early mornings and late evenings. Contrary to Huxley's sentiments, however, as the trek progressed I would often find the enforced boredom of the midday 'siesta hours' harder to bear than the hours of walking. A tourist would have found plenty to occupy them in any of the villages of Extremadura but few pilgrims who have been consistently walking upwards of 30 kilometres per day have much energy left for aimless strolling.

The sound of church bells echoed across the rooftops, convincing me that although I wasn't an 'honest-to-God' pilgrim, I should take a chance to sit in on at least one service during my trek.

The sun was still pounding into the narrow alleyways in any case and it would certainly be wisest to wait until the afternoon heat eased a little before venturing back out onto the shadeless plains. In the delightful coolness of the church, I dropped a handful of coins in the donation box and made my way to the back pew just as the *padre* reached the lectern.

His voice rose above the wheezing of the organ.

'*Vamos a ver,*' he said, by way of a preliminary welcome – Let's see. 'If anyone here doesn't think they can stay for the *entire* service then they'd better get up and leave now.'

I shouldered my pack and left. That was the closest I came to a religious experience – at least in the officially sanctified sense – during the entire trek.

He was probably right. The last time I'd sat through an *entire* church service had been at the First Communion of my eight-year-old daughter in Pamplona.

'I really couldn't think what I was supposed to say, Papá,' she'd told me as she recounted the saga of her first confession. 'They told us we had to think of something to confess to, so I admitted that I'd been *"un poco chuletica con mis amigas"*.'

I wondered if the priest had been able to keep a straight face as he absolved her of the heinous sin of being 'a little bit too cocky with her friends'.

* * *

On the outskirts of Los Santos de Maimona I stopped at a fountain and sifted my last remaining sachet of rehydration salts into my big water bottle. The heat continued to build through the afternoon and by 4 o'clock it was reaching a crescendo. There were still 6 hours of daylight but as the sun sank lower, instead of losing its heat, it became a hot blade that etched tiger-stripes on the dirt track's corrugated surface.

My phone confirmed that it was now 43°C in the shade... but Google certainly couldn't have told me where to *find* any of that shade.

I didn't know it yet but we were entering what would become the hottest Spanish summer since records began in 1916. By the end of the season, the Institute for Global Health (in Barcelona) had estimated that more than 61,000 people died from heat-related causes that summer. More than 11,000 of these deaths were in Spain.

An Algerian Tuareg in the Central Sahara had once shown me how to wrap a turban so that it created a little cool zone (relatively speaking) of circulating air over the crown of the head. I was too exhausted to dig out the sarong that served as my towel and instead rolled a bandana like a donut into my bush hat to create some space for air circulation. I wished I had enough water to dampen the bandana but such wastefulness would have been foolhardy.

I'd heard too that the Tuaregs sometimes carried a stone in their mouths in the desert to provoke saliva. Heirloom sucking-stones – rubbed smooth over generations – were sometimes handed down from father to son. In desperation I tried it, but the hot pebble just sapped what little moisture had remained in my mouth.

Laurie Lee once wrote about a Spanish man who carried a pebble in his mouth to prolong the taste of brandy. Perhaps that would be more effective. But then some of Lee's most delightfully earthy stories were too good to be true: he'd also written, for example, about a pet sparrow that had been trained to steal sips of alcohol which it would then carry to its owner's mouth.

A few kilometres south of Villafranca de los Barros the trail crossed a railway line that marked the start of a sparse forest of spindly trees. There are parts of Spain that have sometimes gone as long as four years without seeing rain and in this desiccated *campo*, only these weak trees stood as proof that rain *ever* fell.

I was anxious to find a shady place to sleep before I reached Villafranca de los Barros because I knew from the map that beyond that town, I could expect no other settlements (and little change in the terrain) for almost 30 kilometres.

But I'd come across nowhere to replenish my water supplies and it would have been folly to camp under this glaring sun before I'd even found a place to refill my canteens.

In all my trudging through that long afternoon I never saw a single shrub that could offer some serviceable protection from the sun. Two or three times I tried to crouch under a scraggy bush but squatting closer to the hot dust made things even worse.

The air shimmered and swayed over the bleached plain and little dust-devils skipped ahead, as if luring me onwards. Twice I zoned out completely as I was walking, overlooking turnings so that I had to double back. I'd walked the equivalent of nine marathons in the last 11 days. There was little doubt now that I'd hit what marathon runners call The Wall. Only later did it occur to me that this state of semi-sleepwalking was probably a symptom of heatstroke.

I remembered that while hiking near Toledo during his midsummer walk, Laurie Lee had his own run-in with that unforgiving *sol de justicia*: 'The Castilian sun caught up with me at last,' he wrote, 'and struck me down with 24-hour fever.'

I was nearing the butt-end of what felt like one of the toughest days of my life when I finally arrived on the edge of Villafranca de los Barros. I'd taken about as much strain as I could manage for one day. I drank my fill at a fountain on the edge of town and then sat on a shady doorstep to peel off my boots. Great bloated blobs of blisters looked – and felt – as if candles had been melted across my heels and onto the balls of both feet.

I had two options. I could either find a corner to sleep rough in town or I could press on and hope to find some shelter on the plains to the north. Neither appealed.

I'd made a grave error in removing my boots. It had aggravated the blisters and, in my flip-flops, I was barely able to hobble the remaining kilometre to the centre of town. At the first bar I came across I ordered a frosty bottle of Mahou. Medically speaking the amber nectar probably wasn't the ideal antidote but it was what my morale was craving. Halfway through the glass I phoned my wife, feeling utterly drained and struggling to keep the shaking out of my voice.

'The old dogs are barking a bit,' I told her, with forced jollity. Narina had lived in London for long enough to know that, in Cockney rhyming slang, 'dogs' meat' were feet.

'I'm less than a quarter of the way through the trek…' I hoped she couldn't hear the quavering in my voice and paused while I fought to control it. 'It's just getting to be such a strain… maybe I'll be alright if I can find a meal before I move on.'

I did my best to mask the strain in my throat, but Narina could tell that I was perilously close to some kind of breaking point.

'You have to listen to your body,' she said.

'I can't do anything *but* listen,' I told her.

It was *screaming* at me.

* * *

I was looking for a sign to tell me what I should do.

The sign, when I eventually found it, read 'Albergue Extrenatura'. The words 'defeat' and 'failure' snarled in my head as I limped up the steps, hauling on the bannister, to enquire after a bed for the night.

Albergue Extrenatura boasted 18 beds, two bathrooms, a kitchen and – joy of joys! – a washing machine and drier. Pilgrims come in many guises but – with no intention whatsoever of visiting the tomb of Santiago – I doubted that I'd qualify in any way. As it turned out, the ten-euro note I handed over for my bed was clearly appreciated at a time when few wayfarers of any description were passing through town.

I soaped myself twice under a hot shower then reluctantly hobbled through the streets to the closest supermarket. It had been four days since my last proper hot meal and, uncharacteristically for a dedicated carnivore, I was desperately in need of fresh vegetables.

A *menestra de verduras* (Navarran comfort food in the form of a hearty vegetable stew) was bubbling in the *albergue* kitchen when the other pilgrims returned. In the whole place there were only two young Spanish men and a middle-aged Dutch woman. I poured four glasses from the bottle of Reserva that I'd treated myself to and, as happens whenever pilgrims get together, the conversation turned almost immediately to blisters and backpacks. I was the only long-distance hiking virgin and the others were all experienced solo hikers: the Spaniards, both veterans of the Camino Francés, had met on the trail that day; the Dutch woman was already familiar with several Camino routes. They all knew how to travel light with just sheet sleeping bags and two sets of clothes and, thanks to the *albergues*, they had the luxury of a fresh change each morning. I was envious to hear that the weight on their backs hovered around 7 kilograms. My own (loaded with hammock, roof, sleeping bag and extra clothes) weighed almost double that with full water bottles.

Of the score of hikers I'd finally meet on the Via de la Plata, every one was a veteran of at least one other long-distance pilgrimage. I was glad that I hadn't been aware before I started out how foolhardy it was to attempt the Via de la Plata without first testing your mettle on a shorter trail.

As the conversation progressed, I developed a new strategy for the remainder of my trek. I decided that Villafranca de los Barros would be a turning point in my psychological outlook. From now on, rather than strive for close to 40 kilometres each day, I'd take the pressure off and be content to average a more manageable 25 or so.

'Don't worry,' said the Dutch woman, 'everybody eventually settles into their own pace.'

'Some hikers walk fast through the morning and then rest for half the day,' one of the Spanish pilgrims explained. 'Others take frequent rests on the trail, easing themselves along all day.'

'But whether the stone hits the jug, or the jug hits the stone,' his friend chipped in, 'it's always bad news for the jug.'

It sounded like a quote from the mouth of Don Quixote's deceptively wise sidekick Sancho Panza.

* * *

I was woken several times during the night by the sound of the old house creaking, contracting after the heat of the day with little cracks and pops and burps. Like an aged body.

'Don't push yourself so hard,' Narina had said. In my new-found sense of acceptance I woke late and enjoyed a slow, leisurely breakfast. After that I pottered around the plaza in a manner befitting my convalescent condition and I even decided to allow myself a second night of comfort in the *albergue*.

Perhaps the mere fact that I'd made this decision helped to reboot my energy and, after a lazy morning sitting around the plaza nursing my wounded feet, I surprised myself with my inexplicable, yet irresistible, enthusiasm to get back on the trail.

'Although my legs were in poor shape,' I remembered the legendary walker John Hillaby writing, 'somewhere else inside a hound still leaped, barking, anxious to get off the chain.'

It was already three in the afternoon – a completely nonsensical time to start a long hike – when I suddenly decided to let my dogs off the chains. I was astounded to find that they carried me out of Villafranca de los Barros with barely any yelping at all.

* * *

'There's no problem so big that you can't run away from it,' the 1960s rebel surfer Miki 'Da Cat' Dora famously said. And Dora should know. He ran all the way from Malibu to carve a new life – and to carve uncrowded waves – in the French fishing village of Guethary.

I'd tried the Dora trick that afternoon. It seemed unlikely that I could outrun my own pain but, to my complete surprise, I found myself 31 kilometres north of Villafranca de los Barros by sunset.

It was almost as if I'd left my rundown self in Albergue Extrenatura and was starting out completely afresh. The terrain north of town was marked on the map as a vast laterite plain, the colour of congealed blood. Near the centre of this expanse was a place marked as Pozo de la Botella – Well of the Bottle. Fortunately I was too experienced by now to place much faith in such desert mirages and was not unduly surprised to find that the well was dry.

For 3 hours that evening I walked along a track that ran arrow-straight, which my compass confirmed was heading directly north. It never wavered even a centimetre to the east or west. In this featureless and barren terrain there was nothing whatsoever to waver around.

Jokers will tell you that when *Extremeño* farmers plough their fields they mark the line along a sighting of flags then, after ploughing the first furrow, they camp for the night before returning on the back-furrow the following morning.

My new resolution to 'listen to my body and take things slower' didn't last long. It was as if the freedom to choose had renewed my enthusiasm and I found myself back on a marching schedule that had me averaging 40 kilometres over the next few days. At last I could convince myself that my feet were toughening up and the pain was far less intense.

While some days were tougher than others, almost every day of walking included pleasant spells when I could almost convince myself that, if I could only switch off my brain, my legs would continue striding indefinitely of their own accord. I imagined what it would be like to slip into a trance so that I could almost levitate across the landscape like one of the *lung-gom-pa* runners, the 'flying monks' of old Tibet who, legend had it, could run 300 kilometres in a single day.

In 1924 the French explorer Alexandra David-Neel became the only westerner ever to witness one of these mysterious 'ironman monks' in action. David-Neel (at the age of 55) was crossing a remote section of the Tibetan plateau on horseback, disguised as a beggar, on her way to become the first European woman to reach the forbidden city of Lhasa.

'I noticed, far away in front of us, a moving black spot which my field-glasses showed to be a man,' she wrote. 'I felt astonished… for the last ten days we had not seen a human being… I noticed that the man proceeded at an unusual gait and, especially, with an extraordinary swiftness… He seemed to lift himself from the ground, proceeding by leaps. It looked as if he had been endowed with the elasticity of a ball and rebounded each time his feet touched the ground.'

David-Neel was desperate to interview the *lung-gom-pa* but she was warned by her guide not to stop the monk: 'This would certainly kill him,' the guide said. 'These lamas when travelling must not break their meditation. The god who is in them escapes… and when thus leaving them before the proper time, he shakes them so hard that they die.'

When the monk passed her, his expression was perfectly calm and impassive, she recalled. Although he passed close by he did not appear to see the French woman and her guides. His wide-open eyes, she wrote, were 'fixed on some invisible far-distant object situated somewhere high up in space'.

Two decades later a German-born Buddhist monk called Lama Anagarika Govinda described the training process of a *lung-gom-pa* in his book *The Way of the White Clouds*. 'He can move with the speed of a galloping horse, while hardly touching the ground', he wrote (although he never actually saw one of these men in motion). *Lung-gom-pa* runners underwent intensive spiritual training that involved solitary confinement for up to nine years during which they meditated and practised levitation. Their aim was not to win races or even to arrive at their destination sooner… but to cleanse the country of demons. Once released from their cells they became *maheketang* (ghost-gatherers) who were sent running each year to far corners of the country to lure evil spirits back to the monastery where they could then be subdued.

* * *

While my pace fell far short of that of the 'flying monks', there was something meditative about the tone of the next week. As I marched across northern Extremadura it was as if my nomadic life was paired down to three basic necessities: eat, sleep and walk.

Hay peligro en la demora, as a Spanish phrase puts it – There's danger in delay.

The most stressful part of my journey was the hour before darkness when I'd scout for a secure place to sleep. I'd delay until as close to nightfall as possible to minimize the chances of being noticed. For the same reason I'd break camp and be gone – leaving nothing but footprints – with the first faint smudge of dawn.

Trees were rare and it was frustrating how often the ideal hammock trees would be just out of reach on the other side of a fence or wall. Despite the temptation I stuck to my self-imposed no-trespassing rule and perseverance almost always led me to a good spot. In the week it took me to reach Salamanca, there were only two nights when I was forced to curl up on a groundsheet.

'Stealth camping' was all well and good as a novelty but trying to stay undetected night after night was becoming a stressful experience. From deciding to slow down I now made the decision to *dale un poco de caña* – give it a bit of stick – and make headway as rapidly as possible. My determination was more likely to falter, I reasoned, under the daily stress of living like a fugitive than it would under the physical strain of the actual hike.

'A journey is like a marriage,' John Steinbeck once wrote, 'the certain way to be wrong is to think you control it.'

I'd find out later that I couldn't call all the shots. Spain herself was determined to have a say in what happened between us.

***

In Spain they say that only people who had known the vast expanses of Extremadura could ever have conquered the New World. Even today it's easy to imagine how the hardship of life in such a wild region during the Middle Ages could have spawned the mix of desperate courage and ruthless ambition that drove so many *Extremeños* to take their chances in a true *terra incognita* on the other side of the Atlantic.

Drifting across the plains towards the ancient town of Mérida I tried to contemplate what it must have been like for such land-locked, insular people to take to the sea. Certainly they were no strangers to endless horizons: the ocean-like stretch of swaying grassland billowed across a landscape where hills appeared like sheltering islands.

My first glimpse of distant Mérida revealed a skyline that would have changed little since the sixteenth century when, according to Spanish historian Juan Lalaguna, 100,000 Spaniards crossed the Atlantic to take part in the conquest of The Americas.

The majority of these desperados came from the poor rural towns of Extremadura. A day's walk to the east of Mérida lay Medellin, birthplace of Hernán Cortés who – with 600 men and, crucially, 16 horses – brought the Aztec Empire to its knees and captured an area that was considerably larger than Spain itself. The conquest of Peru followed ten years later with Francisco Pizarro (from neighbouring Trujillo) at the head of a tiny army of around 200. Thirty-seven of these were from the commander's hometown. In fact, the conquest of Peru was almost a 'family business' with four other commanding positions being held by Pizarro's brother and three illegitimate half-brothers. After the Crown took its share of the spoils, Pizarro received 37 kilograms of gold and 410 kilograms of silver. Each of his men received a tenth of that figure and the majority of these riches poured into previously impoverished Extremadura.

There's a famous story that when Pizarro was asked upon his return what Peru was like he simply took a piece of parchment, scrunched it into a ball and placed it on the table. 'It looks like that,' he said.

For someone who was raised on the plains of Extremadura, the Andes must indeed have looked like that.

* * *

Walking into ancient Mérida I found it hard to imagine that this little city (population 60,000) was once garrisoned by 90,000 legionnaires. Under the name Emerita Augusta, it was one of the great administrative centres of the Roman Empire in western Europe.

The Hippodrome – where chariots once raced and gladiators fought and died – still overshadows the modern *plaza de toros*. The bullring was itself built on the site of an ancient temple dedicated to the god Mithras. In a subterranean cavern under this temple, rituals took place which supposedly rendered the Roman soldiers invincible. They would huddle together under a grating while a bull was sacrificed above them so that the hot blood ran down over them, supposedly bestowing invincibility.

The movie *Gladiator* was based on a fictional character, Maximus Decimus Meridius – a Roman general who, as his name showed, was supposed to be the tenth son of a family from Mérida. I remembered the scene when the character, played by Russell Crowe, galloped back to his plundered homestead and his murdered family. The landscape I'd walked through on the outskirts of the city was vividly reminiscent of the arid plains he crossed. In reality, however, I was fairly certain that the scene had been filmed in even drier Morocco since, in the early 2000s during an assignment in Marrakech, I'd stayed in the same suite that Crowe had occupied during the shooting of that movie.

The route of the Via de la Plata runs right along the front of Mérida's Acueducto de los Milagros. The Aqueduct of Miracles was well named; 2,000 years after it was constructed it still soars in three stacked arches up to a height of 25 metres. You have to wonder if Roman engineers could have been aware that they were creating something that would defy the ravages of thousands of years. It's said that a major incentive was to impress the conquered masses with the enduring might of Rome. Might they ever have imagined that their monuments could endure even after humankind itself has become extinct?

In a bar called El Acueducto, I stopped for a Coke and got chatting with the Ecuadorian bartender. He spoke with the delightfully rich and florid vocabulary which makes so many of his countrymen sound like characters from a Gabriel García Márquez novel.

'*¡Bendito niño!*' he said when I told him where I'd walked from. '*Ni en los sueños*' – Not even in my dreams.

Back in 2007 I was commissioned to write a story for *Geographical* magazine – 'The New El Dorado' it was called – describing how Spain was rapidly becoming more cosmopolitan thanks to influxes of workers from Latin America, Morocco and sub-Saharan Africa. It was said at the time that one in four of all Ecuadorians were working abroad and that almost half of those left behind survived primarily from money that was sent back by these exiles.

'The dream of every young person I know is to go to either the USA or Spain,' one Ecuadorian woman told me at the time. 'After my husband walked out my son and I rarely had enough to eat. When I went to see my husband to ask for money he beat me. Deciding to leave my son with my parents was the hardest thing I'd ever done.'

There was so much money to be made out of the desperation of these would-be emigrants that the mafia set up their own travel agencies. One woman told me that she'd been warned that Spanish immigration officials were wary of travellers coming directly from South America… so the agency advised an infinitely pricier ticket via Amsterdam. Hotels were also said to be extremely expensive so they also sold her $400-worth of vouchers for four nights' accommodation. Only when she arrived did she discover that the vouchers were worthless. Other emigrants paid travel agency representatives for the promise of guaranteed work in their new country, but the mythical 'man in the red baseball cap' who was supposed to meet them at the airport and take them to their new employer never showed up.

The best that many of these immigrants could hope for was agricultural labour. Some might find temporary employment in the orange groves of Murcia and hundreds were hired in the plastic-covered plantations of Almeria – known ironically among immigrants as *el mar de plata* ('the sea of silver').

The people I talked to agreed that cases of outright racism were rare, but those who'd been in the country for any length of time talked of bosses who refused to pay.

'What can you do when you're working illegally?' they shrugged. 'We know that we must just keep quiet and stay out of trouble.'

It was estimated at the time that there were around half a million legal Ecuadorian workers in Spain… but there may have been three times that many working illegally. The government had introduced heavy fines for employers who hired immigrants without papers and it had become increasingly difficult for an illegal immigrant to find work. I asked one recent arrival what he would say to a Spanish employer who expected him to do more work for less than the minimum wage just because he didn't have papers.

'I would tell him that he was my saviour,' he answered without a moment's hesitation. 'And that I would be grateful to him until the day I die.'

The bartender at El Acueducto was one of the fortunate ones. He'd carved a life and a steady job in Spain and his kids had grown up here. Mérida was beautiful but I knew his hometown in the Andes well from previous trips and was not surprised to learn that he hoped to return home one day.

'Vaya usted con Dios, don Marco.' He bid me farewell in the quaintly formal language of Latin America – Go with God.

* * *

The trails were so rarely trodden that hikers in the wilds of Extremadura would come to recognize each other by signature boot-prints in the sand. Sometimes I'd become acquainted with a pilgrim's walking habits for a day or two before I finally met the owners of those boots.

I'd wonder if I was finally gaining on the mysterious hiker who used two walking sticks and had boot-soles that were embossed with little circles. Who was the owner of the boots that were etched underneath with a diamond pattern? For two days I'd been following two sets of tracks which were normally imprinted side by side. I guessed that they were walking as a couple but the next morning I realized that they'd now separated. I could tell this because a cyclist had imprinted his tyre-marks over the larger prints (with an oval in the middle of the sole) but the smaller prints which followed (with a pattern like spaghetti hoops) consistently scuffed through the tyre tracks.

In this way I had the feeling that I knew Gorazd ('the oval') and Katja ('spaghetti hoops') long before I caught up with them at their picnic stop on a burnished hillside of copper-coloured stone. I squatted to chat for a few minutes among clumps of grass that looked like steel brushes, telling them that it was good to match faces to footprints after tracking them for two days.

'It was good finally,' I told them, 'to put a face to footprints.'

They laughed at my detective work and clued me in: they were both walking solo and Gorazd (from Slovenia) had set off earlier from the *albergue* in Mérida but decided to wait for Katja (from Germany) so that they could walk down to Proserpina reservoir together. I didn't want to intrude and three is a crowd, so I hurried on alone to get to the beach.

* * *

The first sight of the gleaming expanse of water that was Proserpina reservoir raised my spirits to an all-time high. Like camels that are said to get drunk with joy at the appearance of water, I danced along the Avenida del Lago singing 'Jerusalema' at the top of my voice. The song had been popular the last time I'd stayed at my wife's family home in KwaZulu-Natal. It was not the religious ramifications but the rhythmic beat (by South African DJ Master KG) that had made it one of the favourites on my Vagabond playlist. I'd listened to it so often that I was now familiar even with the Zulu lyrics.

Drivers on the road from Mérida that hot summer afternoon are probably still wondering who that lunatic was who was capering, jigging, stomping, pirouetting and yelling in what sounded like Zulu.

Gorazd and Katja, following along later, might well have been horrified by the apparently staggering progress of a hiker that would go forwards three steps only to backtrack two, and then scuffle sideways before turning a complete 360°.

But it might have been entirely understandable had they known that I'd promised myself an afternoon at the beach.

With its flat-topped lakeside villas and dry, dusty forests reflected in azure water, it looked more like a Greek postcard than a landlocked Extremadura valley. There were even a couple of picturesquely ramshackle *chiringuitos* (beach bars) on the western shore.

Since it was constructed by the Romans (to supply water, via that miraculous aqueduct, to Mérida) Proserpina reservoir has been a refreshing feature in this otherwise arid landscape.

On Chiringuito Choni's sunlit terrace I relaxed over a tankard of Mahou with a plate of olives and was happily tucking into creole-style chorizo – served in a sizzling iron dish with roasted peppers and fried potatoes – when Gorazd and Katja shuffled past with friendly waves.

I was in no rush. I'd have time enough to follow their footprints after my mini-Roman holiday. The blissful afternoon I spent swimming in the lake and lazing in my hammock, under the gaze of nesting storks on a whitewashed tower, was perhaps the most deliciously decadent experience of the entire trek.

I was grateful that, for once, it had been no hardship whatsoever to wait until the relatively cool hours to get walking again because the route north from the reservoir became arid almost instantly, cutting across low *dehesa* hills of sun-bleached oaks and tinder-dry grass.

Despite my lazy afternoon I covered 30 kilometres by the time I neared the village of Aljucén and found a secluded tangle of vegetation where I could string my hammock across what amounted to a trackside ditch.

* * *

On the sandy plains south of Cáceres the next morning I saw the coaster-sized spoor of a cat. A farmer later confirmed my suspicion that it could only have been a lynx. Pointing south-east towards the Sierra de San Pedro, he told me that conservationists had recently released a number of lynxes in those hills.

The endangered Spanish lynx was making a comeback. From numbers that had dwindled to less than 100 at the start of this century, there are now estimated to be around 1,700 spread across Portugal and Spain. Sierra de San Pedro would be close to the northern limit of their range and now they were apparently spreading northward from there.

'Vaya con Dios,' the farmer said, as we parted ways – the eternal 'go with God' of rural Spain.

V. S. Pritchett had walked over the Sierra de San Pedro in 1928, and the campesinos must surely have been stunned to see a spritely Englishman in tweed hiking togs striding past their homesteads. 'I walked savagely in those early days,' he recalled, 'and men jogging high on bulging mules and donkeys up the long, red loops of road, stared at me in stupefaction and remembered only as an afterthought to say "Vaya usted con Dios".'

My path through Cáceres, Salamanca and Zamora would coincide with the one that Pritchett had taken when he set out on his 480-kilometre walk.

Pritchett spent three days in Badajoz. He recalled that he was still trying to work up the nerve to begin his trek when he was offered a ride: 'There is an exhilaration in breaking a vow,' he wrote. 'For a moment you expect the skies to darken and holy lightnings to whither the clouds… I had sworn to walk: I was riding.'

I had to admit that there was something admirable in Pritchett's rebellion. I knew that if I gave in and took a ride at some point during my journey at least Sir Victor (as he later became known) would have forgiven me.

If I was ever going to be tempted to hitch a ride it would have been on an unnervingly threatening stretch of wasteland near the northern outskirts of Cáceres city. A sign said *Prohibido el Paso* and yet the apparently infallible yellow arrows of the Via de la Plata cut straight across a hobo-jungle of gutted televisions and rusted supermarket trolleys. Rotting blankets testified to the fact that people sheltered here from time to time. Illegal immigrants maybe? Perhaps homeless people who foraged in the city by day? Or junkies? The sun was sinking fast and the sky was already a purple bruise.

I hurried onwards past a collapsed sofa that was slumped in the sour dust. An old fridge lay on its side with the door flapped open like a gasping tongue. Not cool, I thought. Not cool at all.

* * *

Darkness caught up with me that night on the treeless steppes north of Casar de Cáceres. I lay my groundsheet out in a ravine by a wide gravel trail that was marked as a *cañada real*, one of the ancient routes used by migrant shepherds.

Apart from an abandoned barn in the distance there was no sign of human habitation. Worse, from my point of view, there were no trees. I found a hidden sleeping spot among a cluster of vertical boulders that are known as *dientes de perro* (dog teeth). It looked like ideal snake habitat, so I rucked the edges of the hammock up to form a sort of nest and looped my repellent-impregnated ropes around me to dissuade any unwanted bed partners from sharing my body heat. Then I wrapped my green hammock over my bright red sleeping bag for camouflage and extra warmth.

The scrubby undergrowth was pleasantly scented with wild rosemary and, after the day's 42-kilometre hike, I dozed off almost immediately.

* * *

It was that hour of hesitant limbo between night and day. I'd broken camp (such as it was) and, still befuddled with sleep, was sitting on my backpack cleaning my teeth when I became aware of a movement farther along the track. Within minutes I was surrounded by about 100 scraggy sheep, all staring at me with undisguised astonishment.

The trail I'd be following that morning was part of what is officially known as the Cañada Real Soriana Occidental. During the Middle Ages it was commonly used as a migration route by shepherds who drove their precious herds of Merino sheep between seasonal grazing. Although the network of *cañadas reales* trails mostly fell into disuse in the eighteenth century, they'd been protected in perpetuity by the Crown. They were still maintained and kept accessible even today. The Cañada Real Soriana Occidental for example still extended for over 700 kilometres to connect Badajoz with Soria.

Sitting on my pack, surrounded by sheep on a *cañada real*, was a moment of déjà vu that took me back to another migration route much farther north in Aragon, when I'd taken to the trail in the company of Spain's last brotherhood of migrant shepherds. Two decades had passed since that time. My daughter had been born just two weeks before that assignment and I'd been reluctant to leave home. As a struggling freelance writer and a new dad, I needed the *CNN* pay cheque, however, so I'd hit the road in my old Jeep for a rendezvous with the shepherds.

It had taken a couple of hours roaring around the arid plains south of Zaragoza before I spotted the cloud of dust that betrayed the position of a herd of 3,000 sheep.

'*La rodilla esta jodida,*' was the first thing Pelayo Noguero said as he limped up to shake hands – The knee's fucked.

'I've been doing this trek since I was fourteen,' he continued. 'It gets tougher each year.'

Over the course of the next two weeks I walked with Pelayo and his brothers Aurelio and Ramón as their flock – impelled by dogs and profanity in equal measure – was driven from southern Aragon to the Pyrenean peaks around Monte Perdido (Lost Mountain). The Noguero brothers were the remnants of a nomadic tradition that dated back thousands of years and was known as *la transhumancia*.

At an age when Pelayo should by rights have been playing cards and smoking cigars in the local bar, he spent the summer in a cave under the snow-capped peak of the Lost Mountain to be close to their precious animals.

All three brothers were blessed with the sort of icy blue eyes that are rarely seen in the mountains of northern Spain, but 60 years of sun, wind and dust had rimmed them red. Life must have seemed at times to be just a constant flight between bitter Pyrenean winters and the blistering summers that turn the Spanish plains into dust bowls. The bloodshot eyes might almost be the badge of a Spanish shepherd… along with their talent for highly picturesque oaths and the gammy knees that are an unavoidable result of so many nomadic years spent on *la transhumancia*.

It was past midnight by the time the clatter of 12,000 hooves and the hollow clanking of goat-bells began to echo through the historic alleyways of Zaragoza city. Three thousand head on the plains had looked like a *lot* of sheep but it was only when they were compressed into a great woolly river between houses and parked cars that I fully appreciated what such a mass meant.

Surprised citizens came out onto their balconies in their pyjamas to see what was going on.

With a hacking cough and one of the barks of colourful blasphemy that were his trademark, the indefatigable Pelayo would get his ancient caravan underway whenever it showed signs of stalling. His brothers followed suit with oaths of their own and the herd was spurred onwards not only by the dashing dogs but by a dozen huge goats with curving horns and great clanking bells on leather collars. These goats knew the route well, having spent their lives retracing the trail.

'We've been passing this way for more than forty years,' Pelayo told me. 'If we hit the goats with a big enough stick they would probably find the way themselves. The problem comes when we have to use a different route – to by-pass roadworks for example – and then the animals "complain" and try to go the old way.'

In fact, the goats were legally in the right. Regardless of whether the *cañada real* led across desert scrub, precious farmland, or through the heart of a major city, royal decree (dating back to mediaeval times) stated that nothing was allowed to impede the passage of livestock. During the height of the *transhumancia* in the thirteenth century as many as 3 million sheep were crossing the country. The economic importance, in particular of the Merino trade, was such that an organization of gentleman farmers known as *la Mesta* was founded and vested with powers that remained in place for over 500 years. Important privileges for shepherds included the right to bear arms for protection 'against wolves, Gypsies and marauders'... along with the fact that they could never be jailed for debt.

In the years I'd lived in Madrid I'd make a point of going each year to watch the *transhumancia* pass through Puerta del Sol – the equivalent of Piccadilly Circus or Times Square. Traffic was brought to a complete standstill while 1,000 head of sheep filled the city streets from wall to wall. Sheepdogs weaved among the legs of shoppers as they drove the flock onwards through the city centre, keeping the time-honoured tradition alive for another year.

In Zaragoza too, the townspeople were clearly charmed to see one of the legendary migrations underway. It was less likely that we were so popular with the late-night motorists who were stranded behind us for several kilometres. The shepherds had been able to call on reliable reinforcements, however. I walked in the rearguard between the stragglers and the flashing lights of our Guardia Civil escort. Ramón was there with his old Land Rover Defender too. (As the only one who could operate a vehicle, the youngest brother was in charge of logistics and the transport of food, blankets and reinforcement dogs.)

The shepherds had been walking for a solid 24 hours when, shortly before dawn, we finally stopped to camp in a meadow of powerfully scented thyme. Despite their rough country ways, the shepherds were surprisingly tender and caring with their flock. Pelayo had been carrying a young lamb, a weakened straggler, for the last 6 hours. Ramón had spotted a ewe with a swollen eye from a poisoned thorn and his last chore before sleeping was to catch the hapless creature and expertly lance the abscess with his pocket knife. Watching this casual exhibition of veterinary medicine, I was relieved that I'd be well clear of the mountain long before the male lambs needed to be castrated. I'd read that in Spain's rural backwaters the usual way to castrate a lamb still involved biting the testicles off with the teeth.

Trying to block this thought from my memory I figured it was a good moment to prescribe some medicine of my own… and the Noguero brothers were still making use of the bottle of *patxaran* (liquor made with sloe berries) I'd brought as a balm for their battered old knees when a 'mattress' of thyme was already lulling me to sleep.

Over the next few days we followed the *cañada real* north, along migration routes that were being trodden long before the

Romans founded the city of Caesar-Augusta (which eventually became 'Zaragoza'). With the flock dragging its cloud of dust across the landscape and the shouts of the shepherds all around, the scene was timeless. But then Ramón would drive up to hand a chilled can of San Miguel out of the Land Rover window, and I'd give heartfelt thanks for the fact that the lives of today's shepherds have progressed from their traditional diet of stale bread and mutton lard.

All through one long afternoon we dozed – four men and several dogs under a single, lonely bush on the shimmering hillside. The brothers were clearly in no great frenzy to get through the journey: 'Only the bad shepherd rushes,' Aurelio told me. 'The good shepherd travels slowly and allows his flock to arrive in good health.'

There's a mistaken belief that it's cruel to march sheep over such huge distances but, while livestock invariably lose weight during stressful truck- or rail-journeys it's been estimated that the sheep would often gain more than 10 kilograms during the *transhumancia*.

So we lay in the shade for another hour and waited for the Noguero sisters to arrive. Angelita and María Jesús made the long drive down from the highlands with hot meals on days when the track was accessible by road. They took their responsibility very seriously and on the first evening had prepared a celebratory feast with lamb stew, prawns, mussels, strawberries, highly alcoholic stewed apple and great vats of wine.

I began to think there was a risk that I too would put on 10 kilograms during the migration but once we reached the isolated mountain trails, we lived far more spartanly on ham, bread and wine. Dessert was usually more bread, sprinkled with wine and sugar.

Aurelio wore sandals made of recycled car tyres – the sort of 'thousand-milers' that have long since been virtually extinct in Spain – and he was as oblivious to the thick mat of spiky seeds that covered his thick woollen socks as he was to the rocks that we bedded down on at night. We marched from dawn to dusk and at night slept, fanned out across the hillside, to stop the sheep from straying.

When we passed through villages it was as if the circus had come to town. Customers deserted the shops to stare and schools turned out so that the kids could wave. Housewives emerged from their houses with their brooms to stand guard over their geraniums and lapdogs leapt in fear into their owners' arms, their worst nightmares come home to roost.

Maps of the Pyrenean foothills might be littered with place names but these days there are more villages than people in many Aragonese highland valleys. At night we slept in abandoned hamlets that once boasted populations in triple figures.

By the time we were in the foothills of the Pyrenees I was able to convince myself that a few of the sheep at least were mistaking the oaths that came from my wine-rasped throat for those of a real Aragonese shepherd. But then, while we rested at the edge of one backcountry village, disaster struck and the sheep got into a field of young bean-shoots. The mayor and the police were summoned and official complaints were made. There were fears that a fine would probably follow but, as one of the brothers pointed out, 'they were just beans. They didn't come with either bacon or chorizo so why all the fuss?'

Highland folk songs might be filled with tales of beautiful girls who ran away from home to travel south with tough, roving shepherds but the Noguero brothers were not unusual in that they'd remained bachelors. Even if they had someone to pass the flock on to, there were few among Spain's new generation who would be happy to take on such a difficult and lonely lifestyle.

The last I heard of the Noguero brothers they were setting out to do the trek once more the following year. They claimed it would be the last time. After all, the old knees wouldn't hold out forever.

* * *

The Spanish say that Extremadura's climate consists of *'nueve meses de invierno y tres meses de infierno'* – nine months of winter and three months of hell.

In the ten days I'd so far spent crossing the province I'd sometimes had the feeling that even the cycle of individual days could be described in similar terms. The hours just before dawn could be surprisingly chilly. This morning I began my walk along the Cañada Real Soriana Occidental with my jacket zipped up high around my neck and my bare legs goose-pimpled with the cold. I soon forgot to notice the chill in the face of one of the most spectacularly apocalyptic sunrises I've ever seen. It began with a gentle glow, like distant flames, along the eastern horizon. Then suddenly the first slim ribbons of light sliced through the dawn mist – the sun's first sabre cuts leaking crimson pools among the scudding clouds. Apart from the stone wall that lined the trail the only other man-made object visible in the entire landscape was a distant suspension bridge and as the sun rose it gilded the steel cables one by one, as if playing a giant golden harp.

Half an hour later the fiery ball had risen and the daily transition between dew and dust was completed. The trail changed from glowing amber to a monotone cinnamon. The clumps of grass that had appeared like coppery angel hair in the early light were now transformed to steel barbs.

I heard the unexpected sound of an engine long before the trail descended into a shallow valley where a farmer was combing furrows into the rocky ground with a lumbering tractor. *'¡Buenó día'!'* He stopped his engine to greet me and to ask where I was heading. We exchanged pleasantries across the field and he squinted appraisingly towards the sun, as if weighing the strength of an enemy.

'It's going to be a hot one,' I commented.

'*Es lo que hay,*' he shrugged fatalistically – It is what it is. '*Mañana será otro día*' – Tomorrow will be another day.

'All part of the same battle' he could have said, but there was an air of contentment about him as he resumed his ploughing.

* * *

After about 3 hours the 2,000-year-old migration route coincided with the brand-new viaduct over the confluence of the Almonte and Tajo rivers. I crossed the vertigo-inducing strip of tarmac, looking down on the backs of the countless swallows, an entire colony nesting under the bridge. Then I scrambled down the bank for a much-needed bath in the reservoir.

I didn't risk drinking directly from the reservoir. The Rio Almonte was a mere baby – a rural waterway less than 100 kilometres long – but the mighty Rio Tajo (the longest river on the entire peninsula at ten times that size) had flowed all the way from north-eastern Spain, passing through the city of Toledo and countless big towns along the way. Thanks to my potentially life-saving water-filter, however, I was able to replenish my water supply to last me through 4 hours trekking across dry hills that afternoon. The filter was appreciated all the more because I knew that, two years earlier, a 40-year-old German hiker had died of heatstroke (and perhaps dehydration) almost within sight of the town of Cañaveral, my next destination.

I stumbled out of the wilderness, thirsty and sunburned but otherwise in good health, to be greeted by an unexpectedly grand sign: '*Muy Noble Villa de Cañaveral*'.

I shuffled all the way to the end of Calle Real and was still none the wiser as to what aspect of Cañaveral qualified it as 'Very Noble'. Cafetería Avenida (the only bar that was open that Friday afternoon) did at least supply some entertainment, however. Two middle-aged couples were sitting at the bar with their faces turned to an oversized TV screen. Spanish sporting hero Rafa Nadal was in full swing and I realized that this perhaps explained why the other bars on Calle Real were closed for the afternoon. Every point Rafa scored brought mutters of fervent praise from the watchers at the bar while every point scored by his opponent provoked knotted brows and prayers.

It was not the tennis that entertained me, however. At a table, midway between the watchers at the bar and the screen, four old men were playing the traditional card game known as *mus*. This table was centre court as far as I was concerned and I only made the merest pretence of watching the tennis match. The old men also completely ignored the match and the atmosphere around the little table – irreligious and ribald – was typical of any location where Spanish men are playing *mus*.

The game – played with cards that, to the uninitiated, look unsettlingly like tarot cards – was apparently born in the Basque Country at least 300 years ago. Some linguists claim that the name comes either from the Basque word for 'kiss' or the Latin *mussu*, 'to keep quiet' but *mus* is one of the noisiest (and least affectionate) games imaginable. *Mus* is a game of wit. But the wit seems to be less in the cards and more in the way you rile your opponent: casting aspersions on his virility whenever possible, insulting his mother and sisters the rest of the time. It appears to be central to the strategy of the game that you must ceaselessly badger your opponent with banter. The Spanish have a picturesque talent for profanity in any case but a particularly boisterous game of *mus* typically provokes levels of blasphemy that would shock any outsiders who are able to understand. To the Spanish, even the crudest words have often been used so frequently that they have been sapped of their power to offend.

As I sat sipping my beer I pretended to watch the tennis while my ears were simultaneously tuned to the conversation which, in any case, frequently overwhelmed the voice of the commentator.

'I can't believe your luck!' one man bellowed as he threw down his cards with a clatter that made the glasses jump. *¡Que cabrón!* (It was a highly versatile all-purpose insult that could mean anything from 'cuckold' to 'bastard'.)

'Ah, stop complaining,' his friend responded with a smile. *'Cuéntalo a tu puta madre'* – Go tell it to your mother the whore.

They all laughed as one of the men, a comically pious expression on his face, crossed himself: *'Que descansa en paz,'* he said – May she rest in peace.

The cards were shuffled and dealt again and a new game commenced with fresh insults being volleyed across the table as swiftly as the ball on the screen. For the most part the card players never even glanced at Rafito, ignored on the screen, but occasionally slammed their cards onto the table in unison, like a smattering of reluctant applause.

'What the cunt do you think that is?' a sudden cry split the air.

It was followed by hearty guffaws until finally an old man gasped: 'I shit on the mother who whelped you.'

¡Oye tío! the barmaid shouted good-naturedly. *¡Estás meando fuera de olla!* – You're pissing outside the pot, uncle. (It was a typically colourful way of reprimanding a person for tactlessness.)

The door to the street opened and two teenage girls entered wearing tight crop-tops and tight jeans, stretched tighter still thanks to the mobile phones in their back pockets. One of them was apparently the daughter of a pair of tennis fans at the bar: a loan of a few euros, a promise not to be out late and they were on their way. They'd shown no interest in either the tennis or the cards and I wondered how they felt about growing up in the Very Noble town of Cañaveral. Did a Friday afternoon here provoke dreams of life in the big city? If so, did they dream of Madrid or New York? Or would Cáceres have been enough?

As I walked out of the village I passed four other people: a young couple standing at a bus stop with hip-hop music blaring tinnily from a phone and two old men sitting silently on a roadside bench.

A whole row of benches had been stencilled in Spanish with unexpectedly tender slogans: 'Old wood to burn, old wine to drink, old friends to confide in and old authors to read'; 'To sad eyes you should ask less questions and give more hugs'.

Los abuelos tienen plata en el pelo y oro en el corazón read another – Grandfathers have silver in their hair and gold in their hearts. I thought with a smile of the boisterous old card-sharps back in Cafetería Avenida.

* * *

I was now entering a hillier, greener country and the steep climb out of Cañaveral took me through a pine forest packed with perfect hammock trees. I was tempted to stop but there were still 2 hours of sunlight so I thought it best not to give in to temptation.

The road to Santiago might be paved with good intentions but I was about to realize that a pilgrim's temptation might come in unexpected forms.

On the far side of the hill was a lonely building surrounded by a large, empty car park. It was still too early for the neon lights to be illuminated but there could be no mistaking the sign above the door. Two big-breasted silhouettes left little doubt that this was the sort of shady establishment that's known euphemistically in Spain as a *club* (pronounced 'cloob'). Often known as *puti-clubs* (from the Spanish *puta*, a vulgar abbreviation for *prostituta*), I'd seen these establishments beside highways and country roads all over Spain. I recalled one particular *club* that I'd passed often on the highway near Toledo. It was fronted with two towering 15-metre-tall fibreglass legs, complete with fishnet stockings and scarlet high-heel shoes. As if that wasn't startling enough the face of a cartoon rabbit leered at stunned motorists from between the splayed thighs. A huge rodent straight out of some sleazy Wonderland, baring its buck-teeth in an insane grin. It was an incomprehensible sight for passing tourists but hardly cryptic for most Spanish: *conejo* (rabbit) is Spain's vulgar equivalent of the word 'pussy'.

Despite the ubiquity of these establishments, I'd always been happy to let their thresholds remain uncharted frontiers for me.

By comparison with the famous Conejo de la Suerte ('Lucky Rabbit') this place in the forests near Cañaveral was, from the outside at least, positively demure. I was irresistibly intrigued by the complete incongruity of a house-of-ill-repute positioned right on the Via de la Plata. I was a man on a mission though and was not about to let anything distract me…

… I'd walked about 100 metres farther down the road when I finally succumbed to curiosity. I wouldn't forgive myself if I didn't take a chance to investigate. What could be the harm in a quick nightcap before I headed onwards in search of hammock trees?

The shadowy doorway was almost hidden under the looming walls with the sort of narrow, barred windows that I recalled seeing in cloistered nunneries. A sign (no doubt a relic of the pandemic) read *'Mascarilla Requerida'* – Mask Required. I had a bandana tied on my pack, but I had a fleeting image of the newspaper headlines that might be the result of my barging through this particular door disguised as a bandit.

Despite the fact that I was in search of nothing more than a beer, I was nervous as I tried the handle. After the silence and sunlight in the car park, the din of music and flashing neon played havoc with the senses. The glare of blue fluorescence was like viewing the world through an aquarium and I narrowly missed colliding with the billiard table in front of the doorway. I wondered how anyone could ever have played a game in the befuddling dimness.

A glimpse of my own reflection – like an over-aged boy scout with my hiking shorts and backpack – flashed back at me from the mosaic of mismatched mirrors that covered the walls. I wondered momentarily if I was even heading in the right direction as I made my way towards a bar around which several shadowy figures were grouped.

Struggling to deal with this sudden sensory overload and feigning a confidence that I didn't feel, I greeted the barman and asked for a beer. The bottle of Corona reminded me of the fact that, despite the sign outside, nobody here was wearing a mask. In fact, the three buxom women farther along the bar were wearing very little at all. Two dark-haired women were dressed in extremely skimpy miniskirts, stretched almost to breaking point over wide hips. The buttons of their blouses were almost powerless to restrain bulging curves. Subtlety was obviously not in high demand among the local clientele.

The third woman, with peroxide blonde hair, seemed to be wearing only a white fluffy bathrobe. It was hard to be sure and I didn't want to stare too fixedly over the neck of my beer bottle. The joke about the short-sighted man came to mind: 'If those puppies are for sale, I'll take the one with the pink nose.'

Nobody appeared to be unduly surprised to see a hiker and I wondered if pilgrims were a regular fixture. I was grateful for the television over the bar which brought a smattering of natural colour and sunlight into the sickly blue atmosphere. The TV was tuned to a bullfight and the intrusion of the outside world seemed surreal as a lanky matador strutted in his own skin-tight regalia.

Just to make conversation, I asked the barman where the *corrida* was taking place. Realizing that I spoke Spanish, one of the girls strolled over to ask where I'd walked from. I mentioned Gibraltar and wasn't particularly surprised to learn that she knew the area well. La Línea, the Spanish town on the Gibraltar frontier, was a popular base for young women in her line of work.

Médicos del Mundo had recently estimated that there were 350,000 women working in the sex industry in Spain. Since that would equate to one prostitute for every 60 or so adult men in the population it's not surprising that the country is said to be one of the world's biggest markets for prostitutes.

Prostitution is technically legal in the country, but a law had recently been drafted in the Spanish parliament cracking down on people who financially exploited prostitutes. Stricter measures were also to be enforced against people who 'knowingly provide premises for the practice of prostitution' and it was still unclear what this would mean for what the police politely defined as 'hostess clubs'.

It was estimated that around 80 per cent of the women in the sex industry were foreigners without legal papers. I was intrigued to know where these young women were from and how they'd arrived in this unlikely club at the edge of an Extremadura pine forest. Perhaps because it was a quiet evening and they were bored – and maybe because it was clear that I wasn't looking for an *acompañante* (a 'companion') – they were surprisingly open to talking.

The barman didn't suggest that I buy the girls a round of fake champagne or watered-down Chivas Regal. Clearly, nobody was going to mistake me for a big spender but I figured that the bottle of Corona was probably going to set me back considerably more than the tankard of Mahou had back in Cafetería Avenida.

I guessed that the women were in their mid- to late-20s. The one who'd worked in La Linea – Fatima, she called herself – told me that she'd left her home in Marrakech to slip over the border into the Spanish enclave of Ceuta and from there had made it over to the mainland. We talked in French about Marrakech and she went into raptures about the food that she missed. She told me that it was not unusual for pilgrims to stop in for a drink and that, from time to time, they also took one of the women to the back rooms.

As we chatted, I noticed that the other dark-haired woman was grimacing ostentatiously at the bullfight. 'I don't like it at all,' she said. 'It's too cruel.'

Neither did she like Spain, she confided. Andrea (so she said) had arrived here three years ago from Guayaquil, in Ecuador. I'd been in Guayaquil years ago but I refrained from telling her that, although Ecuador was a country I loved, I had no urge to hurry back to her city. Guayaquil had become her dream, she said. She hoped that she could get back when she'd earned enough money to support her aged mother.

I wished her luck in this but, even as I said it, was aware how fatuous it sounded.

'Para eso estamos,' she shrugged – That's what we're here for. There was such a note of resignation in the way she said this that it made me believe she wasn't referring only to herself. It was as if her comment included everyone in the bar and, in fact, all of humanity.

It was time now for me to finish my beer and face the music in the form of the bill. It was a quiet evening, I was the only customer and it was extremely doubtful that I'd ever return. I realized that there was every chance that the barman would charge like the infuriated bull on the television screen.

As it turned out, I felt humbled by my unwarranted suspicion. Before I could even pull out my wallet the barman had flipped the top off another bottle. Apparently it was 'happy hour' and the Corona – although not exactly a bargain at six euros – was on special at *dos por uno* (two for the price of one).

The woman in the bathrobe – from Medellin, Columbia she said – winked and invited me to follow her through the curtained doorway at the back of the room. I held up my hand to show her the tattooed band around my ring finger. 'I couldn't take this off even if I wanted to,' I smiled.

I knocked back the second beer, wished the women luck and swapped the blue fish-tank glare for the fading amber of sunset among the cork trees.

* * *

While the sunbaked plains to the south of Cañaveral had been brutally stark, the rolling hills to the north were almost enchantingly beautiful. Much of it was the sort of ancient *dehesa* wilderness that covered most of Spain in the Middle Ages when, as it was popularly said, a squirrel could have crossed the entire country from Cádiz to Barcelona without touching the ground once.

These cork, oak and chestnut forests, trimmed by deer and furrowed by boar, were connected via wildlife corridors with Monfragüe National Park. Many years before I'd been commissioned to write a supplement on Extremadura for *Wanderlust* magazine and I'd driven to Monfragüe to spend time exploring one of Spain's least known and most pristine wildernesses.

It was already almost dark when I stopped next to two cork trees that were probably well over a century old. They were so thick around their trunks that I was unable to wrap my arms around when I tried to hug them. Technically, I wasn't 'hugging', just struggling to loop my hammock strings around the two forest giants.

The Iberian Peninsula boasts 12,000 square kilometres of sustainably harvested cork forests. This area (half the size of Wales) provides a natural habitat for wildlife and a wonderful variety of other plants – by some estimates around 135 per square kilometre.

Yet many of these areas are under threat thanks to a mistaken belief that buying wine in screw-top bottles or choosing man-made synthetic corks is a way to save trees.

A cork tree must reach at least 25 years old before it can be harvested and the trees (which typically live for 200 years or more) can be harvested, without causing them any harm, about once a decade. Since the cork-cutting season lasts only for two months, it follows that these wild evergreen forests are left undisturbed for the majority of the time.

Rainforest Alliance has estimated that 'a harvested cork oak tree stores up to five times more carbon than an unharvested tree, since the tree utilizes additional carbon in the regeneration of its bark.'

This forest was by far the pleasantest camping spot of my trek. I lay luxuriously in my hammock and promised myself that, once the trek was over, I'd increase my intake of wine and diligently do my utmost to support the natural cork industry.

* * *

I woke once during the night and lay awake gazing through the sparse canopy as shooting stars zipped across the sky like tracer bullets. Once a dark shadow flitted silently past on downy wings and just as it passed me there was a bone-chilling shriek.

Perhaps it's because of this otherworldly shriek that the barn owl has played a devilish part in myth since time immemorial. This bird is known as *la lechuza* and there is even a tradition in far-off Mexico of a witch (also called *La Lechuza*) that takes the form of a 2-metre-tall white owl. Who knows, the legend could even have been imported from Extremadura in the galleons that carried Hernán Cortés and his men. Nobody is entirely sure of the roots of the story but it is said that *La Lechuza* is the evil, owlish manifestation of a woman who was wronged. Perhaps – very likely in fact – she was wronged by a man because the Mexicans believe that she is particularly vengeful towards males... and even more particularly towards drunks.

Gerald Brenan wrote in *South from Granada* that villagers in the highland communities around Sierra Nevada often claimed they'd seen witches 'perching like owls on the poplar trees'. Folk stories from Extremadura meanwhile tell of an entirely different witch called *La Serrana de la Vera*. A local version of an Amazon warrior, it's said that she lured men to her cave where she got them drunk (and, in some stories, has sex with them) prior to killing them. La

Vera region lay less than 40 kilometres from the forest I was now sleeping in, and it is said that *La Serrana*'s cave, hidden somewhere in the Sierra de Tormantos, is still stacked with the bones of her victims.

Some claim that there is some historical basis in the stories of *La Serrana de la Vera* and a statue of this *Extremeña* Amazon stands (clutching a pickaxe, rather than a bow and arrow) on the hill overlooking the village of Garganta la Olla. A plaque on a sixteenth-century house in the village commemorates the fact that María Luisa de Carvajal was born there. Villagers will tell you that she was turned into the psychopathic *Serrana* after a jilted love affair.

As I lay there recalling these disturbing stories, another shadow passed swiftly and noiselessly through the trees. I waited for the hellish shriek but this time only heard a squeal of terror as some small creature was snatched out of this world.

* * *

I was lacing my boots to get going the next morning when I became aware of a movement in the bushes. I sat completely still as a young fox trotted busily through the undergrowth, coming straight towards me. Perhaps it was on the way back to its lair after the night shift. It was within about 10 metres of me when it finally caught my scent. It froze to stare at me for just a moment then took off at an unhurried trot back the way it had come.

Zorra (the Spanish word for vixen) is another vulgar Spanish term for prostitute. Perhaps it was for this reason that the fox reminded me that the women at the *club* would only just have finished their own night shift. I hoped that their nights had not been too intolerable.

I resisted a detour for breakfast into the village of Riolobos (Wolf River), settling instead for cold instant coffee in a sunny clearing and an uninterrupted morning hike across the hills and through lovely belts of *dehesa* woodlands.

Four hours later I began the slow descent onto a plain where a small herd of black *vacas bravas* (fighting cows) clustered around a shrunken waterhole at the foot of a fortress-like hill town. Crenellated battlements gave the impression of a great stone ship, with the spire of a church rising like a mast amidships. Even today, most of Galisteo town lies protected behind the encircling fortifications that date back to the thirteenth century. A few whitewashed houses were clustered around the foot of the wall like a rolling bow wave.

After a hearty three-course *menú del día* in Pensión Los Emigrantes I asked the friendly barman José if there was a room I could rent. I didn't intend to sleep there but I would have happily paid a night's rent merely for the use of a shower. But Galisteo had been offering a warm welcome to pilgrims for a thousand years; José refused to take money and simply showed me a small bathroom where I was able to scrub myself in the first hot water I'd enjoyed in almost a week.

That afternoon my path followed the western bank of the Rio Jerte with the great white ridge of the Sierra de Gredos hovering on the eastern horizon like a desiccated backbone. Those mountains, brutal as shattered knife blades, were the natural bulwark that separated Extremadura from Madrid. They served as timely reassurance that I was approaching the midway point in my trek.

The Rio Jerte (from the Arabic *xerete* – 'crystal waters') was unlike any river I'd walked along so far. I almost regretted my hot shower in the face of so many tempting swimming spots. With banks that were rioting with nettles, mint and basil, the Jerte seemed to belong to northern Spain, much more than to the arid south. Countless storks roosted on raised nesting-posts along the riverbank and I caught a glimpse of gold and azure as a kingfisher dived into the shallows.

Immense buildings, like abandoned army barracks, were relics of a thriving tobacco industry. Their walls had long since been split by fig trees and their windows gaped to reveal interiors that had been colonized by brambles and vines.

After the heat of the day, the oncoming evening was surprisingly chilly. I took this as another promising sign of my progress towards the north. I found a place to string my hammock between two rows of abandoned cottages that must once have housed tobacco workers. Lying with my sleeping bag zipped cosily up to my neck I had a perfect vantage point from which to watch the peach-coloured rays of the sun fade from the flank of the Sierra de Gredos.

* * *

I'd just broken camp when I was startled by a deep bark and a pair of gigantic mastiffs came racing along the dirt track towards me. With no time to run and no handy trees to climb, I hurriedly grabbed a hefty stick that was lying by the trail. It worked like a charm: the two dogs slowed to a trot and their tails started wagging. The biggest of the two, a huge white beast that might have been sired by a polar bear, sniffed meaningfully at the stick... and I spent a very pleasant 10 minutes throwing it for him.

The verdant banks of the Rio Jerte and the cool evening might just have been a hallucination because the next morning I was once again crossing baking hills. The white dust was hard as cement but where the trail dipped into dusty gullies, there were stepping stones to show where walkers had to ford the path during the wetter months.

It was a strange feeling, here in a seemingly uninhabited Extremadura wilderness, to walk suddenly through a statuesque four-sided archway. Like a mini-Arc de Triomphe, it lay right *across* the pathway of the Via de la Plata. I tried to imagine some of the countless wayfarers who had passed under the arch in the 1,900 years since the Roman city of Cáparra was constructed. While the Romans were building fortified cities like this – complete with basilica, temple, forum, thermal baths and underfloor heating – the barbarians of what would later become Londinium still thought that the epitome of art lay in painting your belly blue.

All morning the great whaleback of the Sierra de Gredos basked above a shimmering sea of yellow grass. Then the path climbed towards a region of ragged peaks and brutal ravines. To the north-west lay the so-called Sierra de Francia, named for thirteenth-century French settlers rather than for its proximity to France (still 500 kilometres away). To the south-east, the glacial canyon that is known dramatically as Garganta de los Infiernos (Throat of Hell).

I turned onto an abandoned railway line that would lead me in a steady climb towards the village of Aldeanueva del Camino and the dark gravel of the sidings concentrated the heat so that the whole landscape seemed to shimmer and wobble. Occasionally there was a hint of breeze that rattled the leaves but even this was like a hot breath, as if an oven door had been opened.

As the afternoon progressed my shadow stretched out ever farther in front of me. I was taunted with the realization that, instead of making north-westerly progress, I'd spent the entire day veering towards the east. Although I'd marched 41 kilometres by sunset, I figured that I'd only advanced a little over 20 kilometres towards the north.

* * *

That night the only accessible hammock trees I could find were in a thicket on a big roundabout between the Autovía Ruta de la Plata and a Cepsa service station.

I walked to the blind side of the service station, loitered until there were no vehicles in sight and then scuttled into the trees. Strangely this patch of scrubby bush (barely 60 metres across) was absolutely infested with rabbits. I saw more rabbits as I lay in my hammock that evening than I'd seen on the entire trek. Surely *somebody* else must have noticed this super-abundance. I wondered if anyone had set up snares, or would come around at night to pick a couple off with a crossbow or an air-rifle.

I hadn't given much thought to the fact that I was now taking my 'stealth camping' habit to new extremes. I was more worried as I lay there that somebody might have come up with the idea of 'stealth hunting' on this little rabbit reserve.

It was an unconventional camping spot to say the least, but it was worth the minimal risk of getting caught in a poaching-crossfire because I knew that the 24-hour Cepsa service station would be a great venue for a trucker's breakfast the next morning.

All that was lacking was a place to shower and somewhere to do my laundry. I hoped that Las Cañadas campsite which, according to my map, lay about an hour farther up the road would satisfy both those requirements. As luck would have it two cyclists, a husband and wife I figured, were pushing their bikes out of the campsite gate just as I approached. I tried to find out if there were washing machines in the camp. My attempts, first in Spanish and then in English, met with incomprehension. Realizing that they were French I racked my memory in an effort to dredge up *le mot juste* and then spoke up confidently in my best Parisian accent.

The man and the woman looked at each other, thoroughly mystified. With barely a look at me they cycled quickly away.

'Strange behaviour,' I muttered to myself. 'Must be on a very tight schedule.'

It was only later that it dawned on me that I'd confused the French word *singe* for *linge*.

'Excuse me,' I'd asked them, 'could you please tell me where I can wash my monkey?'

* * *

At the Las Cañadas camp reception I had more success by making my request in Spanish... although ultimately I had no success whatsoever in satisfying my laundry and bathing needs. I asked how much it would cost to use the showers and laundry.

Hospitality fell far short of the standards in the bar in Galisteo; as much as I wanted a wash and fresh clothes, the €30 camping fee was unrealistically exorbitant for an hour's use of the camp facilities.

I toyed with the idea of sneaking into the laundry when nobody was looking but it was nothing more than the passing fantasy of a very reluctant outlaw.

Perhaps it was karmic justice that an hour later I found a bathing spot on the Rio Baños. It was a vast improvement on any campsite shower-block. *Baños* means 'baths' in Spanish and I'd read that in the neighbouring village of Baños de Montemayor there was a thermal spring that had been in use almost constantly for two millennia.

I left my pack propped against the ancient stonework of the elegantly arched Roman bridge and stumbled down the overgrown bank, trying to avoid the nettle leaves that sagged in the heat like the ears of labradors. I wondered how many generations of people had stumbled, cursing, among the brambles and stinging nettles under that bridge over countless centuries.

Once you get past the pain there's something nostalgic about the sting of nettles. I wonder though why the 'dock leaves' that were so common when I was a kid appear to be almost extinct these days. Instead I rubbed my red-mottled wrists with damp riverside grass and consoled myself with the thought that nettles are associated more with northern climes. I'd rarely seen them during my walk through the south.

It was one of the pleasures of a slow trek – something that could only really be appreciated at a pace of around 5 kilometres per hour – that I was ever on the alert for little changes in the landscape that testified to a change in latitude. The previous day, for example, I'd started to notice that bulky two-storey barn-like homes (reminding me of communities in the foothills of the Pyrenees) had begun to replace the white-washed single-storey *cortijo* homesteads of the south. The sparse cork woodlands were now ceding way to denser forests of soaring chestnut trees. That morning too I'd seen my first Basque-style haystack, with the hay forked up high against the tall spindle that formed the peak of the stack.

* * *

I stopped for coffee in Baños de Montemayor and, at a table in the plaza, got chatting to a young man called Juan. He offered me a toke on the reefer he was smoking. I refused the offer, joking that I was going to need all the breath I could muster for the climb ahead.

'It's one thing walking for enjoyment,' Juan pointed out, 'another when you don't have a choice.'

Apparently, he walked down here every day from his home in La Garganta – a 15-kilometre round-trip. From the way he puffed contentedly down to the roach he certainly didn't appear to suffer from a shortage of breath. He was evasive, however, when I asked why he made the journey so regularly: *'Para trabajar uno tiene que manchar las manos'* – To work you have to get your hands dirty.

'People are very narrow-minded here.' He drew a horizontal line with his finger across his forehead. 'Some of them can see through keyholes with both eyes at the same time.'

Juan started rolling another fat one, not going to any pains to keep his vices clandestine. While the cultivation and private use of cannabis had been decriminalized in Spain it was still illegal to sell it or to consume it in public.

I had a long line to walk though and was happy to limit my vices to caffeine.

Despite this, Juan invited me to join him on the walk back up to his village. I was tempted by his description of an ancient *corral de lobos* (literally a 'wolf corral') on the mountainside near his village. Apparently it consisted of a sunken trap dug into the earth, in the form of a sort of amphitheatre. It was about 15 metres across and 3 metres deep, and overhanging stone slabs formed a lip around the circumference. The trap would have been baited with a live lamb. A traumatic experience for the lamb to be sure but apparently rarely fatal: Juan explained that the intelligent wolf would instantly become aware that it was trapped and would devote all its energy to trying to escape. After the farmers had arrived to kill the hapless canine, the lamb would frequently emerge unscathed.

I was morbidly fascinated by these structures and wished I could find the energy to make the 15-kilometre detour.

On my way out of town I passed the ancient thermal baths and a signpost outlining Baños de Montemayor's history. I was astounded to realize that this little town had been the birthplace of the father of a saint. Gaspar Flores (born here in 1525) had died far from home in Peru having first sired the daughter who became Santa Rosa of Lima.

Santa Rosa is the patron saint of gardeners, florists and embroiderers. Also – and this is perhaps thanks to old Gaspar – of 'people who suffer from family problems'.

Apparently when the old man forbade his daughter from becoming a nun she retaliated: 'If Christians are obliged to preach love everywhere,' she pointed out to her conquistador father, 'why did they come to America with wars, destruction and hatred?'

It was, after all, a fair question.

* * *

Crossing into Castilla y León I realized that I was now almost exactly halfway through my hike, smack bang in the middle of Spain. More than a week (and 250 kilometres) had passed since that painful afternoon, in Villafranca de los Barros, when I'd firmly believed that I must surely have taken my last Spanish steps. Yet now I could convince myself that I was feeling stronger with each day. My feet were tougher too and the blisters barely hurt at all.

As if in reward for perseverance, this new region offered a warm welcome in the form of an attractive Roman road lined with tempting resting points under the shade of chestnut trees. I could sit with my back against ancient milestones and, for once, I was able to drink my fill from mountain streams.

The route of the Via de la Plata climbed slowly to La Calzada de Béjar where rickety balconies dangled precipitously over the cobbled road like collapsing shelves. The hamlet had surely changed little over the centuries yet it was easy to imagine that a stiff wind might bring the whole upper level crashing down, leaving only the stocky granite foundations like the milestones back along the road.

It was early afternoon and Albergue Alba Soraya was surprisingly busy with eight South American cyclists and four hikers. It was the biggest group I'd seen on the entire trail but since the *albergue* had a 24-bed dormitory, there were clearly times when it would get considerably busier.

Compared with the €30 campsite I'd visited that morning, €12 now felt like a bargain for the use of a washing machine. I paid up with delight and didn't risk offending the extremely friendly caretaker by admitting that I had no intention whatsoever of staying the night. She showed me where to load my laundry into a machine and pointed out a spotless bathroom. I showered, treated my blisters and shuffled in my flip-flops down to the plaza where, at Bar Manuela, I tucked gratefully into steak, fried eggs and chips.

There was nobody on duty at the *albergue* when I returned later. On the bookshelf there was a dog-eared copy of Hemingway's *El Viejo y el Mar* (a Spanish translation of *The Old Man and the Sea*). It was an old favourite so I sat in the sun reading until my laundry had dried. Then I wrote a thank-you message explaining that everything was fine but that I'd changed my mind and planned to continue to the next town.

The path descended through wooded valleys and farms that reminded me of Spain's northern hills and of other hikes through farming communities with names that clanked like the heavy bells on the Basque oxen: Oroz-betulu, Orbaizeta, Ochagavía...

I thought of the mysterious Selva de Irati, an enchanted forest that's haunted, according to legend, by a form of local yeti. In the ancient Basque religion Basajaun was a benevolent giant who roamed the forests, warning shepherds of coming storms and guarding the flocks from wolves. Some experts have hypothesized that the myth of Basajaun as the great teacher who first showed the highlanders how to construct mills and smelt metals could, in fact, have evolved from the supposedly advanced Neanderthals who had one of their last bastions in the mountains of northern Spain.

I was glad that I'd resisted the temptation of the *albergue* because shortly before sunset I found an idyllic hammock spot under the sprawling boughs of some majestic chestnut trees.

* * *

We were fast approaching midsummer and I felt like one of those desert lizards, scuttling for the shadow of the next boulder. Grasshoppers leaped around my boots like locusts as I hiked towards the village of Fuenterroble de Salvatierra. If Salamanca – lying on its great granite plateau 60 kilometres to the north – was the next significant 'boulder' on my horizon then Fuenterroble de Salvatierra was, despite its impressive-sounding name, barely a pebble.

In a café here I met two pilgrims. Eduardo was a plumber from San Sebastián and had taken two weeks off work to walk part of the Via de la Plata. The other pilgrim was a Catholic from Hong Kong. Unable to speak anything but Cantonese, he communicated entirely through the translation app on his phone and from this I learned that his name was Hong. It was strange to think that Hong's pilgrimage had taken the form almost of a silent penance.

My first day hiking in Castilla y León was an unexpectedly sociable experience. In the late afternoon I detoured into the only bar in Morille, the last 'pebble' in the 20 kilometres before Salamanca.

While I gratefully sucked the froth from the top of my tankard of Mahou, I tuned my ears to a conversation between an old farmer and the barman.

'Pero, hombre, son listos de cojones,' the farmer was complaining about somebody – literally, 'they're clever to the testicles'.

'Que les toman por el culo.' The barman clearly sympathized and just as I was wondering who it was he thought should 'take it up the ass', another customer walked in and I was surprised to hear an unmistakable American accent ordering a beer, albeit in passable Spanish.

This buzz-cut Texan and I took our beers out to a table on the terrace that overlooked the hills. As we chatted I learned that he was now on his eighth pilgrimage. He was a staunch Catholic and, apart from the certificates he'd received in Santiago de Compostela, he'd also commemorated his hikes with seven tattoos on his calves.

Perhaps it was the enforced solitude of our days on the trail that made us talkative. We shared various details about our lives that we might not have done under other circumstances. He told me that his job was to assess PTSD compensation demands from military personnel who had seen active service. From what he told me that afternoon his two tours of duty in Iraq had amply qualified him for such a task.

Tex (name changed because of his military background) had that quaintly polite Texan way of talking – addressing me as 'sir', for example – and he combined it with an idiosyncratic way of recounting all his experiences in the present tense.

'Yes sir. It's like this. I've been six months with the artillery in Iraq.' He pronounced it EYE-rack. 'There we are one night and we've been ordered to light up the field of operation. We fire the parachute flare-lights over the battlefield. It's just to illuminate, ya see? So we're not actually shootin' at anyone.'

He paused to stretch his shoulders and to take a sip of beer. The silence lasted for so long that I wondered if he was going to clam up entirely.

'They're not live rounds and the only risk is that the expended shell-case carries on in an undefinable trajectory.' His right hand – the one not holding his tankard – mimed a parabolic curve over the aluminium table. 'We can project roughly where it lands of course, but normally it doesn't really matter because it's not explosive… It's heavy enough to kill though.'

He fell silent again. Taking a sip of his beer he stared into the dusty glare of the hills we'd both crossed that afternoon.

'It's a particularly hot night and a family of five have come up to sleep under the stars on their roof…'

Another stretch and silence. We both stared into the distance this time.

'That's all she wrote,' he said in a voice that was almost inaudible.

A heavy silence fell between us.

'We're all sinners,' Tex reminded me, after I'd called for another round of beers. 'There's always gonna be a price to pay. But the Pope issued a dispensation and for every Camino you complete, time is deducted from your allotted sentence in purgatory.'

The Camino was considered to be a form of earthly purgatory in other ways too. Even up until the late eighteenth century petty criminals were still being sent on a pilgrimage to Santiago as punishment. If they managed to get through flooded rivers, frozen mountain ranges and to slip through the net of bandits to reach the saint's tomb they were considered absolved upon receipt of a *Compostela* certificate.

Not surprisingly, there were those among the most incorrigible miscreants who found a way around this: for a fee it was possible to buy a counterfeit certificate. With this in hand all you need do was to wait patiently among the bawdy-houses of Seville or Barcelona until sufficient time had passed so that you could present your forged *Compostela* to the judge.

Tex appeared to be more than happy to serve his time in 'purgatory', however. It was his habit, he told me, to start walking while it was still dark each morning and to pray as he walked, counting the rosary in his hand until sunrise. He'd already checked into the *albergue* and was surprised when I told him that my own self-imposed style of purgatory took the form of sleeping out under the stars.

'I have a hammock and will find somewhere to sleep in the hills,' I shrugged. I had a romantic idea of falling asleep with the lights of Salamanca below me. 'Just try not to clack your rosary too loudly if I'm still asleep when you come past.'

* * *

I woke in the predawn darkness to the crackle of undergrowth as some undoubtedly very large creature made its way directly towards my sleeping spot.

Salamanca had still only been discernible as a faint glow in the darkening sky when, after 41 kilometres, I'd finally settled down the night before on a groundsheet. The hillside was covered with some of the biggest trees I'd seen so far but they were so widely separated that stringing a hammock was out of the question. Finally I'd hunkered down on a sort of grassy island amid a sea of corn.

It didn't take long to realize that this crackling and crashing could only have been caused by a particularly big wild boar.

Snuffling noisily through the high corn, it was entirely unaware of my presence. I lay trying to gather my wits. At the last moment – an instant before the last curtain of corn plants separated – one of us let out a terrified squeal.

To this day I'm not entirely certain which of us split the night with that sound but the effect was instantaneous; the boar took off at a gallop, leaving a swathe of flattened corn as wide as a bowling alley.

Once my heart had stopped hammering I lay still, listening to the corn ears nuzzling each other as if snickering.

* * *

Now began the long descent towards Salamanca. I'd assumed that the approach to the big city would be riddled with cafés so hadn't bothered to stock up for my morning caffeine jolt.

I considered a detour to the little town of Arapiles but it would have added an extra hour to my day's hike and, in any case, was almost inaccessible on the opposite side of the Ruta de la Plata highway.

I detoured twice into eerily silent hamlets, straining my ears for the sounds of happy chatter from a café or the blissful gasp of steam from a coffee machine. Every café was closed and by mid-morning I was growing increasingly grouchy with every establishment that had its doors barred against me. It was the bitterest morning of my entire trek and even the momentous event of reaching the 700-kilometre mark didn't improve my morale.

Nevertheless, even at the worst moments that morning, I couldn't help feeling that Pritchett had been exaggerating shamelessly when he described these flatlands as 'the cruellest plain in the world'.

'… I gasp, I bleed, over the cruellest plain in the world,' he'd written, 'past Arapiles, where Wellington's wounded groaned…'

I gasped. I bled a little too. And I groaned a lot but even at the worst moments I was convinced that the planet would harbour crueller plains.

The road curled like a bleached serpent across the plain yet the skyline of Salamanca somehow remained aloof. Several times I felt sure I would see the end of the road from the top of the next hummock and yet it always seemed to retreat deviously, like the end of a flicked rope.

I was struggling with guilt since I'd made the decision to check into the *albergue* in Salamanca. I wanted to take time to soak up the atmosphere of Spain's finest Renaissance city… and perhaps even to give my blisters a chance to heal before I began the second (more mountainous) part of my trek. Now I wondered if karma was exacting revenge and was deliberately keeping the city perpetually out of reach.

Pritchett too had the impression that Salamanca would remain forever elusive: 'If only I could get a sight of the city,' he complained. 'If it would appear out of the burnt plain… I could have shouted Salamanca, but there was no strength in me.'

'I suppose I had no mind left,' he continued, 'the body went on by itself, by its own nervous habit, as a chicken will walk after its head has been cut off. I caught glimpses of my body speeding on like an overwound machine. This bit of flesh and bones and tweed could never cast itself into Salamanca.'

At least I didn't have tweed to contend with.

My forward motion consisted of a trudging head-down slog with my eyes on a ribbon of naked earth, cracked and eroded like the face of death. I moved like a man wading through treacle and the scale of the plain was such that even after I finally caught sight of the city, it was another hour before it appeared to loom any larger.

Even when I arrived in the southern suburbs the city itself was determined to remain out of reach. The Via de la Plata doubled back into a labyrinth of dusty paths that ran alongside the Arroyo del Zurguén. I got over this hurdle and then the wide Rio Tormes also seemed deliberately to be blocking my access to the historic city centre.

Eventually I was forced to make what I considered 'a strategic retreat'. Like a general laying siege to the city, I'd try to sneak up on it like a sapper... during the siesta hour when it was least expecting me.

My problem was that I'd arranged a video conference-call with the publishers of an Indonesian travel book that was due to go to print. I needed to find a quiet café where I could count on an uninterrupted internet connection.

My breakfast was a frenzy of several *cafés con leche*, two large orange juices and a brace of *magdalenas* (sponge cakes). Only after that did I feel human enough to spend an hour discussing marketing strategies with the publisher's PR department.

* * *

I'd visited Salamanca twice in the past and both times had been travelling as a hobo.

One summer back in the mid-1990s an old friend and I had interrupted a hitchhiking trip to Andalucía to spend an evening in Salamanca's *casco viejo* (old town). We'd made a conscious decision to reserve our precious remaining pesetas for *vino* rather than accommodation so, sometime in the early hours of the morning, we left the bars to scout for a place to sleep.

We'd thrown our packs over a wall and climbed into a building site right on the corner of the venerable old Plaza Mayor. We found a place to sleep on the first floor with our heads resting on our packs next to a massive iron girder that ran vertically through the core of the building. It seemed like only minutes later that the entire world erupted in a reverberating clang that echoed like a cathedral bell inside our heads. We leapt to our feet, scrabbled our belongings together and clambered over the wall with the laughter and cheers of the construction team following us. Arriving early for work, somebody had decided that it would be fun to administer a wake-up call courtesy of a sledgehammer walloped against the girder on the floor below us.

Two years later, hitchhiking alone this time, I'd arrived in Salamanca after about three weeks sleeping rough through France and northern Spain. At a bar in Plaza Mayor I had the unusual good fortune to bump into a group of eight English student nurses. They were staying in the city for an exchange programme and offered me a bed in their huge shared apartment. The hospitality of those modern-day Florence Nightingales might have saved my life because a few days later I was diagnosed with pneumonia – likely a consequence of a particularly insalubrious fiesta in Pamplona the previous week.

Unfortunately I could only stay recuperating in Salamanca for a few days. Pneumonia or not, I very reluctantly had to drag myself away to catch a flight back to England from Alicante. In my weakened state the cross-country hitchhiking trip to the Mediterranean was a particularly rough one and I still recall waking in a nook beside the ancient stone walls of Ávila town in a sleeping bag that was absolutely drenched with sweat after my fever broke in the night. I nourished myself almost entirely with oranges purchased with the few pesetas I had left and somehow made it to Alicante airport in time for my flight. (When I returned to England the narrowness of my escape was brought home to me when I learned that a good friend – a healthy mountain-bike enthusiast – had died of pneumonia while I was away.)

Looking back on those early misadventures I wondered if it was a natural outcome of my contradictory character that – midway through a journey where I'd committed myself to a state of 'vagabondage' – I now decided to rent a room and explore the city as a law-abiding tourist for once.

* * *

There were three other pilgrims waiting outside Salamanca's official *albergue* when I got there. Unfortunately, the caretaker – falling far short of the hospitality I'd received from those student nurses – was the most unhelpful person I'd met on the trail so far. He advised us that the place would now be locked and we'd have to wander the streets until he came back from lunch at four in the afternoon. He made it clear that he wasn't obligated to accept bags but that he would let us leave them 'out of the kindness of his heart'. We should be aware though that beds were allocated on a first-come, first-served basis: 'If you wander off and the beds are all taken when you come back, well…' – here he exhibited his first smile – *'mala suerte'* – tough luck.

Spending the next 3 hours limping around the city wouldn't be the best way to cure blisters. Then again, waiting in the sweltering little courtyard was hardly effective use of my brief sojourn in Salamanca.

The caretaker helped to convince me that I'd almost certainly feel more welcome at a private pension. So, I searched the internet and checked into a room at a hostel just two blocks away with the unlikely English name of Sweet Home Salamanca. After a shower, I spent an afternoon limping on flip-flopped feet around that majestic old city of gleaming Castilian stone.

I visited the Gothic cathedral and stood among a group of Spanish sightseers who were marvelling at the mystery of a sculpted astronaut, complete with helmet and oxygen tubes, floating on the facade of the eighteenth-century cathedral. Photos of the figure had circulated widely on social media with bloggers delighting in a mystery which seemed to point towards an extraterrestrial visitation some three centuries ago. As delightful as the story was, I knew that the truth was more prosaic. During a renovation in 1992 permission was given to add not only the astronaut but – perhaps even more mysteriously – the surreal figure of an ice-cream eating gargoyle.

From here I wandered through the cobbled lanes to the Casa de las Conchas (House of Shells), with a facade that features over 300 over-sized scallop shells as icons of the pilgrimage.

At the historic university (commissioned in 1529 and one of the world's oldest) I saw the same group of astronaut-spotting sightseers. This time they were straining their eyes to pick out the form of a small sculpted frog among the tangled stone motifs and curlicues. This frog (perched atop a human skull) has become highly symbolic and tourists are told that it is good luck if they can spot it. For centuries it's been said that students at the university must first spot the frog to have any chance of passing their examinations.

It's sometimes said too that pilgrims on the Via de la Plata must spot the frog if they want to succeed in their own mission.

* * *

The morning I continued my trek onwards from Salamanca, I awoke with the opening lines of a poem marching through my head…

'Not a drum was heard, not a funeral note,
As his corse to the rampart we hurried;
Not a soldier discharged his farewell shot
O'er the grave where our hero we buried.'

My grandfather had taught me 'The Burial of Sir John Moore after Corunna' by Charles Wolfe when I was about 13 years old.

'We buried him darkly at dead of night,
The sods with our bayonets turning…'

At that point my memory invariably failed me. As a cheeky teenager the thought of the toiling 'sods' had contrived to break my concentration every time and I could never for the life of me recall the following stanzas. It was only decades later that I learned the dramatic story that culminated in Sir John Moore's death near the Galician town of A Coruña (as it's properly known).

A hero of military campaigns in France, Corsica, the West Indies, Ireland, the Netherlands and Egypt, General Moore had marched into Salamanca to help free Spain from the tyranny of Napoleon.

Early that same year (1808) Napoleon had exiled the Spanish royals from Madrid to install his own brother Joseph on the throne as King of Spain. On the second of May the people of Madrid rose up against Joseph. The phrase *Dos de Mayo* remains symbolic, even today, of Spanish patriotism since the execution of Spanish patriots was immortalized in Francisco Goya's famous painting.

General John Moore's 30,000 British troops were encamped near Salamanca that winter when the general learned that Napoleon's armies had cut off his retreat with a force that outnumbered him by almost ten to one.

Moore immediately ordered the retreat northward. So began an ill-equipped march over snow-covered peaks to the coast of Galicia where he hoped ships would be waiting for them. That retreat became notorious as the most frantic and undisciplined chapter in British military history.

I wished my grandfather could have known that for the next 300 kilometres or so I'd be walking in the footsteps of Moore and his increasingly desperate army.

* * *

When I stepped out into the streets of Salamanca early on the morning of my departure, I was surprised to realize that it had rained heavily while I'd been curled cosily in my Sweet Home Salamanca bed. I cast a little nod of gratitude heavenward as it crossed my mind that, just maybe, Our Lady of Miracles had contrived to sidetrack me comfortably under a roof on the first night of serious rain in the three weeks since I left Gibraltar.

Puddles flickered like hammered copper under the streetlights as I crossed Plaza Mayor. When I reached the long, straight stretch of Calle Zamora I could see another figure with a backpack dodging puddles as he walked past the Plaza de Toros. I stopped at a Repsol petrol station to fuel up with a triple-shot espresso and – perhaps thanks to this caffeine injection – caught up with the other walker a couple of kilometres later.

Francisco told me that he'd spent the last month walking 600 kilometres from his home in Malaga. He'd walked the Camino Francés the previous year too and told me that he always walked slowly because he considered it part of the pilgrimage to visit every religious building and monument along the route.

'Have you been saved?' he asked me.

I replied that I'd been baptized.

He looked doubtful about the condition of my soul.

'Isn't that enough?' I asked.

He looked more doubtful still.

It was almost daylight when our route led us into a sleeping hamlet with the grand name of Aldeaseca de la Armuña.

Francisco stopped under the belltower on the little Iglesia de Santa Cruz. He gazed adoringly upwards, tracing the sign of the cross over his heart. Then he kissed his thumbnail and pointed to the heavens.

Meanwhile, I – the unbeliever – just gazed.

Francisco clearly had little patience for anyone who walked merely for the sake of walking. He was probably as relieved as I was when we found an opportunity to shake hands and wish each other luck.

'*Buen camino,*' I said.

'*¡Ultreia!*' he replied – Onwards!

It was an almost forgotten pilgrim's salute that had been common in the Middle Ages.

My passage was slowed in the next village (Calzado de Valdunciel) by a row of millennia-old Roman milestones that had marked this as a trading-route and military supply-chain since long before Jesus and his apostles had even been heard of. Francisco would no doubt be waylaid by Calzado de Valdunciel's lovely sixteenth-century church, named for Santa Elena, the village's patron saint. Santa Elena was apparently patron saint of divorced people and people going through difficult marriages. Also of archaeologists, although it's very hard to see what the connection might be.

Later in the morning it was my turn to be overtaken. I was resting near a stile in a dry-stone wall when a tall blond hiker strode briskly across the meadow. I called out *'buen camino'* as he approached and he waved cheerily as he galloped past.

He tackled the stile almost like a hurdle and I saw that, instead of hiking boots, he was wearing a pair of those strange 'barefoot' running shoes that encase each of the toes individually.

At the pace he was moving I very much doubted that our paths would cross again.

I passed through three hamlets before I found an open café where I could get breakfast and when I did, I had to settle for little plastic-wrapped sponge-cakes and a bottle of warm, syrupy apricot juice.

There was nothing memorable about the café apart from an extremely cryptic sign on the wall: 'Don't try to teach a pig to sing,' it said, 'not only will you waste your time but you'll also stress the pig.'

* * *

I walked solidly until early afternoon and then decided to get some rest under a shady tree on the edge of a stubbly hayfield. I reckoned on another 3 or 4 hours of hiking through waterless terrain before my next major waypoint, a town with the poetic name of El Cubo de Tierra del Vino. 'The bucket of the land of wine' sounded like my kind of place but for the time being my mind was focussed less on vino and more on my dwindling water supplies.

As I rested in the hayfield I resisted the temptation to eat either the *jamón serrano* or the cookies I'd carried from Salamanca, since eating would make me thirstier still. I operated on my feet and then lay still, deliberately conserving energy and moisture like some aestivating desert-creature waiting for the sun's strength to weaken.

During the 16 years I lived in Spain I never acquired the siesta habit. Perhaps if I'd done so the long bouts of waiting that formed such a large part of my trek would have been easier to endure. The other solo hikers I'd spoken to also admitted that one of the hardest aspects of the trek were the countless hours they spent in their own heads. Time for introspection was a valuable part of the solo hiking experience but sometimes an escape was necessary. For me an audiobook provided an ideal opportunity to focus on something other than the nagging, muttering soliloquy in my head. I limited the time I could spend on this luxury, allowing myself an hour every now and then as a privilege or as the motivation needed to complete a further hour's plodding.

An audio version of *The Return* (by Victoria Hislop) had proved to be an unexpectedly powerful motivator during the last few days. The novel, with its vivid descriptions of the Republican refugees who walked all over Spain from one bombed-out city to the next during the Spanish Civil War, should be required reading for any long-distance hiker. The descriptions of starving families, bleeding and barefoot, under constant fear of strafing fighter planes often served to remind me that my own trek – plodding contentedly along in state-of-the-art Jack Wolfskin footwear fuelled by an endless supply of first-class ham – was really no hardship whatsoever.

The Return provided such inspiration that (entirely uncharacteristically) I wrote to Ms Hislop's agent to pass on my thanks: 'Victoria's words have carried me a good many weary kilometres along the trail,' I wrote, 'and I feel that I owe a debt of gratitude for that.'

Within a day I received a reply directly from the novelist herself (who was then based in Greece researching another best-seller): 'Just wanted to thank you for your incredibly generous email,' she wrote. 'And from someone who must be one of the best travelled people on the planet it meant even more. What an amazing life you lead! Enjoy every minute...'

If Victoria Hislop could have seen me threading dental floss through my blisters prior to 'aestivating' in a field of corn-stubble I doubt if she'd have considered my life enjoyable in the least.

***

By mid-afternoon I was back on the trail and was by now achingly thirsty. During the next 2 hours I nursed the last of my water and optimistically stopped to check trackside irrigation ditches and even the drainage tunnels for the tiniest puddle.

My water-filter served only to tease me with the possibility of imminent refreshment but the closest thing I came to moisture was cracked mud in the ditches.

Pritchett had written dramatically about this same Spanish steppe and now I could see exactly what he meant. 'Hollow eyed with drought,' he'd said, 'with its rivers dried up and its few trees lilac skeletons among boulders that are a field of skulls...'

The temperature was nudging 40°C and, as I searched for some shade among that 'field of skulls', I cursed my stupidity in thinking that I'd left the dangers of dehydration behind. I tried not to breathe through my mouth in an effort to conserve moisture. My lips were cracked and my lungs felt like they were sucking hot air from a pottery kiln.

I could only keep shuffling forwards – boots scuffing through sump-holes that seemed to be filled with cat litter. I walked over a ridge to find a huge snake blocking the entire dirt track. It was the biggest I'd ever seen in Spain – almost 2 metres long and as thick as my wrist – and was so unfazed that it barely bothered to slither lazily out of my way. It was a Montpellier and a particularly fine specimen of what is said to be Spain's largest venomous snake. It's known locally, with typical colloquial Spanish flair, as *culebra bastarda*. Rather a harsh name for a snake which apparently has such innate decency that it has almost never been known to bite humans. The single recorded case was of a particularly determined French herpetologist who managed to 'achieve envenomation' by inserting his finger deep into the reptile's mouth. (Apparently this dedicated researcher had a week to regret the experiment while he battled with neurological problems before, with the aid of hospital treatment, making a full recovery.)

I waited patiently until the Montpellier deigned to move onwards.

My map showed a spot ahead called Arroyo de la Charca (the Gully of the Puddle) but when I got there, I found very little in the way of a 'gully' and nothing whatsoever that could have been referred to as a 'puddle'.

It was a bitter disappointment and I struggled onwards, increasingly worried about the dehydration that would be likely to set in if I didn't find water soon. Farther along the trail I saw a work van pull into what looked like an abandoned villa. It was almost half a kilometre off my path but it was worth gambling on the detour.

And I was glad I did because the workmen were kind enough to fill my water bottles. I drank my fill, and ice-cold Mahou beer had never tasted so refreshing as that tepid water.

* * *

To a thirsty hiker there was something utterly irresistible about a village with a name like El Cubo de Tierra del Vino yet apparently Pritchett had found no trouble in resisting its allure.

'After twenty miles a sumptuous bus overtook me, and as the inn at El Cubo was filthy I decided to take this bus to Zamora,' he wrote. 'How easily we mounted, how voluptuously we descended…how many hard hours would those winged miles have taken me on foot?'

It was doubtful whether El Cubo de Tierra del Vino's inn had seen a thorough cleaning-day since Pritchett's time but, after the sepia-coloured blaze of the dusty main street, its cool darkness was blissful.

I leaned my sunburned forearms on the aluminium bar and ordered a beer. According to a scrawled blackboard behind the bar the specialities of the establishment were *crestas* (stewed cockerel combs) and *cachuelas* (fried chicken tripe). Just as I was wondering if this knowledge might have endeared the inn to the indomitable Pritchett a blond man came into the bar.

I realized that it was the hiker I'd seen that morning in the strange 'barefoot' shoes, so I called to the barman to make it two beers.

'My feet really hurt,' he told me when we'd taken our drinks to a table. Ronald had left his home in Holland to walk different Camino routes several times in the past.

'I just do it for the sport,' he clarified. 'I'm not religious so I don't care about the certificates.'

Ronald prided himself on travelling extremely lightly and his only extravagance was the extra pair of barefoot shoes: 'I only wear them in the mornings then switch to my walking boots when my feet get tender. Did I mention yet that my feet really hurt?'

'Yes.' I smiled sympathetically.

'No, I mean they really, *really* hurt.'

'Yes. I know *exactly* what you mean.'

'Okay. I think you probably do. When you tell people back home that your feet hurt they just make sympathetic noises but really they have no idea what you mean. Tell a fellow pilgrim and you can be pretty sure that they know exactly what you're talking about. I can see that you know what it's like to have feet that hurt!'

I explained that I was only taking a short break and had some more headway to make that evening. I hoped to get halfway to Zamora by nightfall. While I was speaking Ronald caught the attention of the barman and had signalled for two more beers.

When the barman came over, I asked if I could order something to eat. Unfortunately the inn didn't serve food and El Cubo's only restaurant wouldn't start taking orders until eight in the evening.

Ronald had already checked into the *albergue* and he pointed out that I'd be better off eating there since dinner would be served there at seven. It was the best solution because even if I left at eight, I would still have 2 hours of daylight to cover some of the 30-kilometre stretch to Zamora city.

'So what has the Via de la Plata taught you?' Ronald asked as we both limped towards the *albergue*.

'I think I learned to listen to my body.'

'That can't have been too hard,' he said. 'I can hear it complaining from here.'

* * *

Filiberto Hernández Pablos, owner of Albergue Turístico Torre de Sabre, prided himself on communal dinners. He pointed out that they ought to be a central part of any pilgrimage but that all too often they were overlooked. On the Via de la Plata it was rare enough to find pilgrims gathered in sufficient numbers to constitute a communal meal but whenever Filiberto had a handful of lodgers, he would arrange a casual feast at a long trestle table in a kind of farmyard in front of his house.

That particular evening the *albergue* already had five guests. Besides Ronald there was another Dutch hiker and three cyclists (two Portuguese friends and a solo Frenchman). Filiberto was more than happy to feed one more. His wife had prepared fresh tomatoes in oil and vinegar and delicious chicken stewed in cognac. They refilled our glasses from carafes of the Castilian white that is produced from Malvasia and Verdejo grapes.

'We're now in good company,' Filiberto advised his gathering of thirsty pilgrims, with exaggerated chivalry. 'We know our white wine by the name *doña Blanca*, the white lady.'

Some things had clearly improved immeasurably since Pritchett grumbled his way past El Cubo de Tierra del Vino: 'No man tramping the roads of those yellow and sepia tablelands under the sun, and in that fine, high air, wants to dry up his parched throat with Spanish wine, which is tart as vinegar anyway, or to add the lead of alcohol to his limbs.'

We supped heartily from Filiberto's cellar without a thought for the lead we were loading into our limbs. The chatter around the table was made more interesting by the fact that our host was an expert on all aspects of the Via de la Plata. After riding the route from Seville to Santiago on a 19-year-old purebred Arabian horse called Moha-Hassan, Filiberto had written a definitive horseback guide called *A Caballo hacia Santiago por la Vía de la Plata*.

The conversation – in a mix of Spanish, English, Portuguese and French – flowed as freely as the wine. Long after the meal was eaten we sat contentedly at the table, savouring what the Spanish call *sobremesa*. Best defined as 'beyond the table', this is the period after a meal that typically sociable Spaniards enjoy stretching out – sometimes for several hours – over conversation, laughter and sometimes song. In our case we talked about blisters and backpacks and compared notes on the towns and wildernesses we'd walked through. We recalled pilgrims we'd all met on the Via de la Plata and whom Filiberto would almost certainly meet within the next day or two.

As I'd come to expect by now, I was the only person around the table without any experience of other pilgrimages. I pointed out that I'd been surprised to see that, while some cyclists (like the Portuguese) travelled together, hikers were almost always walking solo. Occasionally a pair of pilgrims might coincide on the trail and walk in tandem for a few days but I'd only met one couple who'd actually begun the trip together. That had been a *Madrileño* couple I chatted to briefly when I stopped to explore the ancient Roman arch at Cáparra. They were uncommunicative when I tried to make conversation and when I overtook them again later, sitting by the trail, the woman's eyes were red-rimmed. Ronald had met them that same evening at the *albergue* in Aldeanuevo del Camino and the husband had complained to him about 'having to stop to rest ten times a day'.

'They must have had a big discussion that night,' Ronald said, 'because by breakfast time they were asking for information about buses to Salamanca.'

The excellent wine and hearty food felt like a real privilege, but the companionship and conversation made me feel that I'd suffered from the solitude of my walk more than I'd realized. It was true that most pilgrims spent their days in solitary walking. In the evenings, however, when other walkers found company and security in villages, I'd deliberately sought refuge in spots that were as far removed from humanity as possible.

That evening at Filiberto's *albergue* was one of the social highlights of my trip. It confirmed my growing suspicion that, in choosing to spend my evenings hidden away alone, I'd been missing out on the communal atmosphere that is a huge part of the essence of rural Spain.

It was about halfway through the third carafe of Filiberto's excellent vino when I realized that there might be some truth in Pritchett's warning about the leaden weight of alcohol. It was already almost 9 o'clock on a midsummer's evening and the dusky sky to the north was heavy with brooding storm clouds.

* * *

By daybreak the next morning the leaden feeling in my legs had levitated to my head.

Feeling guilty about succumbing once again to the temptation of a roof and a bed, I'd grabbed a quick coffee before daybreak in the *albergue* kitchen and slunk out of El Cubo de Tierra del Vino by torchlight.

Filiberto had warned me that there was only one village in the 32 kilometres that lay between his home and Zamora city so I was once again carrying as much water as I could manage, having filled both my 1.5-litre canteen and my half-litre filter bottle. It had rained again during the night and at sunrise I was weaving through puddles on a trail that ran alongside a disused railway line. Dozens of rabbits hopped ahead of me. I assumed that hunting must have been prohibited here because they were incredibly tame and at one point I came almost within reach of a young cottontail. The hoofprints of deer had also been imprinted on the sandy trail.

I'd been walking for about an hour when the French cyclist overtook me. His bike was heavily loaded because he was carrying a tent, although he said that he was yet to use it and had always stayed in *albergues*. The two Portuguese came rattling along an hour later. No doubt they were frustrated to have to squeal to a halt on a rare downhill slope but they graciously stopped so we could shake hands and wish each other '*bom caminho*'.

Around mid-morning I passed two more hikers sitting on their packs by the side of the trail. They were from Asturias and by a strange coincidence both were called Paco – the diminutive of Francisco. I'd seen very few hikers since I left Gibraltar and yet no less than three of them had been christened Francisco. But then again, Francisco (or, more commonly, Paco) is one of Spain's commonest names.

An old joke tells of a father who arrived in Madrid searching for his long-lost son. He posted a message in *El País* newspaper: 'Paco – meet me at Esparteros Café, Friday noon – all is forgiven, Papá'.

They say that the Guardia Civil had to mount a crowd-control operation for the 800 Pacos who turned up at Esparteros.

* * *

I was now at the point where the Via de la Plata passed within a day's walk of the Portuguese border.

Many years ago I'd spent a winter in this area travelling in an old van with some friends. We'd found work on a building site, working for a retired US military colonel building what he said was destined to become a topless go-go bar in a rural Portuguese village. Presumably it had been his lifelong ambition to own such an establishment. According to his boasts he'd registered as a mercenary in the service of Portugal to get the necessary permits. He bragged too that he'd paid off the local police and also that he had the mafia on his side. The first evening we camped on his land the colonel warned us that we shouldn't worry if we heard automatic rifle fire during the middle of the night: 'I go out there and let off a few Kalashnikov rounds from time to time,' he told us. 'That way the villagers think I'm crazy and nobody comes trespassing.'

We thought he was crazy too but since he was mostly in Lisbon 'interviewing' girls for the bar we had the place to ourselves for much of the time.

There were several alcohol-fuelled evenings as the building progressed with the colonel recalling his 'glory days'. Some of his stories might even have been true. (His recollections of fighting in Angola and Mozambique were morbidly illustrated with disturbing snapshots of dead enemies.) Other stories were harder to believe: when he wasn't around we debated endlessly about whether he could really have been a comrade-in-arms with Che Guevara

(Cuba, 1959) or have worked as an advisor during the raid on Entebbe (Uganda, 1976).

We left the property long before the construction was completed and lost contact with the colonel. Several years later I'd been driving through Portugal and – feeling very bitter after the break-up with a French girlfriend – had taken a detour to see if the colonel's go-go bar had finally opened. The property was abandoned and looked very much the same as it had done the day we'd driven away in our van.

Nobody in the village could (or would) tell me what happened to the colonel.

* * *

In the early afternoon the skyline of Zamora appeared through the dusty air. The spires of some of the 14 Romanesque churches appeared so close that I might have been able to hang my hat on them. As I knew by now, the image of proximity was an illusion. The terrain fell away and I found that I was still separated from the city by the meandering green snake of the mighty Rio Duero. A day's hike upriver from here lay Toro, where a bloody battle in 1476 secured the Spanish throne for Queen Isabella and, just beyond that, Tordesillas where poor Juana la Loca (Isabella's daughter) was locked up after being accused of madness. Farther still towards the headwaters of the 895-kilometre River Duero was the Valladolid that Laurie Lee had hated so intensely and described with characteristic poignancy as 'a dark square city hard as its syllables'. The description certainly has a cutting beauty for English readers but it's interesting that it also betrayed Lee's lack of understanding of the Castilian language. On a Spanish tongue there's a definite softness in the name that is pronounced more like 'Vayadolee'.

I crossed the Puente de Piedra (Stone Bridge) over the 250-metre-wide river and, entering the alleys of Zamora's old town, made my way to the *albergue*. I couldn't bring myself to stay another night indoors but I paid for the luxury of a shower and a laundry service before I went in search of a meal.

Eighty-seven years had passed since Laurie Lee padded into the Plaza Mayor on just such a Saturday evening: 'I finally reached Zamora early one Saturday evening after a blistering day through the wheatfields,' he wrote. 'The town stood neatly stacked on its rocky hill. A ripple of orange roofs and walls, somewhat decrepit now but still giving off something of the mediaeval sternness and isolated watchfulness of its past.'

Zamora today appeared well preserved. The decrepitness of those pre-Civil War days had long since been overcome, but that air of mediaeval sternness was clearly petrified forever in the granite walls.

I found a bar with a shady terrace but when I perused the menu my sense of adventure promptly deserted me; I settled for *ensalada de perdiz* (partridge salad) rather than *nuggets de oreja* (pig-ear nuggets) which were described on the menu as 'crusty on the outside and creamy inside'.

* * *

I was somewhere in the middle of a flat plain of stunted vines and lightning was flashing almost continuously on the horizon to the north. I'd passed very few trees in the 2 hours since I left Zamora and, in any case, it would have been foolhardy to tie a hammock to the only tall features in the entire landscape.

Darkness was fast approaching though and although I was making headway every step was bringing me closer to that storm. One way or another I was going to have to find a place to sleep before long, but I could summon little enthusiasm for a wet night on my groundsheet.

Walking through the hamlet of Roales del Pan earlier that evening I'd looked for abandoned barns or even a bus-shelter or doorway where I could potentially stay dry. I'd even pondered the advisability of declaring myself a vagrant and asking to sleep at a police station, just as Laurie Lee had done in Gibraltar.

Hobo-ing across the US in the late 1800s, the Welsh 'Super-Tramp' W. H. Davies often availed himself of the corrupt system of 'boodle jails' in order to pass the winters in warmth and relative comfort. You could always break a window or get into a fight to gain a few nights' free accommodation, he explained, but in these 'boodle towns' there was no necessity to actually break a law; a hobo could make an illicit arrangement with a law enforcement officer to spend an agreed number of weeks, or even months, in voluntary incarceration. Benefits could be thrown into the bargain (complimentary tobacco for example) if you agreed to contract for a substantial time. Governors of county jails received funds for each prisoner in residence and a good part of these funds were pocketed also by the police. Standards had to be kept up, however, because a jail would lose 'business' if word circulated among discerning hobos that levels of comfort had slipped.

Regular work was never an option for Davies. He subsisted largely by begging and it's clear from his classic *The Autobiography of a Super-Tramp* that the winters spent in these boodle jails 'card-playing, singing, smoking, reading, relating experiences and occasionally taking exercise or going out for a walk' were among the pleasantest periods of his time on the road.

In 1899, on his way to join what later became known as the Klondike Gold Rush, Davies was attempting to hop a train when his foot was crushed. His leg had to be amputated below the knee.

'All the wildness had been taken out of me,' he wrote, 'and my adventures after this were not of my own seeking.'

As darkness began to close in, I felt that some of 'the wildness' had been taken out of me too. I had no option but to push onwards and yet was aware at the same time that each step was bringing me closer to the storm. Ahead lay an apparently treeless landscape, offering nothing in the way of shelter apart from the stumpy vines.

Roales del Pan was way too small to have a police station but on the main street there was a bar with a canvas awning over the terrace. I decided to grab a gin-and-tonic nightcap and take time to scout this potential shelter out. A group of farm-workers – three-quarters pickled after a Saturday afternoon boozing – invited me to drink with them. It might have led to a covered place to sleep – a barn maybe – but I'd walked 40 kilometres that day and didn't fancy trying to keep pace with them until closing time.

The television over the bar was tuned to a weather report discussing the wildly erratic conditions that were hitting the country: Murcia had been sweltering in 37 degrees that day while Torrevieja (just a day's walk to Murcia's east) was only 27. While so much of the country was simmering in a drought, I was horrified to hear that the city of Lugo (which I expected to pass through within two weeks) was battling with floods and devastating hail storms.

The northern horizon was even more menacing by the time I left the bar. Billows of sooty clouds and slanting rain swept across the landscape in grey curtains. The steely air was so charged with electricity that it seemed to leave a metallic taste on the tongue. Regretting the time I'd wasted in the bar I hurried along, spurred by the dark army that gathered around me like an ambush.

It was almost dark when, with infinite gratitude, I saw two trees on the leeward side of a small barn. Faded writing on the wall read *'Bodegas Armando, Quinta Duri'* but the barn was deserted. Raindrops were now speckling the dusty soil so I hurriedly tied my plastic roof up for a shelter before stringing my hammock underneath.

By stringing the roof with a very shallow pitch I could maintain visibility in all directions around me. If the wind increased or the rain began to encroach, all I needed to do was to clip the carabiner of one of my water canteens from an eyelet on the edge of the roof and the weight would tug the roof lower. Tonight I unscrewed the lids from the canteens so that the rain washing off the roof would replenish my water supplies during the night.

As I lay cosily listening to the patter of rain on my plastic roof and watching the flash of lightning over the hills, I promised myself that I'd order a case of Quinta Duri's finest by way of repayment after the trip was over.

* * *

I was woken at first light by the hissing hydraulic brakes of an articulated truck stopping on the dirt track.

I broke camp and, driven by curiosity, went to talk to the driver. The huge rig was full of thousands of racing pigeons from Porto which would be released at precisely 8 o'clock to fly back home across the Portuguese frontier. The driver told me that the birds could make the 250-kilometre flight in about 2½ hours.

'So they'll get home before you do,' I joked.

'Oh, they'll be back in their coops before I even get out of Spain,' he laughed.

I wished I could stick around to watch the release. The storm had passed and I was determined now to make as much headway as possible under a sky that once again threatened rain. As I walked briskly onwards I figured that (having crossed the 800-kilometre mark) I would by now have taken my millionth Spanish step since crossing the border at Gibraltar. I didn't normally pass the hours of walking in mathematical calculations and the thought was inspired more by something I'd recently read about an entire cadre of intrepid Indians who accurately charted some of the world's wildest regions solely by counting their paces.

Back in the days of the British Raj, government surveyors were naturally viewed with distrust by the inhabitants of the highlands.

These Indian explorers – forbidden to carry surveying equipment or maps which might fall into the hands of bandits or rebels – were sent to the remote border areas on what was called the Great Trigonometrical Survey. Unfortunately, their incredible story had remained largely untold because the real names of these fearless geographical 'spies' never appeared on their reports. One particularly intrepid explorer, codenamed Hari Ram, set out from Darjeeling in 1871 and circled Everest alone on foot, memorizing the route and counting his steps as he walked. During his explorations near the village of Choksum he reported a unique man-made walkway that stretched for 775 paces (about half a kilometre) across the sheer face of a cliff, 450 metres above a river. It was no more than 'a shelf' Hari Ram wrote, 'formed by bars of iron and slabs of stone stretching from peg to peg and covered with earth.'

I might not have possessed the geographic descriptive abilities of Hari Ram but through the course of my trek I'd subconsciously become a minor expert on trail surfaces. The worst walking surfaces of all for a footsore pilgrim were the stone-slabbed humpback bridges that crossed so many rivers on the Via de la Plata. The cobblestone alleyways too could have been commissioned by the Spanish Inquisition specifically to maximize suffering for pilgrims who were serving penance on the trail.

After stone slabs and cobbled lanes, the worst surface was the sort of newly covered gravel road that I was walking over. The sharp, knuckle-sized pebbles, yet to bed themselves into the surface, dug painfully into my blisters. I looked forward to curves – very rare on this flat terrain – where the spinning tyres of farm vehicles had shot the loose stones to the side.

I walked into Montamarta village just as the church bell was tolling for Sunday morning Mass. After the welcome I'd received during the last service I'd attempted to attend the previous week (in Los Santos de Maimona) I decided that I'd rather pass the next hour over a leisurely breakfast in Bar Valdegoda.

I nodded *buenos días* to two farmhands who apparently had their own ideas of the ideal Sunday morning. They were playing billiards and, judging by the shot glasses lined up around the table, I thought that maybe they'd been there since Saturday evening.

I ordered *café con leche*, a fresh orange juice and a *croissant a la plancha* (grilled croissant) and settled down at a table where I could charge my mobile phone and power bank and still watch the pool game.

I noticed now that one of the men had a mangled hand. It lay raw and burned-looking against the green baize when he played a shot. He was clearly not at any disadvantage, however. His friend had an unlimited supply of oaths ready for each ball that clunked decisively into a pocket: *¡leche de tu madre!* (your mother's milk!); *¡hostia puta!* (fucking host!); *¡concha de tu hermana!* (your sister's shell!)...

It was all water off a duck's back to the 'singlehanded' sharpshooter who did a little dance of victory at the end of the game, waving his mangled hand in the air.

'Haga el favor de no tocarme los cojones,' his friend muttered bitterly – Do me the favour of not touching my balls.

* * *

I walked through Montamarta village, stopping only to check out a life-size bronze statue to El Zangarrón that stood beside the church. The bizarre figure of a human with a hare's ears was draped in ribbons and cowbells and carried a trident. While El Zangarrón dates back to pagan times, it has long since been incorporated into Christian ceremonies in this area. Twice a year a young man, masquerading as this demon, invades the village. On New Year's Day he appears in his more diabolical form in a black mask and on the Day of the Three Kings (6 January) he appears with a red mask, decked in flowers. For reasons that have been completely lost in the mists of time he smacks young men on the back and skewers heaps of bread on his trident. As he capers through the church he draws circles on the floor, into which only he is allowed to step.

The statue of El Zangarrón didn't waylay me for long because I was excited to see Montamarta's spectacular reservoir. According to the map a large body of water stretched right across the entire northern side of Montamarta and, although the morning was overcast and cooler than usual, I had my heart set on a blissful bathing opportunity.

Even before I stepped beyond the shade of the last building, the reservoir had been revealed as nothing but a dustbowl. A sparse fringe of scraggly yellow reeds showed that presumably, once in a blue moon, there was actually some water here. Even the storm of the previous evening had barely dampened the parched earth and I walked straight across a cracked mud basin that had more in common with a Kalahari salt pan than with a European lake.

Then just as I was passing the Virgen del Castillo hermitage, on the opposite 'shore', raindrops started to patter into the dust. It was as if Our Lady of Miracles was pointing out that I should be careful what I wished for. I pulled the hammock-roof poncho out of my pack and slipped the hood over my head. This was the first time I'd been rained on during the day but after 20 minutes, the sun came out again and I could shuck the sweaty plastic off my body.

I was now climbing into the rolling hills of Zamora Vieja. This region, known as Old Zamora, is famous among the Spanish primarily for the fact that it's so spectacularly uninhabited. As I crested a scrubby hill the immense walls and soaring towers of a mighty fortress appeared, like a mirage rising over the deserted hillsides. It was hard to imagine that 800 years ago a large community thrived behind the monumental battlements of Castillo de Castrotorafe.

Built in the late twelfth century (on the site of an even earlier Roman fort), this fortress was a stronghold of the Knights of the

Order of Santiago which by that time was already becoming a major competitor of the flourishing Templars. I imagine the relief that a mediaeval pilgrim might have felt to see those protective walls rising out of the lawless wastes. Trekking in complete solitude across the abandoned hillsides, the sight struck me as an oddly unnerving one.

'Even the finest scenery loses incalculably when there's no one to enjoy it with,' Mark Twain wrote in *A Tramp Abroad*.

Yet I could feel the tingling of excitement that I used to get when I first started travelling and found myself in what felt like impossibly remote locations. I might be alone on horseback searching for jaguars in the northern Guatemalan rainforest perhaps, or hitchhiking solo across Botswana's Kalahari Desert. There would be a moment of almost dizzying excitement in the sudden revelation that I'd been fortunate enough to find myself in a place that I might only have dreamed of.

The immense ruin of Castrotorafe seemed so secretive that I could almost convince myself that I'd had the privilege of discovering it for myself.

Fontanillas de Castro (a village with a population of about 50) was just a frail shadow of the ancient fortress. It was easy to imagine that those great stone towers would still be standing tall long after the crumbling brick and cracked plaster of the village was just dust on the Castilian wind. I steered optimistically for the church steeple, like a drifting mariner making for the security of a lighthouse. The church was empty, the *albergue* was locked and, like most other buildings in the village, both appeared to be almost abandoned. I'd hoped to buy lunch and to escape the sun for a few hours but it didn't take long to confirm that there was no bar or café. Finally I accosted an old man – midway through his furtive dash between the coolness of one house and another – to learn that my only chance for sustenance was at a Cepsa service station on the southbound highway heading towards Zamora.

Feeling thoroughly dejected I retraced my steps southward, anticipating a miserable snack sitting on the curb of a fuel station. Then things took a marked turn for the better when I saw, directly opposite the service station, a gently creaking sign that read Bar Restaurant 107. I breathed a sigh of relief when I tried the door, it swung open and a very friendly barman handed me a menu.

Since it was a Sunday there was no set *menú del día* but the à la carte selection offered more – far more – than I would have hoped for. The hearty bowl of *garbanzos* (chickpeas) stewed in rich tomato sauce with thick chunks of chopped chorizo was exactly what I needed. Second course was succulent *pancetta* (marinated pork loin) with fried potatoes. I finished with *natillas* – very similar to English custard and usually served with cinnamon and a soggy Marie biscuit floating, like a deflated raft, on top.

The meal, served with a carafe of red wine in the cool tiled dining room, was a timely boost to my morale. Still, I needed to take time for the afternoon heat to diminish so I moved out to a table on the terrace and wrote for 2 hours, while I sipped a string of *cortados* that I hoped would provide a jolt of energy to counterbalance the laziness of a full stomach and the 'leaden legs' caused by the wine.

* * *

The landscape was still shimmering in the steely haze of early afternoon when I left the roadhouse. I felt heavy and slow with food but the caffeine put a temporary spring in my step.

I was glad to veer off the melting tarmac but after an hour squinting along the glaring white ribbon of the dusty dirt track, it felt as though nothing existed in Zamora Vieja but reflected sunlight.

I walked into Riego del Camino where even the barn doors had buckled like longbows under the sun. Farm buildings that had been built generations ago from packed mud had gaping cracks like the remnants of a volcanic disaster.

Although I was prepared to march through the village without stopping, I was lured into the town's only bar out of curiosity rather than thirst. Intriguingly it was called La Biblioteca (The Library). Sleepy little Riego del Camino was unexpectedly proud of its literary history. The prolific Castilian novelist Miguel Delibes based some of his hunting stories here and the townspeople weren't about to let anyone forget the fact.

'Everybody calls me Lalé,' the elderly barmaid introduced herself then pulled me a tankard of Mahou – *'Toma m'ijo.'*

Lalé, whose real name was Pascuala, had a clipped way of abbreviating *mi hijo* (my son).

She explained that Miguel Delibes was born in Valladolid but he used to drop into the social club for a warming brandy or two during his winter hunting trips in the 1950s and 60s. So when Lalé's son renovated the building he'd named it La Biblioteca in Delibes's honour.

'I've lived in Riego del Camino all my life,' Lalé told me. 'My husband used to bring me to this same building when we were courting and I remember don Miguel drinking here. There are only about seventy people left in the village and life here is very different now *m'ijo.'*

* * *

Late that afternoon I reached a momentous point in my journey. I stood at a junction in Granja de Moreruela, facing two blue signs emblazoned with yellow arrows. The western route, favoured by virtually every Via de la Plata pilgrim, was the direct route to Santiago on what is known as the Camino Sanabrés. The northern route pointed towards Astorga, a major waypoint on the famous Camino Francés.

As befitted such an important junction, Granja de Moreruela had, in the twelfth century, boasted a Cistercian monastery which housed around 200 monks. These days, however, this was surely the road less travelled. I was aware that I'd be very unlikely to see a single other hiker on the 110-kilometre trail that led from here to Astorga, official end of the Via de la Plata.

There were still 3 hours until sunset, so in Granja de Moreruela I looked for a bar in which to toast my impending deviation from the path of the righteous pilgrim. In three or four days I'd reach Astorga and from there my westbound path would converge with well-trodden Camino Francés for about 150 kilometres. Then I would veer off, alone once again, on the homeward leg (about another 150 kilometres, I figured) to my final destination on the most northerly tip of Galicia's coast.

As I walked into Bar la Espiga I finally allowed myself to believe that the plan felt achievable.

'Why the devil are you hiking in this weather?' an exasperated voice bellowed as soon as I dropped my pack by the bar. I just smiled sheepishly and the man turned to his friends: *'Hay que tener huevos como el caballo de Santiago para andar en un día como esto,'* he said – You'd have to have balls like Santiago's horse to hike on a day like this.

A group of four younger men at another table laughed. There was a bottle of Osborne Veterano on the table and one of them sloshed amber liquid into a stumpy glass: *'Toma algo de algo.'* He offered me the glass – Take something of something.

I'd ordered a bottle of Estrella Galicia beer (a promising sign that I was nearing the north). I didn't want to seem antisocial though: *'Gracias,'* I nodded. *'Un traguito na' mas'* – Just a swallow.

I slugged the brandy back – *'Salud, pesetas y amor'* – Health, money and love.

Then I took my beer out to a streetside table. Although it was now in the shade the aluminium table was still almost too hot to touch and the wall behind me radiated the heat of the day. The four young men emerged from the bar too and pulled up chairs at a neighbouring table. The one who'd offered the brandy introduced his friends and we shook hands.

'... and they call me El Rubio,' he concluded as, with the care of a casino croupier, he dealt a little sheaf of cigarette papers onto the table.

With his russet goatee El Rubio (The Blond) could just as easily have been described as El Pelirrojo (The Redhead). He reminded me of stories I'd read of a mysterious red-headed tribe whose homeland was centred in the mountains to the north. We sipped our drinks in silence while we watched El Rubio create a miniature patchwork quilt from his papers and crumble a block of tarry hashish onto a heap of tobacco. Then Juantxo – a short, stocky man with an arrow-straight Basque-style fringe – asked where I planned to sleep that night.

'I'm not sure. I just plan to make some more distance before nightfall and then see what I find.' Even now, after almost a month on the road, I still felt that there was something pretentious about my refusal to sleep under a roof. I had no idea what 'stealth camping' was in Spanish or whether the practice would even be familiar.

By the time El Rubio's joint was finished it looked like the fuselage of a miniature Airbus. He lit the end with a shallow puff and a billow of hashish smoke wafted over the table. He flicked a speck of tobacco off his lips with his tongue, making him look strangely like a lizard shaking a mealworm, as he waggled the spliff across the table at me.

I refrained. There was no denying the inadvisability of taking sociability to such extremes if I still wanted to cover some ground before sunset.

The joint continued its circumnavigation of the table as El Rubio pointed out that the next town with accommodation was almost 30 kilometres away. They could certainly come up with a sofa for me to crash on, one of the others said.

The offer was generous and, in the face of such hospitality, I felt vaguely embarrassed again about my silly insistence on sleeping outdoors.

'I have a hammock. I usually just stop when I get tired.'

'Aren't you afraid of wolves?'

One of the other men laughed.

The reefer had made a full circuit of the table by now and El Rubio was becoming more gregarious by the moment. He had the perfect solution, he said excitedly. His family owned an abandoned plot at the edge of the village. I could tie my hammock up in the lean-to shelter and there was even water for me to wash. We could stay here until the bar closed, he suggested, and then he'd show me where it was.

I was tempted but, having spent the midday hours waiting for the coolness of evening, I now wanted to make use of the last 3 hours of daylight. To appear sociable and to buy some time to consider options I went back into the bar to order a round of Estrella Galicias for my new friends.

When I returned to the table a middle-aged woman was talking to the group. El Rubio introduced her as his mother and she smiled proudly as another perfectly engineered doobie made the rounds. She nodded politely – but in a noticeably non-committal way – when El Rubio told her about his plan for my night's lodging.

Juantxo, perhaps slightly less stoned and perceiving that I was keen to get moving, now suggested a viable alternative. There was an abandoned restaurant, he explained, about an hour's walk up the road. The men all agreed that nobody had been there for years and that I'd certainly be safe sleeping there for the night.

When I shook hands half an hour later El Rubio was already dealing fresh cigarette papers onto the table with all the finesse of a poker pro revealing a royal flush.

* * *

Almost as soon as it left Granja de Moreruela, the Via de la Plata entered a shadowy woodland that could have dropped out of the pages of *Peter and the Wolf*.

It was dusk when I saw a huge breezeblock building up ahead. Rags of striped awning clinging to the veranda betrayed the fact that this was once a restaurant. Every pane of glass had been smashed. The tiled roof was perforated with holes and when I stuck my head cautiously through one of the broken windows, I could see that most of the plasterboard ceiling tiles had warped with the damp and fallen to form piles of soggy grey porridge on the floor.

More worrying was the graffiti and tendrils of soot that had crept up the wall, testament to a series of fires. Somebody had sheltered here relatively recently and I was naturally reluctant to intrude on their refuge, especially if they were to return 'home' later that night.

I trusted El Rubio, Juantxo & co but I figured that the story of my trek and, more importantly, my current whereabouts would very likely become common knowledge during a sociable Sunday evening in Granja de Moreruela. I could imagine someone suggesting after closing time: 'Hey, let's head up and say hello!'

So I avoided the restaurant and instead walked far enough back into the darkening shadows of the trees so that I couldn't be spotted from the road.

The roof of my hammock was coloured silver on one side for optimal coolness and black on the other for secrecy. I chose 'stealth-mode' and hurried to set up my sleeping spot before it grew dark enough to require a headtorch.

It was only when I was lying back reviewing the events of an incredibly varied day on the trail that I remembered that light-hearted remark about wolves.

Was it foolhardy of me, I wondered, to string myself up like a meaty fajita in 'wolf country'?

And if there was anywhere in Europe that could still be described as 'wolf country' then this was certainly it. Of the estimated 2,500 wolves that are still running wild in Spain, almost all of them are concentrated through this wild region to the north of the Rio Duero. The forest in which I was now camping was connected by 30 kilometres of wildlife corridor with the almost completely uninhabited forests of the Sierra de la Culebra ('the Snake Mountains').

Few people recall that the closing chapter of *Robinson Crusoe* takes place in Spain, but Daniel Defoe has his Crusoe and Friday leaving Pamplona to do battle with a pack of 300 wolves during a winter crossing of the Pyrenees.

Of course that was mere fiction but it can be accepted as fact that there are likely to be less than ten wolves surviving on the Spanish Pyrenees these days. Most of them were here, in the neighbourhood of my camping spot.

I tried to take my mind away from visions of blood-dripping jaws and to reassure myself that, despite their fearsome reputation in literature, it's extremely rare for an adult human to be attacked by a wolf. There's something about wolves that speaks to a primal fear for humans and I've known people who were brought up in Africa – where a far more real concern might have been lions, hyenas or even packs of African wild dogs – and yet were traumatized as kids by fairytale wolves. Stories get passed on and the truth gets passed over, as the saying goes.

In the first two decades of this millennium only 26 fatal attacks by wolves on humans were recorded. More than half took place in Turkey, Iran or India and the majority of those were attributed to rabies.

Despite the legends and fairytales, attacks in Spain have been almost unheard of. In an online database of wolf attacks (dating back to the 1600s) only three attacks are listed. In 1957 and 1959 two attacks on toddlers took place (one fatal) in Galician villages. The fact that the victims lived less than a kilometre apart would indicate that the perpetrators were the same wolves – or at least from the same pack. Two wolves were killed after the second attack and that was that. Then, in 1974 in Ourense, a wolf killed and carried off two small children in the course of a single week. When it was finally hunted down the wolf was found to have a severe parasitic infection and was struggling to feed two pups.

In 2021 the Spanish Ministry of Ecological Transition passed a law ending culling and making wolf-hunting punishable with up to two years' imprisonment. The Partido Popular political party had tried to overthrow the ruling, claiming that the cost of compensation paid to farmers for the estimated 10,000 head of livestock that are killed by wolves each year was financially unsustainable. The debate was particularly 'rabid' between the livestock farmers who considered wolves a pest and naturalists who were anxious to preserve one of Europe's most iconic natural treasures. In one bizarre *Godfather*-style incident, pro-hunting activists left two wolf heads on the steps of a town hall in Asturias province.

In my hikes in Spain I'd often dreamed of seeing a wild wolf but – with an estimated 290 packs roaming the mountains I'd be crossing during the next week – I hoped now that any sightings wouldn't be too dramatically close.

* * *

The night passed peacefully, without a visit either from the wolves of Snake Mountain or from El Rubio and the boys.

I set off the next morning and, after an hour, noted with gratitude that for once my compass showed that I was steering an almost perfect course towards Estaca de Bares. The path was ascending steadily but the Galician mountains remained stubbornly out of sight somewhere to the north-west.

Near the village of Barcial del Barco the sight of a majestic three-storey Osborne bull put an extra spring in my step. It's strange that what was essentially a vintage example of corporate graffiti has evolved into such a powerful icon of travel in Spain.

Soon I'd join the army of hikers on the Camino Francés and my endless hours of solitary hiking would be over for at least a few days. I'd decided that I should embrace that change and be prepared to ease my rules and spend nights in towns so that I could experience the unique communities that lay along that trail.

The Osborne reminded me that for now I should enjoy the solitude of my trail while it lasted. I took advantage of the fact that I could see a good way in all directions to spend an hour wailing in accompaniment to the Vagabond playlist on my phone. I roared 'Walk on the Wild Side', 'Bright Side of the Road' and 'Stuck in the Middle with You' until my throat felt wrenched.

Whenever I indulged in one of these bouts of caterwauling I never failed to recall, with mixed emotions, a reminiscence from my early Spanish travels. It was an incident that, despite its cringe-worthy nature, encapsulated the most joyous morning of hiking I'd ever had. I'd set out to explore Cabo de Gata National Park (near Almeria). I'd slept on a building site and I was hiking towards the coastal mountains. It was a bright and sunny Sunday morning and I was walking along a country lane that was deserted for at least a kilometre in either direction. In pure high spirits, I was singing (for want of a better term) at the very top of my voice.

I'd just hit the second verse of Dusty Springfield's 'Son of a Preacher Man'. I was jigging down the centre-line of the road yelling when I became dimly aware of a faint buzzing sound. I was in full swing – 'bein' good isn't always easy... no matter how hard ah try...' – and it was only when I did a full 360° pirouette in the middle of the road that I realized that a cycling club was coasting along just behind me. As they shot by, they cheered my performance – a standing ovation from the entire club. I could do nothing but bow deeply and turn 50 shades of crimson as they sped away.

It might have been highly embarrassing but, at the same time, there were few moments in my life when I'd felt so utterly carefree and contented as I had that Sunday morning near Cabo de Gata.

* * *

The Via de la Plata ran alongside the Rio Esla, following the route of the historic railway line that once ran from Plasencia to Astorga. I'd been hoping to have a swim but the banks were so overgrown as to make the river almost inaccessible.

The proximity of the Esla had diverted my thoughts from wolves to an even rarer and perhaps even more fabulous creature. I sat on the Puente de Hierro railway bridge, legs swinging high over the river, and strained my eyes for over an hour, yearning for a glimpse of the strange rodent known as the Iberian desman.

'C'mon Des,' I pleaded under my breath. 'Where are ya, mate?'

This bizarrest of creatures sounds like a part of highland mythology rather than a living animal. It's somewhat like a smaller European version of a platypus, that has been redesigned during a committee brainstorming session. Its duck's feet are propelled by kangaroo legs and tipped with cat's claws. At the other end it has a perpetually fidgeting 'snorkel' like an elephant's trunk. Its powerful back legs allow it to stand upright and the thick fur gives it the appearance of sporting dreadlocks.

The rare Iberian desman – found in the Pyrenees as well as the north-western part of the Iberian peninsula – is one of only two members of the tribe *Desmaninae* (along with the Russian desman).

Very few people have ever seen one in the wild... but this didn't stop me from pleading.

'Don't be shy, Des,' I begged. 'Step into the light, old mate...'

* * *

On the riverbank, somewhere near the town of Benavente, I came across a woman who was using garden shears to cut weeds and brambles around what looked like a Christmas tree. It had been created from dead branches, shrouded with white linen and decorated with pale blue ribbons. There was a hand-written sign: *'Todos queremos paz'* – We want peace.

'The school children made it,' the woman told me. 'They were praying for peace in Ukraine.'

She told me that the children chose this part of the riverbank because people had always said that there were fairies here. It was such a pretty little clearing that it could be easy to believe. Perhaps there were even desmans here, I thought.

* * *

My grandfather's old hero Sir John Moore had arrived in Benavente on 29 December 1808, during his forced march from Salamanca. The British rearguard cavalry were able to delay the mounted chasseurs of Napoleon's Imperial Guard just long enough so that the ancient bridge over the Rio Esla could be dynamited. The French, however, found a ford and 600 chevaliers roared into Benavente... straight into an ambush of British hussars. About 50 men were killed on each side but in the end the French broke and ran, leaving General Charles Lefebvre-Desnouettes (a personal favourite of Napoleon's) and about 75 men as prisoners.

This fleeting moment of victory was soon forgotten amid the chaotic mayhem of the mountain crossings (and several other frantically dynamited bridges) in the coming weeks.

I too scuttled hastily through Benavente, pausing only for a swift beer at Bar La Bodeguilla. I extended my liquid lunch with a litre of clementine juice and a huge tub of passionfruit yoghurt, consumed on a park bench, then I returned to my trail along the abandoned railway line.

Two hours later I detoured into Villabrázaro to replenish my water supply and to grab a coffee. Señor Dionisio, the owner of the village bar, told me that the virtually unused *albergue* had closed during the COVID-19 pandemic and that it was currently serving a more laudable purpose as a refuge for three Ukrainian refugees. I wondered what it felt like for people who had been forced to flee their country to find themselves relocated to somewhere as dusty and foreign (mostly dusty) as Villabrázaro.

Señor Dionisio told me that he'd walked the Camino Francés seven years ago and still walked for 2 hours each morning. He'd like to do it again, he said as we stood in the otherwise empty bar, but work kept him 'busy'.

'Es lo que nos toca,' he shrugged – Those are the cards we're dealt.

While we chatted, a television screen above the bar showed images of a huge wildfire that was devastating Sierra de la Culebra, just 50 kilometres to our west. The hottest summer on record had exacerbated the surge of wildfires that annually ravage much of Spain. Almost four times the usual area (over 3,000 square kilometres) would have burned by the end of the year and a whole string of conflagrations were rampaging through Extremadura.

I was relieved now that I'd made that last-minute decision to leave my little camping-cooker behind. My campsites would have been made even more memorable by the addition of a 'bush-telly'. Now, however – watching footage of the raging bushfires that were ravaging entire mountains back along my route – I was immensely grateful not to have to wonder if there was even the smallest possibility that I'd left an errant coal dangerously smouldering.

* * *

An unusually strong evening breeze had picked up by the time I said goodbye to Señor Dionisio and started walking again. Tractors were still busily ploughing the fields and I hunched my shoulders and pulled my bush-hat low to keep the flying dust out of my eyes. I wondered how the farmers felt to see their precious topsoil flying westward on the breeze.

I remembered the sharecroppers in John Steinbeck's *The Grapes of Wrath* sifting the poor Oklahoma dirt through their fingers. Squatting on their haunches and drawing figures in the dust they worried about the impending evictions: '... yes, they knew, God knows. If the dust only wouldn't fly. If the top would only stay on the soil, it might not be so bad...'

But the forefathers of the Castilian farmers I was now passing among had ploughed here for many centuries. The names of villages along this valley – Vecilla de la Polvorosa ('Dusty Vecilla') and Fresno de la Polvorosa ('Dusty Fresno') – betrayed the fact that this was probably just a typical evening.

Perhaps, I thought, it was the perpetually flying earth that had convinced earlier inhabitants of Maire de Castroponce that it was better to live underground. What I'd first taken for tombstones randomly scattered over hills like slag-heaps at the entrance to the village turned out to be chimneys, and the doorways of dozens of cave-shelters peered out of the rock like suspicious eyes as I passed by.

Maire de Castroponce these days is a village of about 200 people, 250 dogs and 200 million flies. I tried to drink a rum-and-Coke nightcap on a table in a sort of gravel car park but the flies drove me into the bar. If not the dust, perhaps it had been this plague that forced the people to live underground.

Only later did I realize that the caves were actually excavated as cellars in which to store wine.

Just before I crossed the little Rio Órbigo a road sign advised me that I was now entering León province. For days now I'd been expecting the path to steepen on its way up to the peaks, but the trail continued its lazy meandering and the high peaks remained just out of sight. I wondered if they were just waiting for their chance to pounce.

I'd covered the 160 kilometres from Salamanca in four days and as I hobbled across the stone-slab humpback of Puente de la Vizana I was already scanning the banks for hammock trees. All that remained of the old village of La Vizana was the ancient bridge and the abandoned eighteenth-century post-house. I explored the western bank of the river, just in front of the post-house, and found an idyllic little pebble beach. The crystal waters of the Rio Órbigo cascaded under the bridge into a little tannin-stained pool that served as a natural jacuzzi. I dropped my pack on the beach and within moments was happily soaking in the cool water.

A little stand of stately trees, hidden from the road, was perfectly positioned for a hammock bedroom. It seemed too good to be true and I never did come to understand why this well-watered spot (just 2 kilometres from the dry, fly-blown village) was almost completely free of insects.

As I lay luxuriously in my hammock I tried to picture some of the dramatic events that must have taken place here in the two thousand years since the bridge was first constructed. I imagined the scuff of leather sandals as the ghosts of Roman legionnaires, loaded with armour and weapons, marched over the bridge to camp beside the water at the end of their gruelling marches.

I lay awake picturing the spectre of El Cid trotting his ghostly charger across the bridge. I'd once spent ten days travelling on horseback in the hoofprints of the legendary knight and warlord. He'd skirmished far and wide across Spain and there was every chance that he'd ridden this way at some point. During the eleventh century El Cid's fame spread, like a bushfire in the harmattan it was said. While he's traditionally celebrated in Spain for his victories over the Muslim occupiers, he was equally celebrated in his time for his fighting prowess as a soldier-of-fortune in the service of various Moorish rulers.

More recently the increasingly ragtag troops in Sir John Moore's retreating army had crossed the Rio Órbigo here and part of the bridge had to be rebuilt after the British general, true to his habit, blew it up in an effort to stall his French pursuers.

As it turned out both the flies and the ghosts left me alone that night and my camp beside Puente de la Vizana turned out to be one of the most perfect of the entire trek.

* * *

I'd just started making headway into the foothills of León early the next morning when I was startled by a young deer. It bolted away, bounding gazelle-like across a field of ripe corn. The swaying stems were tall enough to cover it entirely when it landed and, with the white flash of its tail showing like a splash, I was reminded of a dolphin I'd once watched leaping across a shimmering lagoon.

By midday I'd followed pretty country lanes through a whole chain of villages with poetic names: La Nora del Rio, Quintana del Marco, Villanueva de Jamuz, Santa Elena de Jamuz... My plan was to make it to La Bañeza for lunch and the first notable landmark I saw on arrival in the town was a beautifully painted three-storey mural of Grand Prix motorcycle-racer Ángel Nieto. Every August the town of La Bañeza is transformed into the only motor-racing circuit in Spain that's entirely within a town. According to a quote painted on the portrait, Nieto had once said: 'To become champion of the world you first have to win in La Bañeza.'

The great racer won 90 Grand Prix victories during his 23 years racing… only to be killed in Ibiza in 2017 when a car hit the quad bike he was riding.

As I neared the town centre there were more murals. And they were some of the most spectacular I'd ever seen. The entire wall of an abandoned lot was covered with hauntingly beautiful female eyes. A colossal druid goddess towered five-storeys high across the facade of another building. There was a gargantuan image (a self-portrait presumably) of a young man wielding a pair of spray-cans. Having spent the morning walking through the parched hills of southern León province, I shouldn't have been surprised to see that some of the most evocative works of art betrayed a local obsession with water. A 20-metre-tall tap dripped a single droplet of water onto a thirsty rose. The intense shadow around both tap and rose threw that entire image into mind-spinning 3D but also emphasized the brutal sunlight of the Spanish interior. I stared up at a two-storey image of Neptune proudly displaying a bottle in which a scuba diver was trapped. Another even more surreal painting depicted a young woman bathing in the open beak of a pelican.

Cervecería La Penúltima gave me a memorable opportunity to continue my lucky streak of fulfilling lunches. The name of the bar appealed too: while, in other parts of the world, people who are out drinking at night would have 'a last drink before bed', in Spain someone is very likely to suggest *la penúltima*. In other words, 'let's have the one before the last'.

Since I'd been hankering for vegetables I ordered *revuelto de espárragos* (scrambled eggs with asparagus), then I sated my carnivorous instincts with *secreto a la plancha* (literally 'grilled secret' but best translated as armpit of pig). The waitress generously paired the *menú del día* meal with a full bottle of local Pago de Rozas red wine so I took my time before ordering custard-like *natillas* and a *cortado*. It was delivered to my table with a complimentary shot of *licor de hierbas* (herb liqueur flavoured with aniseed, coriander, rosemary and cinnamon).

At eight euros it was the best-value meal that I'd enjoyed on the entire trip.

When I went up to the bar to pay, two old men were passing the afternoon with their bar stools twisted towards the window. Outside a pair of white-haired women were crossing the road. They carried shopping bags and one wore a short skirt that was stretched taut across her hips.

'*Aunque hay nieve en el monte, sigue el calor en el valle,*' one of the men winked – There might be snow on the mountains, but there's still heat in the valley.

His friend was still guffawing when the waitress emerged from the kitchen.

'I don't know what's going on with these crazy temperatures,' she said, wildly misinterpreting the subject matter, 'it should be in the twenties now and yet we're sitting here in thirty-seven-degree heat.'

* * *

Perhaps it was a combination of the Pago de Rozas and the herb liqueur that convinced me to rest for a while longer before striding forth to brave the sun. From where I was sitting on a low wall, I could see one of the incredible murals. It was extremely tall so I figured that I could admire it just as well if I lay down on the wall.

Two hours later I woke with relief to find that my head was, mercifully, still resting on my pack.

'To awaken quite alone in a strange town is one of the pleasantest sensations in the world,' travel writer Freya Stark once wrote. I, however, felt dazed and utterly bemused as I tried to figure out where I was and what time of day it might be. Moreover, I was vaguely surprised that the *guardia* had not been summoned to deal with this undesirable hobo.

I didn't expect to have another opportunity to reprovision in the 25 kilometres before I reached Astorga, so I replenished my canteens in a fountain and I bought some ham, bread, biscuits and a packet of dried dates.

I remembered a Tuareg leader I'd travelled with on a camel-train in Algeria explaining how desert nomads could live for ten days on three dates.

'On each of the first three days they eat the skin of one date,' he explained. 'Then, on the following three days, they eat the flesh of a date. And on the final three days they suck the three stones.'

'What happens on the tenth day?' I'd asked.

'On the tenth day they die,' the Tuareg told me.

I'd carried a lightweight plastic camping trowel in the side pocket of my pack throughout the trek. I figured that it was a workable (though far from perfect) solution to some unavoidable metabolic needs but thus far I'd had no necessity for it. I rarely missed an opportunity to take advantage of a toilet and it seemed that I'd long since trained my bowels to activate at will.

I've heard it said that 'travel broadens the mind and loosens the bowels' but this was the only day in the entire trip when I had to dig a makeshift toilet. I threw the dates in a bin... and a few days later the obsolete trowel met the same fate.

Dusk found me walking along a red laterite dirt track of the sort that, once again, reminded me more of African landscapes than of Spain. The stunted oaks, reminiscent of acacia thornveld, made me subconsciously more fearful of leopards than of wolves. The only signs of wildlife that I noticed, however, were in the rasped bark of trunks used as scratching posts not by black rhino but by wild boar.

This would be my last night of solitude before joining the Camino Francés and I was delighted to find an idyllic hammock spot in a 'hobo-jungle' that, according to the map, stretched unbroken for almost 100 kilometres into Spain's 'Wild West'.

CHAPTER 3

Over the North

Estaca de Bares

Vilalba

Asturias

Lugo

Triacastela

Sarria

O Cebreiro   Cacabelos

Ponferrada

Astorga

Galicia   La Bañeza

Rabanal del
Camino

Castile and León

The sun had only just risen and I was faced with less than 3 hours hiking to Astorga and the end of the Via de la Plata.

I took the opportunity for a morning bath at the spot where El Puente de Valimbre (one of the most beautifully proportioned Roman bridges) looped over the Rio Turienzo in four elegant arcs. Somehow, this bridge had been spared General Moore's relentless dynamiting and has remained almost unchanged since the days when this was part of a Maragato trade route. During the Middle Ages, this mysterious tribe of red-headed *arrieros* (muleteers) formed a well-coordinated network, transporting dried Galician fish (via their home-base in Astorga) to the interior and returning to the Atlantic coast loaded with olive oil, wine and flour.

There are still an estimated 4,000 Maragato people living in the highland villages around Astorga. Their origin remains an enigma but some historians claim that they're descended from Berbers who emigrated here from the Rif Mountains in what is now Morocco. Nobody's entirely sure of the truth but, having travelled through the Rif with Berber guides (where red hair is surprisingly common and where mules are a way of life even now), it seems like a plausible explanation.

As I passed the village of Celada, another Osborne bull appeared and I greeted it like an old friend.

Unlike the domineering bovines of the south, this one peeked shyly from behind a large mountain ash. It was the fourth Osborne I'd passed along my trail and I realized with sadness that it would almost certainly be the last.

My boots were scuffing over the gravelly crest of the very last hill on the Via de la Plata when they kicked something soft.

Stooping to look more closely I saw that it was a severed rabbit foot. A strange thing to see lying on the hillside without the rest of the rabbit attached. Perhaps it had been amputated in a snare, I thought. Or gnawed off.

Perhaps I was getting overly superstitious but who could help wondering in this context whether such a rabbit foot should be considered good luck or bad?

I shoved it gently under a bush with the toe of my boot, muttering an apology to the poor rabbit.

But it must have been good luck because when I looked back up it was to catch my first glimpse of the historic skyline of Astorga.

Known as Asturica Augusta to the Romans, this city is less famous today for its link to Via de la Plata than it is for being one of the seven historic cities on the celebrated Camino Francés.

I was intrigued – and a little nervous – about what I'd find. While the sleepy villages I'd passed through in the last few days would be lucky to see a hiker once every two weeks, Astorga would frequently see well over 600 in a busy month.

* * *

For once I'd sailed through the morning trek without even stopping for one of my instant cold coffees. I'd been saving my appetite for a celebratory breakfast in Astorga and, when I arrived in the Plaza España, it was worth the wait.

In the short time it took for my croissant to be toasted I counted 20 pilgrims walking across the plaza. And by the time I'd luxuriated over my second coffee another 40 had passed. This was three times the number of hikers I'd seen since leaving Gibraltar almost a month ago.

Any year in which the Day of Saint James (25 July) falls on a Sunday is termed an *Año Xacobeo* (a Jacobean Year). In the eyes of the Catholic Church these years – falling on average 14 times each century – are considered particularly propitious times in which to complete the pilgrimage. In layman's terms a pilgrimage undertaken in an *Año Xacobeo* compensated for more than the usual allotted time in purgatory. Since the 2021 Holy Year had been disrupted by the COVID-19 pandemic, the Catholic Church had decided to extend the privilege for another year... and 2022 was shaping up to be the busiest year on record for the Camino Francés. (By the end of that year a record 438,182 *Compostela* certificates would have been issued. The vast majority were for completion of, at least part of, the Camino Francés but the figure, of course, ignores the many 'recreational' pilgrims who were walking for non-religious reasons.)

I'd been based in Spain during the *Año Xacobeo* of 2004 and was commissioned to write a magazine article on the rapidly increasing numbers of pilgrims who walked the Camino each year. A priest at the monastery in Roncesvalles had told me that as many as 500 pilgrims were arriving in his little mountain hamlet (population less than 250) in a single day at the height of the season. During the *Año Xacobeo* of 1993 the Spanish army had to be called in to erect a tented 'refugee camp' to accommodate the pilgrims.

The priest had described the strict adherence of so many hundreds of thousands of pilgrims to this single well-trodden route as *una tontería*: 'It's foolishness,' he told me. 'There's no *single* Camino. Traditionally the path led from the individual pilgrim's home and the only fixed point on the route was the final destination. People would start from absolutely anywhere.'

Also, he pointed out, few people spare a thought for the fact that in mediaeval times pilgrims used to walk twice as far: there was no public transport and, having arrived in Santiago, few had any option but to turn around and walk back home again.

Sitting over a slow breakfast in Astorga it was easy to spot the spritely hikers who were only covering short sections of the trail. The veterans who had hiked the 510 kilometres from Saint-Jean-

Pied-de-Port (the French border), or from the highland town of Roncesvalles (25 kilometres less), shuffled along. Many of them limped, in obvious pain, like refugees from some natural disaster. After descending the Pyrenean slopes they'd have walked directly below the balconies of the house I'd rented in Pamplona for several years after my divorce, so that I could stay close to my daughter. They'd crossed Navarra province and the vine-covered hills of La Rioja before this army of the walking wounded finally climbed into the highlands through Burgos province.

The first section of the Camino Francés (across the Pyrenees, Navarra and La Rioja and up to Burgos) is said to challenge the body. The second section (across the hills to Astorga) is said to open the mind. The hikers crossing the plaza in Astorga were now embarking on the final section (through the mountain ranges of León and Galicia), which is said to elevate the soul. This ragtag army of hikers still had 257 kilometres to go before 'salvation' in Santiago de Compostela, but it was easy to see that many of these Christian foot-soldiers were still heavily invested in the 'body challenging' section of their walk.

The weariest of the pilgrims I saw in Astorga looked like they were taking that earthly purgatory analogy to extremes. Dusty and bandaged, some hobbling with the aid of sticks, it was easy to imagine what John Moore's defeated army had looked like as they dragged themselves through Astorga two centuries earlier.

In *Iberia*, James A. Michener described how the already frantic retreat sank to horrific depths in Astorga. It was here that the British army, with discipline and uniforms in shreds, looted the city before shamelessly abandoning their Spanish allies to the vicious retribution of Napoleon's troops.

'Technically it was the French who were the enemy,' Michener wrote, 'but the English were worse.'

The French dictator was detested by the Spanish but, in the face of brutality, plunder, murder and rape from the uncontrolled

British troops, it was impossible for the people of Astorga to look upon their fleeing 'allies' with anything but bitter hatred.

Historical novelist Bernard Cornwell described the typical British infantryman of that era in his excellent *Sharpe* series: 'They were the despised of England, Ireland, Scotland and Wales,' Cornwell wrote, '… the drunks and the thieves, the scourings of the gutters and jails. They wore the red coat because no one else wanted them, or because they were so desperate that they had no choice. They were the scum of Britain, but they could fight.'

By the time they reached Astorga the crucial discipline that had reined this rabble in had collapsed and 30,000 of Britain's toughest hoodlums were on the rampage. They were hungry, armed and desperate. And the Spanish peasantry were entirely at their mercy.

To make matters worse Moore's flanking attack on Napoleon's army had been expected to be such a God-given success that on their departure from Lisbon, many English soldiers brought their wives and children along in the spirit of a family outing. Things became so dire that some of the British soldiers even abandoned their own families in Astorga. After plundering the town, what was left of the routed army headed for the highlands along the route that I'd follow in the coming days.

And as they climbed to the high passes of Galicia they began to realize (as I too would soon see) that things were going to get a lot tougher.

* * *

I'd promised myself a rest day in Astorga. A chance to explore this historic city and, even more important, a much-needed opportunity to get some laundry done. I'd also decided to treat myself to a night in a bed. What El Emigrante Luso hostel lacked in atmosphere it made up for with hot water, soft bedding and friendly staff.

It was one of only two rest days I'd allowed myself on my five-week trek and, in an attempt to replace some of the 5 kilograms of bodyweight that I'd lost, I spent most of it trawling the tapas bars of Astorga's old town. Rafters were hung with cured hams and there were glass cabinets filled with *tortilla*, octopus and marinated pig-trotters. There were sizzling terracotta dishes of garlic mushrooms and heaps of shrimps with filmy pink skins which the diners shucked onto the floor.

The cordillera I was entering now separated the lush, wet coastline known as 'Green Spain' from the dry, distinctly *yellow* Spain I'd been walking through so far. There was a good reason why Galicia (famous among the Spanish primarily for octopus and rainfall) was the part of the country that I had least experience of. I was always happy to encounter octopus but habitually did my best to avoid rain.

I would be traipsing along the Camino Francés for the next four or five days. I had no idea what to expect and it was unnerving to think that, having covered 900 kilometres from Gibraltar, I was now going to attempt the particular section of the Camino Francés that was notorious as the toughest on the entire route between Roncesvalles and Santiago.

All I knew was that pilgrims referred to the climb from Astorga to O Cebreiro as *Rompepiernas*. Leg-breaker.

* * *

I left the hotel in the dark and by first light had already slipped into the ranks of the refugee column that was marching out of Astorga. The city is a popular starting point for Spanish pilgrims, who were easily spotted, even at this early hour, by their jaunty step and chatty demeanour. Honest-to-God pilgrims complained about the hikers who did the pilgrimage simply in a spirit of adventure. The 'fitness freaks', meanwhile, looked down upon the 'slackpackers' who made use of vans to relay their packs (and when the going got tough sometimes themselves) between *albergues* or hotels.

In the Middle Ages any crowd of pilgrims would also have included people from wildly diverse walks of life. Many among the Catholic faithful walked the trail as an act of thanksgiving or penance, or to seek salvation at the tomb of the saint. There would also have been monks, priests and nuns walking primarily to show their devotion. There would have been soldiers and knights living up to a promise made in the heat of battle and there would have been petty criminals, 'condemned' to this form of earthly punishment by some provincial judge. There may even have been the occasional wealthy penitents – a mediaeval form of slackpacking – walking with supporting entourages and hired porters.

We'd meandered out of Astorga in single file, almost forming a queue so that you felt that you had to apologize as you stepped into the gutter to overtake. By the time we reached Murias de Rechivaldo an hour later the line had thinned and we were strung out across the open landscape like a column of Matabele ants.

Just up the hill was Castrillo de los Polvazares where, it is said, Napoleon spent a night during his pursuit of the fleeing General Moore. Two centuries later this little village – just a cluster of houses that was once a base for Maragato muleteers – would become notorious for one of the region's most gruesome murders.

One morning in April 2015 an American woman left Astorga during a solitary pilgrimage that had begun in Pamplona. It seems that she took a wrong turn near Castrillo de los Polvazares. Her attacker beat her with a stick before killing her with a knife. The motive, if there was one, was unclear but according to Spanish newspapers a bank-teller in Zamora (1½ hours' drive away) later alerted authorities about a suspicious man who tried to change US$1,200 in cash at about the time of the woman's disappearance.

After being interviewed by the police the main suspect (who lived alone in a prefabricated house on the hill above the village) went on the run. He was finally arrested five months after the murder. He admitted that he'd cut the woman's hands off and – although he led police to the spot where he'd buried the body – the hands were never found.

El Pais newspaper revealed that other women had reported being harassed in the same area by a man who was masked with a balaclava. Diabolically, the murderer had painted a fake yellow arrow on the trail to lure hikers towards his home.

* * *

Every café that I passed that morning had a queue for refreshments and a separate queue waiting for access to the little pad of ink and the rubber-stamp imprints that pilgrims gathered in their *Credenciales* (Camino passports).

Trying to quell a feeling of claustrophobia I continued onwards. Then the village of El Ganso provided what was certainly the strangest breakfast stop of my entire trek. The front of the bar, like any other along this route, was lined with shucked backpacks. A sign advertised the fact that pilgrims' passports could be stamped here. Next to it a stencilled silhouette of a six-gun packing cowgirl in a miniskirt advised patrons of the fact that this 'cantina' had been serving pilgrims since 1991. The name above the door told me that I was entering 'Mesón Cowboy' as I stepped into a barn that was decorated with Stetsons, bandanas and a tangled assortment of rusty farm implements.

The owner was Señor Ramiro: 'Everyone just calls me Ramiro "el Cowboy",' he told me as he poured my *cortado*.

I asked Señor Ramiro how many pilgrims visited the bar each day.

'When it's busy I might serve two hundred in a single morning,' he said.

Some of the artefacts that decorated the cantina were relics of Ramiro's lifetime as a cowboy fanatic. Others had been donated by passersby and well-wishers. There was a pith-helmet hanging from the ceiling and a painted cow-skull. Pictures of Buffalo Bill and Pancho Villa decorated the wall. A table football game took up most of the floor space. Presumably someone had imagined that it would be exactly the sort of activity that pilgrims would be craving.

Some of the Wild-Western imagery seemed entirely authentic. Bottles of tequila were lined up behind the bar. Dying flies kicked their legs feebly on the dusty table tops.

Bizarrely, there was apparently also an *albergue* in El Ganso called 'Indian Way' where pilgrims had a rare opportunity to sleep in Native American teepees.

As far back as the eleventh century there had been immense investment in tourist infrastructure along the Camino routes. It was one of the earliest instances of what could be called a tourist trail and by the twelfth century there was already a guidebook for pilgrims, known as the *Codex Calixtinus*. The 225 parchments (currently in Santiago de Compostela cathedral) were full of useful logistical advice, along with some bizarre warnings about giant wasps, murderous ferrymen and the supposed penchant of the 'barbarous Navarrese' for copulating with mules and horses.

This obsession with 'Cowboys and Indians' appeared to be taking things to unusual extremes and I had the bizarre feeling that I'd stumbled upon a Costa del Sol-style theme park high in the mountains of León.

I tried to convince myself that I should feel privileged to experience this pedestrian tourist trail while I could. After all, in three or four days I'd once again veer off on my own solitary path. The popularity of the route made the hardships of the hike a lot easier to bear: every village had functioning fountains where pilgrims could refill bottles and most had farm stalls or shops advertising ice cream and cold drinks in hand-painted signs spelled out in English, German, French and Dutch. There were even quaint antique shops and souvenir stands selling pilgrim memorabilia to day-trippers who would drive out to the country to watch a procession that had continued almost without ceasing for over 1,000 years.

Holier-than-thou purists complained that the religious spirit had been sapped out of the pilgrimage and it was indeed hard to see anything very spiritual in the scrummages for passport stamps… or in a pilgrimage where every night could be a party.

It was, however, a highly sociable walking experience and I struck up conversations throughout that first morning with hikers from at least six countries. They had one thought in common: 'wasn't the Via de la Plata an intensely lonely experience?' they asked.

I had to admit that there had been lonely days on the trail. But the sense of solitude had been amplified in my case because I'd restricted myself to nights in the wilderness. Spanish villages and towns are, after all, inhabited by some of the most easy-going, hospitable and friendliest people on the planet.

'I would rather be a foreigner in Spain than in most countries,' George Orwell wrote of his first reactions to the country in 1936. 'How easy it is to make friends in Spain!'

Words that were written more than 80 years ago still hold true.

The sociability of the Camino Francés called for smiles and *'buen caminos'* whenever one pilgrim overtook another. Occasionally it also made for unexpected meetings in this cosmopolitan crowd made up of zealots, nature-loving hippies, gung-ho adventurers and solemn penitents.

Near the town of Rabanal del Camino I caught up with one of the most pitifully hobbling figures that I'd seen on the trail so far. He was leaning on two walking sticks and limped so badly that I had the impression that his ankles were shackled. As I came closer I could hear his boots whispering over the stony trail with each step – shhhh-shhhh-shhhh – like the last sorry straggler in a zombie apocalypse crowd scene.

When I finally caught up I was amazed to recognize him as a young Japanese man I'd met the previous day on an Astorga terrace.

This was only his third day on the trail and I was horrified that he was clearly suffering so badly. We talked in a confusing mix of Spanish and English because, although he'd told me that he lived in Granada, he wanted to practise English: 'Never in a bunch of Sundays had I imagined it would be so tough.'

We walked together until he stopped to rest on a grassy bank. He obviously wanted to take his time so, making sure that he had enough water and checking if he needed painkillers or bandages, I wished him luck.

'I'll be okay,' he said with a weak smile. 'I just need to rest for a lilly bit.'

* * *

Most foot-pilgrims, having started out from Astorga in the morning, tended to cover 20 kilometres before stopping for the night at Rabanal del Camino, which was founded by the Knights Templar as a base from which they could skirmish out to protect pilgrims.

Stopping here for the night was a logical game-plan since it saved the hard climb to Cruz de Ferro (the Iron Cross) for fresh legs the following morning. Despite the fact that it was now mid-afternoon I'd decided to continue walking, and halfway up the slope to Cruz de Ferro I stopped at a coffee wagon. The only other customer was a Dutch-Surinamese woman who'd already cycled 2,500 kilometres from Holland and – in the style of old-time pilgrims – planned to cycle back home once she'd reached Santiago.

The so-called Iron Cross was erected by an eleventh-century hermit named Guacelmo who was famous for his charitable work in protecting pilgrims as they crossed these heights. These days there's an ever-growing heap of stones and rocks around the foot of the cross. This cascading pile could potentially provide rich pickings for a geologist since it's become a Camino tradition for pilgrims to carry a stone from home. The idea is that by placing the stone on the cairn they also remove any spiritual burdens.

While the mornings were frequently full of chance encounters on the trail, most pilgrims were ensconced in their *albergues* by early afternoon and from then on walking would be a relatively solitary experience. Now, in mid-afternoon, I had the Iron Cross to myself but I'd been told that the morning rush-hour often sees dozens of pilgrims queuing for a chance to offload their metaphorical burdens and snap a spiritual selfie.

I crossed Foncebadón Pass, the highest point on the Camino Francés at 1,504 metres above sea level, then continued onwards along the mist-shrouded ridge. Our Lady of Miracles had done an incredible job of keeping me dry so far but I was aware that it would take nothing short of a grade-A miracle for her to shelter me for the next few days on these high passes. I'd spent the last month entirely in shorts but on Foncebadón Pass I stopped by the deserted trail to pull on the thermal leggings and thick jacket that I'd bought in Astorga.

The ridge dropped away at Alto de Cerezales (Heights of the Cherry Trees) and I clambered down the rock-strewn hillside to El Acebo de San Miguel (San Miguel's Holly Tree) where ramshackle balconies were bracketed onto the narrow cobblestone canyon.

The sky was gloomy by now but I grabbed a table on the terrace outside a tavern called Mesón El Acebo and ordered a glass of *crianza*.

I'd already discovered another monumental difference between the Via de la Plata and the Camino Francés: whereas the Via de la Plata had been a trail of frosted beer, the Camino Francés was most definitely destined to be fuelled by full-bodied *vino tinto*.

As a traditional Spanish refrain puts it: *Donde hay vino beben vino. Donde no hay vino, agua fresca* – Where there is wine, drink wine. Where there is no wine, fresh water.

The only other customer at Mesón El Acebo was a middle-aged Venezuelan pilgrim. She explained that in her opinion the cordiality of the Camino was both a curse and a blessing: 'The problem,' she said, 'is that everybody tends to walk at about the same rate, stopping at the same *albergues*...'

It could be wonderfully sociable, she admitted, but unless you were careful you could end up walking the *entire* route with the same crowd simply because everybody tackled the challenge in identical stages. Ana had found that it was preferable to 'mix things up every once in a while' by throwing in an extra-long day and effectively leap-frogging ahead into a new group.

For this reason Ana had completed 36 kilometres from Astorga that day, to bring her to this little mountain town that effectively fell between stages.

I had a decision to make too. I realized that to attempt the extra 8 kilometres mountain crossing to Molinaseca that afternoon would mean completing one of my longest hikes. It would be tough going in this mountainous terrain but to fall short of Molinaseca could mean a night spent out in the open and I couldn't imagine anything I'd enjoy less than a night on a groundsheet on those bare, treeless mountain slopes. I could feel the icy presence of the mountain pass up ahead and imagined that before long I'd be cowering in some highland squall. It was this highland section of my route – and the inclement weather that I might encounter here – that had worried me far more than the hot days on the plains.

I was still thinking about this when dark storm clouds came rolling over the ridge and fat drops of rain started to slap onto the table. I grabbed my pack and wine glass and scurried into the tavern as the wind began to whip silver curtains across the hillside.

Once I saw the cosy beds and the hot showers there was no returning to the street that evening.

* * *

I overtook an elderly couple as they hobbled along El Acebo's cobbled main street at dawn. Inexplicably they also carried an extra backpack swinging between them, even as they limped under the weight of their own packs. It was impossible to imagine that they needed so much stuff. Could it have been their own form of penance, perhaps? An extra backpack filled with bricks would serve the purpose admirably. More likely they were doing it out of an act of love or solidarity. Perhaps that third backpack belonged to a sick or departed loved one. Or perhaps to a comrade of the Camino who had been forced to retire.

I'd have dearly loved to know what their motivation was for carrying this third pack but, whatever it was, I had no doubt that it would be very personal. I certainly didn't feel that I could impose on them with busy-body curiosity. I simply smiled and wished them a heart-felt 'buen camino'. I hoped that it wouldn't be too long before they (and their precious cargo) were shuffling through the so-called Portal of Glory into Santiago de Compostela's cathedral.

On the outskirts of El Acebo there was an ugly granite edifice resembling a 1970s ski-lodge. A sign told me that it was Albergue la Casa del Peregrino and that it had 88 rooms, a swimming pool, a spa and even offered massages. At this hour of the morning the car park was packed with jostling slackpackers loading their suitcases into a fleet of vans.

I scrambled down a rocky hillside that was slippery with miniature cascades carrying the night's rainfall. Twice I had to clamber over fallen trees that had been victims of the storm. The thought that I might have tied my hammock to such a tree made me even more grateful that I'd decided to sleep in the *albergue*. The craggy mountaintops rose ahead of me. Every time I crested a peak I'd stare towards the north hoping – though it was far too early – for a hint of the ocean.

The mountains here were sparsely populated and the few highland farms I passed were dominated by ancient fortress-like *casona* homesteads. Extended families would have slept on the upper floor while the precious livestock lived below making the house cosy with their body-heat and adding to a sense of homeliness with sounds of contented snuffling that carried up through the floorboards like muffled lullabies. Many of these homesteads might have been worked by the same family for many generations and every once in a while their ploughshares still turned up pieces of ancient pottery and coins dating back to the Romans.

The trail converged with the banks of the Rio Meruelo and just as I realized that I was hankering for breakfast, a road sign advised me that I was entering 'one of the most beautiful villages in Spain'. Molinaseca translates as 'dry mill' but a dammed section of the river just next to the so-called Pilgrim's Bridge had created a popular swimming spot that tempted pilgrims and lured day-trippers from the neighbouring town of Ponferrada. Molinaseca was indeed a lovely town, full of the sort of cobbled alleyways that offered picturesque allure to sightseers... and sheer torture to a footsore pilgrim. I stopped for breakfast at a café beside the bridge and was served by a very friendly Venezuelan woman whose lilting South American Spanish was sweeter than the condensed milk that she drizzled into my *cortado* coffee.

***

It was Saturday and the weekend market was in full swing when I reached Ponferrada. A motorbike club was having a meeting next to the castle and dozens of modern-day chariots in the form of three-wheeled trikes were parked on the spot where, eight centuries before, the horses of the Knights Templar would have grazed.

Ponferrada's castle is one of Spain's best-preserved Templar fortresses and it played a particularly dramatic part in the strange tale of honour, bravery, religious fanaticism and betrayal that formed the Templar myth.

The brotherhood was already well established on the Iberian Peninsula by 1178 when their great castle at Ponferrada was built. They were an order of warrior-aesthetes who shunned riches. Their temples were adorned with weapons rather than jewels and no distinction was allowed between the richest and the poorest among them. Each knight was allowed three horses and one squire (whom they were expressly forbidden to beat).

Their white tunics symbolized purity and chastity and the red cross on their chest was the mark of the blood of Christ. It was also a symbol of the blood that they were willing to spill (or, if it came to it, to shed) for their faith.

'The numerous fast days of the Church calendar were to be observed', wrote Dan Jones, in his exhaustive 450-page book *The Templars: The Rise and Spectacular Fall of God's Holy Warriors*, 'but allowances were to be made for the needs of fighting men. Meat was to be served three times a week, on Tuesdays, Thursdays and Saturdays.'

The Templar's official charter stated that they could kill 'enemies of the cross' with impunity. Their detractors claimed that they were homicidal maniacs but the charter made a careful distinction between homicide (the act of killing a man) and 'malicide' (the act of killing evil itself).

They were reminiscent of the Samurai with their code of honour and martial fearlessness. They dutifully established fortresses throughout the wildest sections of the pilgrim routes to protect the devout from the bandits who found easy targets among unarmed and exhausted wanderers.

The Templars might have shunned riches but, thanks to numerous donors and the support of the Pope, the order's network of properties all across Europe and the Holy Lands had provoked envy among some extremely powerful enemies by the beginning of the fourteenth century. Their naval base Château Pèlerin (in what later became Israel), for example, could accommodate 4,000 troops and had stairways that were ample enough to ride horses up and down.

In 1306 Philip IV of France evicted the Jews from his kingdom, purloining all their wealth in the process. It turned out to be a great way to boost the royal coffers and was likely a major incentive in his sudden ambition to do the same with the Knights Templar. Philip (who, according to some historians, was in debt to the Templars) put pressure on Pope Clement V to investigate the order for three unthinkable abominations that had come to his attention: it was said that the Templars had appropriated funds that were due either to the Pope or the King; that they held blasphemous rituals where they said the Mass backwards as a mockery; and that they sodomized new recruits as a form of initiation. It's hard to imagine which of the three charges would have been considered worse in the eyes of the Church. (Some historians have since pointed out that King Philip seemed to have quite an obsession with sodomy – anyone who offended him could normally expect to end up being accused of it sooner or later.)

The king's ministers – under the command of William of Paris (who was not only the Chief Papal Inquisitor in France but also private confessor to the king) – had acquired testimonies from several disgruntled ex-Templars. These were believed to have been knights who had been evicted from the order or who had otherwise left under a cloud.

It's unlikely that the knights were guilty of *any* of the charges but the form of interrogation was such that it very rapidly produced an entire chain of witnesses who would admit to *anything* whatsoever rather than undergo the bodily torment of further 'interviews'.

Fear – a stranger to the knights on battlefields across Christendom – quickly became very palpable indeed wherever members of the order congregated. Some brothers went into hiding. Any who were caught were submitted to questioning and before long the accusations became increasingly bizarre. It was said that recruits were forced to spit upon an image of Christ. They had to remove their clothes, the royal report read, and were then kissed three times, 'first on the lower part of the dorsal spine, once on the naval and once on the mouth'. They were then obliged to sodomize one another.

The first mass arrests took place on Friday 13 October 1307. Even today it is sometimes said that the event inspired the 'Friday the thirteenth' tradition.

Within a terrifyingly short time the Templar Knights became outlaws. Their leaders had been tortured and burned at the stake, minor members got away with mere hanging and all the order's property rested in the 'rightful hands' of Church and state.

Walking below the crenellated battlements and archery-slitted towers of the great castle in Ponferrada it was easy to imagine that such edifices might have inspired envy in the minds of the mighty. It's poignant too to imagine how things might have been when the black-and-white piebald banner of the Templars was hauled down all across Spain for the last time and the last warrior-monks fled as cloaked fugitives, fearful even of the mere mention of the word *Templario*.

The myth of the Templars has revived in unexpected ways over the centuries. Some claim that the Templars continued to exist as a secret society which eventually evolved into the Freemason organization. Seven centuries after the demise of the order it was revived in a very disturbing way in far-off Michoacán State when Mexican drug-lord Nazario Moreno González founded *Los Caballeros Templarios* (The Knights Templar Cartel). It was said that Moreno, known for good reason as *El Más Loco* (The Craziest One), required his recruits to eat the flesh of their victims as part of their initiation. He faked his death and instigated his own beatification in the eyes of his followers. By the time he was gunned down (for real this time) in 2014, shrines had been erected all over Michoacán State to the killer that many still refer to as Saint Nazario.

* * *

After Ponferrada's Church of 'Santa Maria of the Oak' – built on the spot where, according to Templar legend, an image of the Virgin was discovered in the hollow trunk of a tree – two mediaeval Caminos diverged to approach Santiago de Compostela from different angles. A separate and lesser-known trail, the Ruta del Invierno (the Winter Route), still runs 209 kilometres along the Rio Sil which avoided the high snowbound passes.

But I would need to traverse the entire mountain chain sooner or later, so I crossed the Sil valley and headed directly north-east to catch the first clear view of the peaks from the heights of Fuentes Nuevas. It was disconcerting to realize that I'd be walking downhill all day, descending to an altitude that was actually *below* the average I'd maintained throughout my crossing of Extremadura. It would clearly all have to be repaid with interest in the coming days.

The climate had changed dramatically since my path coincided with the Camino Francés. The nights were now bitterly cold and I reluctantly decided that it might be wisest to sleep indoors, at least until I started the descent towards the coast.

Camponaraya turned out to be a lively little village on a Saturday afternoon so I stopped at a bar and ordered a glass of *crianza* and a plate of the traditional shepherd's dish known as *migas*. Literally translated simply as 'crumbs', the bread (aficionados will tell you that it should be four days old) is fried in lard with garlic, pork belly, serrano ham and mushrooms. Good *migas* are best served with cured *txistorra* sausage, roasted peppers, *campesina* bread... and plenty of wine.

The bar was so friendly and the Camponaraya locals so chatty that I considered staying here rather than slogging onwards to the town of Cacabelos. But then the juke box in the corner of the bar jumped to 'Should I Stay or Should I Go' by The Clash. As a song that's guaranteed to put a spring in anyone's step, it had become one of the great motivational anthems on my Vagabond playlist. By the time the last chords had echoed away I'd already paid my bill and was slipping back into the shoulder straps of my pack.

As I strode on that afternoon I passed the time reading the graffiti that lined the route. Apparently some pilgrims habitually travel with thick permanent markers because the majority of the Camino signs on this section were defaced with motivational slogans: 'Silence is the greatest of all masters'; 'Take a breath, and be here now'; 'What if your biggest power would be your vulnerability?'

Perhaps the habit had rubbed off on local kids since one rebel had defaced a 'Castilla y León' signpost so that it now read '*Puta* Castilla y León *Solo*' (Fucking Castilla and León Alone).

'Camino injuries are God's messages,' one sign warned me, '– listen to your body.'

'God loves you,' another told me.

'Have faith. Even when it's hard – that's when you're tested.'

Across another sign, informing pilgrims that there were still 198.5 kilometres to go before Santiago, one tormented soul had simply written 'OH SHIT!'

* * *

'One September, just before the first rains,' Gerald Brenan recalled in the classic *South from Granada*, 'I took it into my head to walk home from Granada...'

Brenan left at three in the morning and arrived at his home in a village in the Alpujarras region at 10 that night.

'It was a long walk,' he admitted, 'scarcely if at all less than sixty miles – but on high mountains one can keep going for ever.'

I'd finally arrived in the high mountains myself, though at the opposite end of the country to Brenan, but I certainly didn't feel that I could keep going forever. In particular a disconcerting niggle in my left leg had started to bother me increasingly. For the last week my left thigh had occasionally felt strangely numb. From time to time I felt the urge to slap my leg, trying to beat some sense of feeling back into it. Paradoxically the skin would, at other times, feel so sensitive that I couldn't bear to touch it. Occasionally, when the hem of my shorts brushed it, I had the startling sensation that it was either scalding hot or icy cold. It was the beginning of a condition known as Meralgia paresthetica. Attributed in particular to overworked thigh muscles, it's common among workmen who use heavy tool-belts. It seemed that the waist-belt of my backpack had trapped a nerve and many months after the trek ended, I'd still feel the occasional need to slap my thigh like a Bavarian dancer with obsessive compulsive disorder.

John Moore's retreat column was irreparably fractured by the time it reached Cacabelos. After I'd covered another 35 kilometres and found a bed in a dorm in Calle Angustia (the 'Street of Anguish'), my left leg felt that way too.

Only about 2,000 British soldiers reached Cacabelos on the night of 3 January 1809 to face as many as 10,000 French. The majority of Moore's column was busy plundering the nearby town of Villafranca. A whole division of other troops were busy drinking themselves into oblivion in Bembibre. They'd stumbled across the wine harvest in storage and decided to make an extended New Year's celebration of it. Moore's entire army had gone to pieces and, supply chains completely shattered, they now survived entirely by looting and plundering.

'I could not have believed, had I not witnessed it,' Moore reported in a letter to his superiors, 'that a British Army, could, in so short a time, have been so completely disorganised. Its conduct during the late marches has been infamous beyond belief... I cannot think, after what has transpired, that there can be any intention of sending a British force again into Spain.'

'Whatever discipline did appear in the ranks seemed to come from German mercenaries...' James A. Michener wrote in *Iberia*, 'what personal courage and good spirits, from the Irish.'

It was a rare stroke of luck for Moore that sharp-shooting Irish rifleman Thomas Plunkett happened to be on hand by the bridge in Cacabelos that January day. Military correspondents – hard put to report anything very positive at all – joyfully recorded how Plunkett put a bullet in the head of Brigadier General Auguste-Marie-Francois Colbert of the French cavalry. The shot was estimated to be at a distance of almost half a kilometre. Then, with uncommon dexterity, Plunkett reloaded his unwieldy Baker rifle (normally a 30-second process) and also brought down the officer who rushed to Colbert's assistance.

The facts are unverifiable and perhaps the military propaganda machine was quick to capitalize on a rare incident of exemplary British soldiering amid what many historians have described as one of the most lamentable chapters in British military history.

The footnote to the Thomas Plunkett legend makes sad reading. Apparently he survived the retreat to be evacuated finally from A Coruña. He may have been with Wellington at the Battle of Quatre Bras (present-day Belgium) in 1815 because contemporary accounts recorded that Plunkett married a woman who was unfortunate enough to have had her *entire* face blown off when an ammunition wagon exploded during that battle.

Plunkett himself received a head wound during the Battle of Waterloo and after retirement traded his pension for an offer of land and emigrated with his 'faceless' wife to Canada. The property turned out to be useless, however, and the Plunketts returned penniless to England. They ended their days as roving tinkers and the old soldier finally keeled over dead in Colchester in 1851.

* * *

I crossed the bridge that had made Plunkett famous the next morning just as the bell on the Church of Santa María began to toll for Sunday Mass.

It was strange to think that, by regional standards, this 900-year-old church was a relatively recent construction. This area had been inhabited since Palaeolithic times and had seen Bronze and Iron Age settlements long before the Asturian tribes were conquered and the Romans established their province of Gallaecia. Later came the Suebi people (a mysterious Germanic tribe who started an insurrection against the Roman Empire in 406 CE) and then, later, the Visigoths. The region had seen countless incarnations by the time the name Cacabelos first appeared in manuscripts during the tenth century.

As I climbed through hills beyond the Cúa Valley the flat, leaden light was oppressive after the steely glare of the plains. On the edge of a vineyard of Mencía grapes (harvested here since the Middle Ages) I stopped for cold coffee to celebrate reaching the 1,000-kilometre mark in my trek. It had been exactly a month since I walked out of Gibraltar and this would be the hardest day climbing on the entire trek as the path rose steadily towards the village of O Cebreiro. The long walk that was behind me had strengthened my legs and by now covering 30 kilometres or more each day was becoming a natural part of my daily habit. Nevertheless, there were steep sections of the trail where, rather than actively walking, I doggedly trudged onwards putting one foot mechanically in front of the other like a high-altitude mountaineer with eyes fixed on the summit. (I later calculated the total elevation gain and found that, since leaving Gibraltar, I'd ascended 15,300 metres – an amount equivalent to four ascents from Everest Base Camp to the summit.)

'At first I'd hobbled,' Laurie Lee had written at the end of his first month on the road. As his blisters hardened he was able to walk without pain and developed what he described as 'a long loping stride which could cover some 20 miles a day.'

Even now I still hobbled, especially towards the end of a day's trek. It was a boost to my morale, however, to realize that my average daily distance had outstripped the strapping 19-year-old trail-blazer, even if only by a mile or two.

I stopped to rest in the plaza in Villafranca del Bierzo, a pretty mediaeval town that carries the dubious distinction of having been sacked by the British no less than three times during the Peninsula War.

'If our march had been an atrocity so far,' a British army doctor in Moore's column reported, 'from Villafranca onwards it can be said that the death march began.'

It was on the summit before O Cebreiro – the most desolate stage on the pilgrimage route – that the retreat reached its most nightmarish point. Women and children froze by the wayside and exhausted horses were killed so that they wouldn't fall into enemy hands. To save ammunition they were driven off the cliffs to their deaths. Here the paymasters were ordered to back their wagons up to the precipices and a fortune in gold coins (over £2 million in today's money) was tipped into the canyon. The starving soldiers could only watch but, in that bitter January of 1809, there was nothing that could be bought anyway in a region that had already been exhaustively plundered.

It is said that General Moore was overseeing the retreat when a British infantryman nearby had his leg torn off by a French round-shot. Not surprisingly the wounded man screamed horribly.

'My good fellow, don't make such a noise,' the general admonished him. 'We must bear these things better.'

Biographer Janet Macdonald quoted the general: 'They [the French] have taken or cut to pieces many hundreds of drunken British cowards – for none but unprincipled cowards get drunk, nay, in the very sight of the enemies of their country; and sooner than survive the disgrace of such infamous misconduct, I hope that the first cannonball fired by the enemy may take me in the head.'

It was an unusually accurate prophecy because on 16 January 1809, Moore was within sight of the port of A Coruña when a French cannonball missed his head by a matter of centimetres. Unfortunately, it passed so close that it carried away his left shoulder exposing his heart and lungs.

Sir John Moore's burial, in an unmarked grave, was later immortalized in Charles Wolfe's famous poem:

'Slowly and sadly we laid him down,
From the field of his fame fresh and gory;
We carved not a line, and we raised not a stone,
But left him alone with his glory.'

Opinions are divided among historians concerning Moore's leadership. There's little doubt that the three-week retreat had been one of the most shameful campaigns in British military history. More lenient historians have speculated, however, that the retreat might have served as a shrewd diversionary tactic, drawing Napoleon's fire at a time when the French would otherwise have been in a position to occupy the entire Peninsula.

The majority of Moore's 30,000 men lived to fight again and a few of those veterans were with Wellington four years later when he finally drove the French out of their last stronghold at San Sebastian.

* * *

By mid-morning I was walking among a procession of pilgrims under the shade of giant chestnut trees along the banks of the Rio Valcarce. The clank of cow bells brought a feeling of déjà vu, recalling the goats that had woken me among the Roman ruins at the start of my trip.

An icy drizzle drove me into a crowded bar in Las Herrerias where other pilgrims were already shucking waterproof hiking jackets and ponchos off in the doorway. Most of these hikers would stop for the night here, having completed almost 30 kilometres since leaving Cacabelos that morning.

I hoped that the rain would hold off and that a plate of ham and fried eggs would provide the necessary sustenance for a final 2-hour climb to O Cebreiro. Although tiny, Las Herrerias was a place of cruel temptations: five or six *albergues* and hostels beckoned as I passed and, an hour later, I saw a convoy of the sturdy white horses that are hired out each day during the hiking season to carry pilgrims to the top of the mountain. Although it struck me as a more picturesque version of slackpacking, it may have been a sensible decision that had perhaps even saved lives over the years.

Many of the 8,000 men who died on Moore's retreat breathed their last on this stretch of the trail and an online database of fatalities on the Camino shows that at least five pilgrims have succumbed to heart attacks on the climb to O Cebreiro. I was horrified to read that several of them were about 20 years younger than I was.

The weather is notoriously unpredictable in these mountains and once again afternoon rainstorms were forecast. I feared for the worst as I gazed up at a granite sky that was as brutal and hard as the fortress walls of Ponferrada. While this trail would clearly have been well-trodden in the mornings, it struck me as an unimaginably wild and desolate country in which to be hiking solo.

These mountains were once notorious for packs of feral dogs... and even more feral bandits. The latter were long gone but wolves are still occasionally seen on the slopes and I'd heard that two more of those *corrales de lobos* (wolf corrals), now fortunately decommissioned, lay along the ridges to my west. Laurie Lee must have wondered what he was getting himself into when he found similar conditions on the day he arrived in Spain and spent his first sleepless night fending off a pack of feral dogs in the Galician hills.

The bruised sky grew increasingly threatening as I hiked up to a tiny hamlet with the unlikely name of Laguna de Castilla. It was hard to imagine anything *less* like a 'lagoon' than this wind-battered and desolate frontier community on the Galicia border. Any villagers that might have been in residence very wisely remained cosily ensconced indoors on such a grisly afternoon. I saw nobody as I shuffled through the village and then crossed the border in true Galician style, with thermal leggings under my shorts, a jacket zipped to under my chin and with a bandana tied over my face against the chill mountain air. This was not shaping up to be a good night for 'stealth camping'. A hammock and a sleeping bag that was suited to midsummer in Extremadura would not provide much protection in these mountains.

As the afternoon progressed a low fog blocked out the sun, belying the fact that we were heading for the longest day of the year. By the time I walked into O Cebreiro the little village was almost hidden in a thick pea-soup mist. I felt like a sailor steering a course into a mysterious port as the granite slabs of cottages drifted towards me like floating hulks in the swirling mist. The stumpy steeple of Santa María la Real church (at almost 1,200 years old, supposedly the oldest church on the Camino Francés) loomed like a blacked-out lighthouse and the traditional circular houses known as *pallozas* looked like rock outcrops as the rain dripped steadily from their thatched roofs.

The shroud of fog seemed to deaden sound so that the village was hauntingly silent. My footsteps shuffling over the shining cobbles were the only noise until a door in an expanse of grey granite opened with a creak and two cloaked figures scuttled across the road like villains in a Sherlock Holmes mystery. In the instant before the door closed I glimpsed the fiery orange interior and heard the promising clatter of cutlery and conversation.

I forced myself to continue onwards to the hangar-like building that was the municipal *albergue*. I hadn't phoned ahead to book and was nervous that it would be full and that I'd have to find somewhere to camp after all. Fortunately this 100-bed *albergue* was the biggest I'd seen on the entire trip. It was a veritable night-shift production-line dedicated to converting weary and weakened waifs into serviceable pilgrims by morning. It was as efficient and soulless as any other factory but eight euros a night bought me a hot shower and a bunk with clean sheets.

The Camino from the French border had already been described stage-by-stage in 1135 CE, in Book V of the *Codex Calixtinus* but it was in O Cebreiro that the decision was taken to raise the profile of the Camino on a global scale. Parish priest Elías Valiña Sampedro was the visionary who spent most of the 1980s travelling in his little Fiat van while he painted the yellow arrows that have become icons of the trail. It's said that he was once stopped for questioning by Basque separatists who were suspicious of his toing-and-froing past their mountain strongholds. When they searched his van they found only countless canisters of yellow paint.

'I'm preparing for a great invasion,' the curate told the group's commander.

Father Elías died in 1989 and his memorial in O Cebreiro, permanently decorated with flowers and scallop shells, is now a place of homage for pilgrims. You have to wonder though how he would have felt if he could have seen how the French Way has become so famous that it's now considered to be the one and only Camino.

As the priest in Roncesvalles had pointed out to me, there is no single Camino. In fact, there are now 49 official Spanish Camino routes, covering a total of about 15,000 kilometres. Of the 400,000 or so hikers and cyclists (and horseback pilgrims) who traipse along the Camino Francés each year, only a tiny fraction are aware that other, blissfully uncrowded, alternatives even exist. While pilgrims queue to have their passports stamped in tiny O Cebreiro or line up for refreshments at isolated mountain cafés, other routes remain almost untrodden. It was only when I passed through Zamora on the Via de la Plata that I realized that the city was also a point of convergence for two other Caminos: the Camino Portugués de la Plata (which cuts through a corner of Portugal); and the virtually unknown Camino de Levante (which starts in Valencia). Even among dedicated aficionados of the Camino, the route known as Camino da Geira e dos Arrieiros (connecting Braga in Portugal with Santiago de Compostela along trails once used by mediaeval muleteers) is almost unheard of. At just 236 kilometres long, yet taking in spectacular scenery in two countries, it ought to be one of the most popular hiking trails in Europe.

O Cebreiro's *albergue* felt like an immense orthopaedic clinic since the vast majority of the 'in-patients' were limping and most had bandaged feet and taped knees. There was a fully equipped kitchen and dining room but there was no grocery store in the village, so I reluctantly donned my flip-flops and ventured back into the icy drizzle. I splashed across the puddled cobbles making straight for the welcoming glow of the bar I'd glimpsed on my way through the village. La Venta Celta ('Celtic Trading Post'), with its heavy stained-timber furniture and glowing orange lamps, was surprisingly empty. I had the feeling that I was on a different planet from the land of chilled gazpacho and sangria that I'd hiked across the previous month. The *vino tinto*, in its stumpy glass, was as fortified as the thick stone walls of the bar. The *caldo gallego* soup came in a heavy terracotta bowl and the timber table creaked under the weight of the basket of country bread that accompanied it. *Caldo gallego* was the hearty cabbage soup, made from the tall Galician cabbage, with leaves as big as dustbin lids, that is known as *berza*.

I also took a chance to sample the almond-flavoured *tarta de Santiago* pastry that is said to be one of the required experiences of the Camino. It was surprisingly cloying and hard to swallow. The first mouthful convinced me that *tarta de Santiago* could have been created to add to the trials of the Camino; a pilgrim who breakfasted on it in Roncesvalles might still be chewing when he or she finally walked into Santiago de Compostela.

When the waitress came to clear my empty dishes, I asked her how life had changed for the villagers in the face of visitor numbers that increased each year. She wouldn't know, she said, since she'd come from Venezuela just a few years ago looking for work. There was no point in asking the barman either – he was from Ecuador. It was very unlikely that O Cebreiro would have lured such a cosmopolitan workforce back when Father Elías was planning his invasion.

I could see through to the kitchen where an old woman with a cleaver was chopping cabbage as if settling an old grudge. She was probably Galician, I thought, but she didn't look like she was in any mood for conversation. Over in the corner – occupying prime position by the fire – an old farmer was moodily nursing a glowing glass of amber-coloured liquor. I didn't feel that I could ask him whether life had changed for the better.

Every once in a while the door would open and dripping figures would shuffle in, shaking the fog off their shoulders as if they were trying to detach particularly tenacious ghosts. In the moody spirit of the evening I decided to have a nightcap. Perhaps feeling a little homesick for my daughter at her home in Pamplona I decided that the 'spirit of the evening' ought to be a *patxaran* (the traditional Navarran liquor made from sloe berries).

The old farmer, in his watchful position by the fire, reminded me of the Miracle of O Cebreiro. The legend had boosted the village's fame during the fourteenth century almost as much as the efforts of Father Elías would later. There were several versions of the story, but James A. Michener recorded what is probably the most entertaining in *Iberia*. During a long, bleak winter a lone priest was stationed here to perform Mass. No pilgrims braved the snowy trail but every day the priest was forced to leave his cosy seat by the fire and venture out to the chilly chapel to offer communion for a single lonely shepherd. One day the priest cursed that he had to leave the warmth of his fire for this 'idiot shepherd' who came every day, no matter the weather, so that he wouldn't miss out on a sip of communion wine and a tiny hunk of bread. There was a clap of thunder and a flash of lightning, and the priest fell to his knees before a chalice that was now filled with real blood and a hunk of bread that had turned into the body of Christ.

'I too have come to attend Mass,' a voice boomed, 'for I too am a shepherd.'

The tale of the miracle echoed through the Catholic world turning the sleepy village of O Cebreiro into one of the holiest spots on the Camino Francés. That legend lives on in the host and chalice which still form a central motif on the flag of Galicia today.

* * *

The sun had already risen when I left O Cebreiro the next morning after what had been a very restless night.

I'd climbed onto my upper bunk about 9 o'clock to take my place midway along a row of sleeping bags. It was like gazing along a row of monstrous cocoons on a laboratory shelf. Judging by the snores and farts that kept me awake until the early hours it clearly wasn't going to be butterflies that emerged in the morning. Of the 40 or so pilgrims in the dorm at least 30 of them snored. And they did so with surprising coordination; just as one fell silent another took up the tune, like a choir of mournful Welshmen belting out a close-harmony ballad.

I put my pillow over my head in an effort to cut out the noise. Then I furled my ears, like the stiff canvas of a sailing ship, bending them double so that I could batten them down with my bandana. Even that didn't block the sound. Of the ten pilgrims who weren't busy snoring, at least five talked in their sleep. This was at least a little more entertaining and I spent much of the night trying to decipher which of the dozen or so languages represented in the dorm that night were being used.

The chrysalises began to hatch, with a zipping sound, an hour before dawn. It was still pitch-black when I became aware of bright red fireflies, flitting across the room at head level. These were the headtorches (on the relatively subdued red-bulb setting) of early risers as they rustled their belongings together. From the communal bathrooms below came the sound of hacking coughs as smokers' lungs were shocked into action by the chilled dawn air.

Why did they rise so early, I wondered. We were a few days short of midsummer and they would have 15 hours of daylight for walking. From the way the chilly mist swirled beyond the window I doubted that they were intent on dodging the power of the sun.

Father Elías had worked so conscientiously towards establishing this invasion that some pilgrims now considered it necessary to leave in the dark; only those who arrived in the next village ahead of the crowds could be certain of securing a bed. The Camino Francés tends to have an *albergue* every 15–20 kilometres yet some villages can barely cope with the influx. Many pilgrims are grateful merely for a warm shower and a clean bed but the places with rave reviews are often impossible to secure unless you book ahead or arrive well before lunchtime. Some establishments, perhaps for administrative ease, preferred to stick to the time-honoured first-come-first-served system... but for these you'd need to wake up early to get the drop on your fellow pilgrims.

I was aiming for another tough 40-kilometre day but I figured it would be worth every centimetre if I could somehow descend back to what I thought of as Spanish weather. I was frustrated at having abandoned my hammock and was in a hurry to get to more comfortable climes where I could sleep under the stars again. If I could reach the city of Sarria it would mean that by tomorrow my route would splinter from this army of westward-bound pilgrims and I'd start on my solitary hike to the north coast.

Was I being shallow, I asked myself, wanting to avoid Santiago just because that was where everyone else was going?

Of all the people I'd spoken to, only Tex the artillery officer had said anything that made me curious to see Santiago from a pilgrim's viewpoint: 'Yes sir,' he'd said. 'I'm sitting watching the pilgrims stumbling, limping towards the cathedral and it's one of the most powerful experiences imaginable. Many are crying tears of relief... or just tears of pain.'

I decided that I should witness that one day. And, if I could only complete my own trek, I could even drive there and still be able to watch without guilt.

Although I'd maintained about the same pace right through the trek, I was finding the Camino Francés unexpectedly hard going. The reason was less to do with the mountainous terrain and more because the unseasonably stormy highland afternoons had conspired to thwart the walking schedule that I'd finally accustomed myself to. I'd developed the habit of waking at first light and covering at least 15 kilometres before lunch. Then walk again in the cool of the evening (ideally from about five in the afternoon until nine). In this way I'd managed an average of around 35 kilometres per day.

With violent rainstorms forecast for the afternoons I was now doing my best to get to some form of shelter as soon as possible after lunch. It turned out that tackling 30–40-kilometre days in two separate sessions was infinitely easier than trying to complete what amounted almost to a marathon every morning. I now understood why most pilgrims on the Camino Francés considered 20–25 kilometres an ideal daily goal.

I was among the last to leave the *albergue* but by eight in the morning I was already crossing the 1,270 metre Alto de San Roque pass. Named for the patron saint of pilgrims and dogs, the pass has the reputation of offering spectacular views but it seemed that I was destined to number among the great many hikers who are cheated of this privilege by the impenetrable fog that typically clings to these high passes.

'The rain in Spain falls mainly on the plain.'

Whoever first coined that nonsensical phrase certainly never visited the mountains of Galicia.

* * *

It's hard to imagine that the tiny hamlet of Hospital de la Condesa (population less than 30) was once the site of the most famous hospital on the Camino Francés. The hospital itself has long since ceased to function and these days it is O Tear café that provides the greatest boost to pilgrim welfare. Much of the space inside the café was taken up with a statuesque old handloom that's said to be over a hundred years old and the few tables that occupied the rest of the dark little tavern were packed with pilgrims sitting elbow-to-elbow. I took my coffee outside to a stone step by the back door, pulling my legs in to make space when a small herd of cows passed by on their way to the milking shed.

I later learned that the local bovine breed is known – apparently without a hint of innuendo – as *Rubias Gallegas* (Galician Blondes).

The trail from Hospital de la Condesa continued past slate-roofed farmhouses, presided over by gnarled trees that had witnessed the passing of many millions of pilgrims. Dogs barked territorially at one another but completely ignored the constant procession of walkers. Experienced hikers on these trails say that if a farm dog starts barking at you, it's probably wise to double-check that you haven't inadvertently strayed off the route.

The rainfall had provoked a plague of spectacularly huge slugs that lay strewn across the track like obsidian daggers. Some of the hills had burned patches showing that, even in this waterlogged landscape, wildfires had been a problem already this summer.

I walked for 3 hours then stopped for a breather at the Chapel of San Pedro do Biduedo. It was founded by the Knights Hospitaller of the Order of Saint John, more fortunate comrades-in-arms of the persecuted Templars. The chapel boasted a carving of my old friend San Roque, as usual hiking up his tunic to show a well-turned limb. It occurred to me that he looked suspiciously like he was trying to slap some feeling back into a deadened thigh. I diagnosed a mediaeval case of Meralgia paresthetica.

Whereas the early days of my walk recalled African landscapes, I was now reminded increasingly of Olde England: the sunken lanes, scoured out by the scuffling of countless pilgrims, reminded me of the ancient smuggler routes of the Dorset coast; the rustic Galician barns could have been built of Cotswold stone; the dank, misty oak forests (known locally as *carballeiras*) could have been the Sherwood Forest of Robin Hood fame. Yew trees and chestnut groves became a sign that I was arriving on the outskirts of the villages. While experts claim that the chestnut had been growing here for at least 20,000 years it is also believed that the Romans were chiefly responsible for promoting its cultivation through the chain of their settlements. Chestnuts became such an integral part of the Galician diet that it's said that when potatoes were first brought back from the Americas, people in this area referred to them as 'earth chestnuts'.

The poisonous yew tree also played a large part in local history. Roman historians claimed that after the Galician warriors were defeated by Roman legions in a battle (around 22 BCE) the vanquished warriors, rather than face the shame of surrender, took their own lives by ingesting yew tree poison.

In a crowded roadside bar in Fonfria I ordered a ten-euro *menú del día*, featuring fried 'earth chestnuts' (potatoes), mushrooms and ham, sardines and a carafe of *vino tinto*. The only dining space left was at the bar so I sat looking at a wall loaded with framed photos of good ol' boy local hunters kneeling proudly with dogs, guns and carcasses. In one group photo I counted no fewer than ten dead wild boars.

* * *

Mediaeval pilgrims invariably breathed a profound sigh of relief upon reaching Triacastela. The little town signified the end of the toughest mountain passes on the Camino. From here I could hope that the terrain and perhaps even the climate would be more benign. Triacastela has more than 15 *albergues*, hostels and hotels that cater to pilgrims.

You can still see the buildings that, in mediaeval times, housed a hospital for pilgrims and a prison which was used to detain incorrigible criminals who'd been condemned to the pilgrimage but were found to have backslid into old habits along the way.

I walked through Triacastela without stopping, racing a stormy sky that grew moodier still as I continued through the chain of sleepy villages that ran down the ridge: A Ferrería, A Balsa, San Xil de Carballo, Fontearcuda, Furela... At the crest of each hill I optimistically strained my eyes towards the north, for the first glimpse of the Bay of Biscay.

In a farmyard in Montán I was astounded to see that some rural entrepreneur had installed a vending machine. I treated myself to a can of Red Bull and a chocolate bar. Then, just 3 minutes later, I came across a place that encapsulated the spirit of hospitality that has traditionally been central to the Camino Francés. Tierra de Luz (Land of Light) was the name given to what had once been an old blacksmith's barn by its new owner. Australian pilgrim

Simon Keenan had fallen in love with the spot eight years ago and had turned his back on life in Murray River. Simon had installed tempting sofas and armchairs in the barn and he kept a table loaded with coffee, fresh fruit, juice, nuts, eggs, tomatoes, avocados, preserves and the makings of sandwiches. Nothing was for sale. This was what is known to pilgrims as a *donativo* and pilgrims were free to take what they needed and leave what they could afford.

The spirit of hospitality had clearly won Simon a lot of friends throughout the world and grateful messages from well-wishers, scrawled on pieces of slate and timber, covered the walls of the barn and surrounded an old black-and-white photo of the blacksmith and his wife.

'Some people stop by for a quick coffee and end up staying for a month,' Simon told me in his quietly spoken yet energetic way.

I could understand why.

Some were lured also by Simon's interest in yoga and meditation. More than just a place of relaxation and refreshment, Tierra de Luz was designed to be a creative space. Another hand-painted sign invited guests to 'write words of wisdom, paint creations, inspire fellow companions to remember that we *together* are travelling on the Camino of life'.

'What's the hurry?' Simon asked me when after a half-hour or so of chatting I began to make signs that it was time for me to move on.

He convinced me to visit the 'labyrinth' that he'd created among the trees. Inspired by a 3,000-year-old petroglyph that was discovered nearby at Castro de Formigueiros, Simon's labyrinth consisted of ankle-high rocks and what he described as 'powerful' quartz stone. Connecting ancient worlds with modern worlds, it was a meditational walkway that was designed, perhaps, as a sort of pocket-sized pilgrimage. An old door had been turned into an info board (in English and Galician) explaining that *el laberinto* was created to be walked 'with purpose and intention'. The walk inward was a process of 'RELEASE – releasing what you don't need'. The centre was the place for 'RECEIVING clarity, inspiration and guidance' and the RETURN was about 'opening your heart and applying what is learned'.

Simon claimed that his labyrinth had strange powers.

'A friend of mine wanted to film it from above with a drone,' he told me, 'but it was impossible. He tried to fly over it from all angles but the drone was completely unable to enter the airspace above the labyrinth.'

It was the one and only time during the trek that I wished I'd made space in my pack for a drone.

Simon's enthusiasm and generosity of spirit was infectious and I was sorely tempted to stick around for longer. My own 'purpose and intention' was, by now, wholly directed towards reaching Sarria before the storm broke.

***

It was early afternoon when my route joined the highway that ran into Sarria city.

Up ahead was a roadhouse with three highway maintenance vehicles parked outside. I took this as a recommendation more compelling than an entire army of pilgrims and stopped for lunch.

The shadowy granite dining room – misty with garlic-scented steam – was brightened with the reflective luminous jackets of the highway workers. Through the door of the kitchen I could see smoked chorizos hanging from the ceiling and strings of red peppers hung like fairy-lights. Pots and pans were clattering busily amid the sizzle and pop of frying olive oil.

'Cuisine is culture,' Paul Theroux once wrote, 'and traditional cooking persists in places that have been ignored by gourmet chefs or high-end restaurants.'

Callos (tripe) was the special of the day but I ordered a starter of *arroz a la Cubana* (essentially Cuban fried rice with a fried egg), followed by *zorza* (spicy mince created from what might be described as deconstructed chorizos). It was served with fried potatoes that were sprinkled with the brick-dust of paprika.

There was a full bottle of vino: *'Vitamina V para el camino,'* the waitress smiled.

I refilled my stumpy glass several times in the knowledge that I had less than 2 hours' walk to Sarria and the end of my own personal Camino Francés.

For dessert I ordered a double espresso and a little terracotta dish of *flan casero*. I was pleased to see that this crème caramel showed the dimples of little air bubbles – incontrovertible proof, so Spanish chefs say, that it must indeed be homemade.

The storm that had hovered, like a dark predator, along the horizon all day finally pounced when I was about 5 kilometres short of Sarria. The rain began to pound in heavy drops, a miniature bombardment that raised little explosions of dust in the ground around me. I squatted on my haunches under a tree, reluctant to dig out my poncho and trying to stay dry amid the steamy odour of roots and wet moss. It was only the second bout of rain that had caught me in open country in almost five weeks of walking. It only lasted for about 30 minutes and then, for the first time that day, the sun broke through the clouds. The land was bathed in silver light, and the tip of every leaf dripped with diamonds in the afternoon glow. A rainbow thickened, luminous stripes stretching across the hills like a threadbare tapestry.

* * *

The Church stipulates that for a pilgrim to be issued with a *Compostela* certificate he or she must be able to show, upon arrival in Santiago, a *credencial* passport with two stamps per day for a minimum of 100 kilometres of hiking (or 200 kilometres of cycling). The city of Sarria lies exactly 113 kilometres from Santiago so it is logically the most popular starting point for thousands of pilgrims each year who are determined (whether by necessity or inclination) to do the absolute minimum.

Roughly one in four of all pilgrims on the Camino Francés begin their trek in Sarria. I would later see that the *Wise Pilgrim* app lists no less than 28 *albergues*, hostels and guesthouses for pilgrims in Sarria. The app also had a warning, luridly highlighted in red, to the effect that the route into and through the city was a gathering point for 'beggars, buskers and the occasional scam artist'.

I didn't meet a scam artist there, but I did catch up with an old man who was dawdling down the last stretch of the highway into the outskirts of the city who, even from a distance, didn't look like a regular pilgrim. He trudged so aimlessly that I thought to myself that he would *never* get to Santiago at that rate. His beard was grey and ragged and his plaid lumberjack shirt and backpack looked like they might have been through *several* Caminos.

In fact, by his own reckoning this old man had walked more than 20,000 kilometres – through France, Italy, Greece and even as far as Syria – during the last 13 years.

Perhaps anxious that he shouldn't be taken for a scam artist, the old man made me take a note of his full name: 'When you have a connection later search Andoni Moreta Hernández on the internet. Some newspapers have published my story.'

We chatted in Spanish as we dawdled into town and he described his endless walking as an act of penance. He'd been a school teacher in Bilbao, he told me, until he retired to dedicate his life to living permanently as *'un pícaro del camino'* (rogue of the road).

He seemed to be a more troubled and haunted version of the old vagabond I'd met so many years before on a train near Badajoz. I'd eaten well and was anticipating a comfortable bunk in Sarria so I slipped enough cash into his hand so that he too could afford a meal and a bed somewhere (if he so chose).

Later, I googled a news report from 2018 on *La Voz de Galicia* website: 'On February 16, 2008 a 12-year-old autistic student fell from a high school window,' it read. There was a photo of Andoni Moreta Hernández looking considerably younger and with a less bedraggled beard. The reporter wrote that señor Andoni had been the girl's teacher. The girl was in a coma when he set out to walk the Camino Francés and he promised to continue until she recovered. Two months later the girl died and, true to his word, señor Andoni never stopped walking. He simply gave the house that he'd inherited from his grandparents to his ex-wife after he made the decision to become a vagabond. His three daughters had grown to adulthood by the time he entered his second decade tramping around Europe.

'I don't know how to steal or beg,' he told the reporter. 'But I *do* know how to talk. If I do it correctly and touch the sentiments that we all have – something we call goodness. Well, if I do it right... then they give.'

He did it right and his story tugged at my heartstrings. I thought of him often afterwards.

* * *

I awoke before daybreak in a dorm room in the charming old Casa Peltre hostel and lay still for a while as the pilgrims around me packed their bags. They probably needed to get moving promptly if they were going to get the drop on other pilgrims for tonight's accommodation. I had little reason to rush, however.

It was Midsummer's Day and 16 hours of daylight would be ample time to cover the 33 kilometres that led to the city of Lugo.

I stepped through the hostel's garden gate and turned into Rúa Maior to find myself swimming against the tide of Santiago-bound hikers. I revelled in their confused expressions and frantic conferring over maps as I sauntered confidently in what appeared to be *entirely* the wrong direction. One German couple emerged from a café and instinctively followed me until I stopped and gently shooed them back in the other direction.

I was not quite as confident as I might have looked, however. The obvious way to Lugo was along the Carraterra Lugo-Monforte highway, but as I zoomed in on Google Earth it looked like there were several viaducts that appeared to be impassable for pedestrians. The smaller LU-546 also ran directly north, meandering through a chain of villages before entangling itself with the web of junctions and flyovers to the south of Lugo. With a population of around 100,000, Lugo would be the biggest city I'd passed through since Salamanca and, as had happened in Seville, I didn't want to find myself on the outskirts with no way to reach the city on foot.

The grey, overcast morning I spent traipsing down the hard-shoulder of the LU-546, buffeted by the slipstream of trucks, led me through a region that was more industrial than I'd anticipated. I passed factories, warehouses and car dealerships and stopped for refreshments in service stations along the highway. It was the least interesting day of hiking but by now walking had at last become painless. The 7 hours that I hiked along the LU-546 passed almost as if I was sleep-walking – one foot in front of the other. Impelled forwards by sheer habit.

On the outskirts of Lugo – almost within sight of the monumental Roman walls that were constructed when this was known as Lucus Augusti – I stopped at a Repsol service station and grabbed a chocolate bar to celebrate the 1,100-kilometre mark on my trek.

I'd hoped that, now that I was clear of the mountains, I'd be able to string my hammock somewhere along the banks of the Rio Minho. By the time I'd crossed to the northern edge of Lugo, however, it was drizzling faintly in the style characterized as *calabobos* in Galicia. The name translates literally as 'soak the stupid' because it is the sort of deceptive rain that leads the uninitiated into believing that it's not enough to get you wet. I searched on my phone for accommodation and was surprised to find a hostel that was named (in English surprisingly) Roots and Boots.

I hadn't realized until now that Lugo was located about two-thirds of the way along the so-called Camino Primitivo, the 350-kilometre route which connects Oviedo (the mediaeval capital of the Kingdom of Asturias) with Santiago de Compostela. But in comparison with the Camino Francés the Camino Primitivo was definitely the road less travelled and, on this drizzly evening, I had Roots and Boots all to myself.

Lugo is famous among the Spanish for cuisine that centres in particular upon octopus so I dined on *polbo á feira* (paprika-tinged octopus), soaking up the rust-coloured olive oil with heavy slabs of Galician bread. I tried to imagine that I could almost catch the scent of the ocean. I knew though that it was likely to take another three or four days of walking before I could step onto a beach. A lot could happen in that time.

As a Spanish saying has it, 'until the tip of the tail has gone by it's *still* a bull'.

* * *

Early the next morning I stood on Lugo's historic Ponte Vella bridge watching the great, grey, green, greasy Rio Minho running under stone arches that have withstood seasonal floodwaters for almost two thousand years.

A wealth of legends surrounds Galicia's biggest river and the Romans themselves believed that this haunted river was the gateway to *finis terrae* (the ends of the Earth). Beyond the wall of mist at the extremes of the river there was a cliff that dropped away into the void. The Gallego highlanders had a strong tradition of *meigas* (the generic name for any one of a dozen or more types of witches) and the Minho valley was the domain of *feiticeiras*, diabolically charming witches who were forever listening out for young men who they could lure to their death by drowning.

Tradition had it that boatmen on the Rio Minho would carry a stone in their mouths to remind them not to speak and so alert the *feiticeiras* to their presence. There were also *chuchonas* who sucked the blood of children and used their tender bodies to make potions. (In Mexico it is sometimes said that *La Lechuza* – the giant owl-witch – does this.)

The Basque highlands might be the home of *lamia* (golden-haired fairies with duck's feet), but Galicia was haunted by *lobismullers* (female werewolves) and *xacios* (a type of Galician mermaid that lived in highland tarns).

In a few days it would be Saint John's day (24 June) and, according to ancient folklore, witches of all persuasions would by now be flying from all over the region, bound for the gatherings that take place annually. Galician villagers used to place wild garlic and spiny thistles between their roof tiles at this time of year, as a deterrent to hellish nocturnal pilots. Apparently Spanish witches don't rely on the traditional broomsticks of their northern counterparts as a mode of aviation. When they're not zipping around on airborne ploughshares they are carried aloft, helicopter-style, powered by the traditional spools that are used for winding wool: 'Putting it on their heads they drew their skirts up over it and took to the air,' Brenan reported in *South from Granada*.

This part of Spain is also said to be the land of the Santa Compaña, a candlelit procession of damned souls. It was said that they filed out from the cemeteries chanting morbidly as they announced the roll call of those who will soon be summoned. Occasionally unfortunate witnesses might hear their own names reeled off as they paraded past.

I had no disturbing encounters and even the *nubeiros*, hairy long-tailed creatures who control the crop-destroying summer storms, were kind to me that day. It was a perfect morning for hiking and remained cool enough to continue walking right through midday. Descending into the Rego de Xoibán valley I squatted down to watch a lone stag browsing at the edge of the forest. At a spot where a stream gurgled through a little wood I stripped off for a wash that gave me an instant ice-cream headache and left me shivering.

I'd only just begun walking again when a pine marten poked its head out of the roadside vegetation. It turned towards me and stared for a moment, displaying the creamy-white bib on its chest, and then trotted nonchalantly across the lane.

I stopped for a lunch of garlic mushrooms and grilled sardines in a village bar. Then I sat for a while studying the choice of several routes that would lead me to the coast. Walking again without the benefit of those yellow arrows, I was becoming obsessive about checking and rechecking my location. I wanted to find a route that would lead me as close as possible to due north while avoiding busy roads.

Naively I'd imagined my walk down from the northern slopes of the mountains to be a steady descent towards the coast. For several days now I'd been hoping to get a glimpse of the sea, or at least the mist that hovers over the Galician coastline. But when I stopped for the night in a hostel in the village of Vilalba I saw on the map that the coast was still barricaded behind yet another mountain range.

There was something more promising about the name of this last range, however; Serra do Xistral seemed to echo the whisper of sand blowing across a Galician beach. Google Earth showed a very tempting dirt track that followed the ridgeline directly across those mountains. Leading due north and sticking to the high ground rather than weaving along the valleys, it had the potential to save me a day's walking. Zooming in on the map I could see that the track appeared to be a service road for a chain of countless wind-turbines that threw their shadows across the hillside like gigantic crucifixes. The trail appeared to be accessible but what if it fizzled out or was blocked by private land just short of the coast? Then I'd have to backtrack and, even allowing for Galicia's reputation for rainfall, there could be no guarantee of water on those highland trails during midsummer.

Logistical decisions of this sort would continue to haunt me for months after I'd completed my journey. Night after night I'd dream of scribbly red lines on a map – the breadcrumb marks of potential routes that might lead me into a dead-end in remote Spanish wilderness.

'May your brother's El Camino run forever,' went the lyrics of a favourite song on my Vagabond playlist ('All Your Favorite Bands', by Dawes). In the months after the trip ended, I'd wonder if I was perpetually cursed to wake to the nightmare of a route that could never be figured out to my satisfaction by daybreak.

I stuck to the safe option, avoiding what might be a tempting trap and sticking to a chain of country lanes that wound their way down the valleys and up over the flanks of Serra do Xistral. Although it was undoubtedly longer I was reassured by the certainty that it would ultimately reach the coast. So, rather than making a beeline across the hills heading directly for the coast, I spent two days meandering 80 kilometres across the countryside.

Crossing the last mountain pass to the west of Monte Xistral, I stopped for lunch in the village of Viveiro. A group of farmers was sitting at the bar in Casa Cándida watching a television screen that showed one of the endless gossip shows that make up the bulk of Spanish day-time television – interminable bickering about celebrity divorces and the affairs of soccer-stars and pop-idols. But after the brisk mountain air the bar was warmly welcoming and the periodic hiss of the coffee machine was like the purr of a house cat.

I sat in the dining room at the back – beyond the irritating television – and dined on *carne estofada* (hearty beef stew) with a carafe of Ribeiro vino.

An icy wind was blowing as I stepped back into the street and I was glad for the warming effect of the stew... and for the fact that I'd left half the carafe undrunk. I was determined to do my utmost to get off the mountain before nightfall and prayed that an afternoon squall wouldn't force me to string my hammock up here among the pine forests that lined the road.

It seemed that the bull still had more than enough time for a last lunge at me.

I hurried onwards into the late afternoon, my heart sinking with each hill that I crested only to find another ridge rising beyond. Finally the road began a winding descent into Barreiros valley. It was evening when I arrived in Vilares. More a sprawl of roadside holiday homes than an actual village, Vilares nevertheless boasted a friendly bar where I ordered a tankard of Estrella Galicia and enjoyed a tapas of octopus salad.

The word hobo originates from 'homeward bound' and now I could finally admit that I was on the last downhill stretch. I'd covered 46 kilometres since dawn and yet I felt surprisingly strong and extremely happy with life as I strode along that evening looking for hammock trees. There were some stands of trees in the distance but the fields were all fenced off. Then, barely an hour before sunset, I passed a dilapidated barn. Doubtless it belonged to *somebody* but for the moment at least it was deserted and possibly forgotten. The cracked concrete forecourt was unfenced and part of the roof had caved in. I stepped through the crumbling wall and there, parked inside under the only section of the roof that appeared still to be more or less watertight, was an old timber hay cart. Complete with a rusty pitchfork, it would have been instantly familiar to Laurie Lee. Unfortunately my hammock would once again go unused but I realized that I couldn't have asked for a more appropriate sleeping spot for my last night on the trail.

I hefted my pack into the cart, wriggled into my sleeping bag and did my best to stay awake until the first stars appeared through the broken roof of the barn.

I failed miserably.

* * *

It was one of the best night's sleep I'd had in the last month and a spring had returned to my steps as I walked out that last midsummer morning down the Landro Valley where hydrangeas of every shade – from deepest blue, to scarlet to subtle pastel-pink – were sprinkled with diamonds of dew.

Today was the day of Saint John when, according to Spanish tradition, the spirit of John the Baptist blesses the dew which in mediaeval times was believed to have dropped from the stars. In Mexico this was the only day on which lepers (traditionally prohibited from touching water) were allowed to bathe.

'There are villages in the province of Soria and in Navarra,' wrote Gerald Brenan in *South from Granada*, 'where the girls roll naked in the dew.'

I was disappointed to see that sensible Galician girls don't go in for such nonsense these days.

Approaching the tidal wastes of Ría de Viveiro I caught the unmistakable tang of seaweed in the air but even now, the tall buildings hid Playa de Covas until I was already on Viveiro's promenade. As fate would have it the tide was low so, having covered more than 1,200 kilometres since Gibraltar I was now forced to slog an extra hundred metres through soft sand before I could finally let the first ripple of salt water touch the toes of my boots.

* * *

A gusty wind buffeted me as I clambered along the knife-edge ridge that formed Spain's northernmost outcrop. For the first time I was grateful for the weight of my pack. Without the added ballast, I'd be in danger of getting blown right off the ridge. A far from ideal end to my trek.

The last stretch along the winding country lane that leads the length of Estaca de Bares headland had been a pure buzz of adrenalin. I'd whooped with joy over the phone to my wife as – bursting with anticipation – I jogged towards the lighthouse.

'I can see the end of Spain!' I shouted over the hammering wind. 'One thousand, two hundred and twenty-five kilometres lie behind me... and absolutely nothing in front but sea!'

'There is no moment of delight in any pilgrimage like the beginning of it,' American essayist Charles Dudley Warner once said.

On the toughest days I'd thought that finishing this walk would come a close second – but after 35 days of living life to the rhythm of my footsteps there was also a definite feeling of regret that it was all over. Habits are formed in much less time, after all, and it was strange to think that when I went to sleep that night it would not be as a hobo but as a regular tourist.

I wondered if mediaeval pilgrims ever had the same feeling when, having reached their longed-for destination in Santiago, they simply turned around and started limping home.

Looking back on the hills of Andalucía, the seemingly endless plains of Extremadura and the Galician peaks I struggled to comprehend the fact that I'd finally made it to this northernmost tip of Iberia. The thought was almost dizzying – more vertigo-inducing than the narrow, windblown ridge upon which I balanced. The only way I could fix the scale of the journey in my mind was to conjure up an image of the map of Spain. A finger-hold for my brain to grab onto. The great difference between the clean-shaven hiker who left Gibraltar and the bedraggled vagabond who arrived on the Bay of Biscay was that the latter knew the brutality and beauty of every footstep that was so prosaically hinted at on paper.

Postscript

As luck would have it, the closest accommodation to Estaca de Bares is a little hotel in O Porto de Bares, a fishing village a 3-kilometre hike back down the road from the tip of the headland.

When I awoke the next morning, rain was streaming down the window and running off the roof in cascades. It was the only rainy morning in the five weeks since I'd left Gibraltar.

As I shuffled my flip-flops through the puddles I thanked my lucky stars that I need only walk as far as the café for breakfast.

ACKNOWLEDGEMENTS

Thanks firstly to my sponsors Jack Wolfskin and Polartec for believing that I could complete this trek (even when I secretly doubted it myself).

My gratitude also goes to Debbie Chapman, Claire Plimmer, Claire Berrisford, Ross Dickinson, Imogen Palmer and the wonderful team at Summersdale who believed that there was a book to be chiselled out of those 1,225 kilometres of Spanish granite.

Thanks to Blanca Montes whose enthusiasm for Spanish history and grammar saved me from many embarrassing errors and the arrows and slingshots of a barrage of Spanish accent-marks and tildes.

Thanks to my friend Filiberto Hernández Pablos, who gave me a copy of his book *A Caballo hacia Santiago por la Via de la Plata* and whose *albergue* at El Cubo de Tierra del Vino was the setting for one of the pleasantest meals I've ever enjoyed.

Love and thanks, as always, go to my daughter Lucía whose enthusiasm is an endless boost to her old papá and to my soul-mate and life-partner Narina who, through endless support and love, makes even my craziest schemes seem imminently achievable.

Most of all I'd like to pass my thanks to the nameless *vagabundo* who inspired me with his love of roaming on a vaguely remembered train somewhere near Badajoz. And to Andoni Moreta Hernández – the old 'Rogue of the Road' – who's still going strong, proving to a disbelieving world that there can still be something romantic and swash-buckling in the life of a Spanish *vagabundo*.

ABOUT THE AUTHOR

Mark Eveleigh has been a full-time magazine writer and author for 25 years. A British citizen, he grew up in Ghana and Nigeria and has spent more years based in Spain and Indonesia than he ever did in the UK.

As a travel journalist, Mark (a fellow of the Royal Geographical Society and The Explorers Club) has published more than 850 full-length travel features for more than 120 international publications, including *BBC Wildlife, BBC Earth, BBC Travel, CNN Travel, Condé Nast Traveller, The Telegraph, The Independent, The Guardian, Boston Globe, Travel Africa, The Sunday Times, Africa Geographic* and *National Geographic Traveller*. He's written for the in-flight magazines of countless national airlines, including KLM, Qantas, Etihad Airways, Qatar Airways, Korean Air, Malaysia Airlines, Oman Air, Brussels Airlines, Kenya Airways, Uganda Airlines, Philippine Airlines, Gulf Airlines and Garuda Indonesia.

He co-authored the *Secret Bali* and *Secret Bangkok* guidebooks along with several *Lonely Planet* guidebooks including Borneo (2023), Tanzania (2023), Madagascar (2023), Ecuador (2024) and Spain (2024). His Indonesian travel book, *Kopi Dulu* (Penguin Random House SEA, 2022), was listed among the best books of 2022 by *Jakarta Post*, and his debut novel, *Driftwood Chandeliers* (2023), was set in Bali.

When he's not on assignments he can often be found in West Bali where he has some well-stocked bookshelves and a small shed that's crammed with surfboards.

Website: www.markeveleigh.com
Instagram: @markeveleigh

GLOSSARY

A la plancha – anything cooked on/under a grill.

Albergue – a pilgrims' hostel, with dorms (and sometimes private rooms), that might be charged by the night or sometimes on a *donativo* (donation only) basis.

Berza – Galician cabbage, with leaves as big as dustbin lids.

Brava – literally 'savage'. Can refer to fighting bulls/cows (*toros bravos* or *vacas bravas*) or to potatoes served in a particularly fiery chilli sauce (*patatas bravas* are literally 'savage potatoes').

Cachuelas – fried chicken tripe.

Café con leche – espresso served with steamed milk.

Calabobos – Galician drizzle known as 'soak the stupid' because it is the sort of deceptive rain that leads the uninitiated into believing that it's not enough to get you wet.

Caldo gallego – hearty cabbage soup, made from the tall Galician cabbage.

Carne estofada – beef stew.

Casona – big farmhouses common all over northern Spain. Extended families slept on the upper floor while the precious livestock lived below.

Chiringuito – a bar or restaurant styled like a beach shack (although not always on the coast).

Chuchonas – witches who sucked the blood of children and used their tender bodies to make potions.

Corral de lobos – literally a 'wolf corral' but more accurately a wolf trap.

Cortado – espresso with a dash of hot milk.

Cortijo – southern Spanish homestead.

Crestas – stewed cockerel combs.

Dehesa – the traditional mixed pasture-and-woodland areas.

Feiticeiras – diabolically charming Galician witches who lure young men to their death by drowning.

Flan casero – crème caramel. Dimples of little air bubbles are incontrovertible proof, so Spanish chefs say, that it must indeed be homemade.

Gitano/a – the Spanish Gypsy/Romani community.

Hostia – Communion bread used in sacrament. (Frequently used also as a swear word.)

Jamón serrano – cured mountain ham (which comes in various categories).

Jarra – literally jug but better described as a tankard.

Lamia – golden-haired fairies with duck's feet (part of Basque mythology).

Licor de hierbas – herb liqueur flavoured with aniseed, coriander, rosemary and cinnamon.

Lobismullers – Galician female werewolves.

Meigas – the generic name for any one of a dozen or more types of Galician witches.

Menú del día – the daily set menu that is the most cost-effective way to eat in Spain. It is usually sold as three courses with a drink but sometimes a *media menú* (half menu) is available, i.e. starter and main.

Migas – literally translated simply as 'crumbs' that are fried in lard with garlic, pork belly, serrano ham and mushrooms.

Natillas – very similar to English custard and usually served with cinnamon and a soggy Marie biscuit floating on top.

Nubeiros – hairy long-tailed mythical beings who control the crop-destroying summer storms in the Galician highlands.

Nuggets de oreja – 'pig-ear nuggets' that are occasionally described, very unappealingly, on menus as 'crusty on the outside and creamy inside'.

Pancetta – pork loin or thick-cut bacon (best *'a la parrilla'* – i.e. barbecued).

Patxaran – the traditional Navarran liquor made from *encinas* (sloe berries).

Polbo á feira – paprika-flavoured octopus.

Rabo de toro – bull-tail stew.

Revuelto de espárragos – scrambled eggs with asparagus.

Romería – a festive pilgrimage.

Salmorejo – a thicker version of *gazpacho*, typical of Cordoba and often served with shreds of ham and chopped boiled egg.

Secreto a la plancha – literally 'grilled secret' but best translated as armpit of pig.

Serrana de la Vera – an Extremadura version of an Amazon warrior. It's said that she lured men to her cave where she got them drunk prior to killing them.

Sobremesa – best defined as 'beyond the table', this is the period after a meal that typically sociable Spaniards enjoy stretching out – sometimes for several hours – over conversation, laughter and sometimes song.

Tapas – traditionally a saucer of food that was placed on top of a glass (literally as *una tapa* – 'a top') to keep a drink fresh. *Una tapa* was often offered complimentary with a drink and in many places (especially around Granada) they are still often incredibly generous free portions. A northern trend for very fancy bar snacks (known in those areas as *pinchos/pintxos*) has led to these exquisite morsels often fetching quite high prices.

Tarta de Santiago – traditional almond-flavoured pastry that is considered a speciality of the Camino.

Tinto de verano – literally 'summer wine', cheap wine mixed with Casera (a sort of soda) as a refreshing – and low alcohol – hot weather drink.

Tortilla española – Spanish omelette which, so purists say, should contain nothing but eggs, potatoes and onions.

Venta – traditionally a trading centre but these days usually applied to a roadside tavern or restaurant.

Xacio – a type of Galician mermaid that lives in highland tarns.

Zorza – spicy mince created from what might be described as deconstructed chorizos.

BIBLIOGRAPHY

Boling, Dave *Guernica* (2010, Bloomsbury USA)

Brenan, Gerald *South from Granada* (1963, Penguin Travel Library)

Brenan, Gerald *The Face of Spain* (1950, Turnstile Press)

Cornwell, Bernard *Sharpe's Fury* (2006, HarperCollins)

Davies, William Henry *The Autobiography of a Super-Tramp* (1908, A. C. Fifield)

Defoe, Daniel *Robinson Crusoe* (1719, William Taylor)

Govinda, Lama Anagarika *The Way of the White Clouds* (1988, Shambhala)

Hemingway, Ernest *Death in the Afternoon* (1932, Charles Scribner's Sons)

Hemingway, Ernest *For Whom the Bell Tolls* (1940, Arcturus Publishing Limited)

Hislop, Victoria *The Return* (2009, Harper Perennial)

Jones, Dan *Powers and Thrones: A New History of the Middle Ages* (2021, Apollo)

Jones, Dan *The Templars: The Rise and Spectacular Fall of God's Holy Warriors* (2018, Penguin Books)

Lalaguna, Juan *Spain: A Traveller's History* (2001, Interlink Books)

Lee, Laurie *As I Walked Out One Midsummer Morning* (1969, André Deutsch)

Lee, Laurie *A Moment of War* (1991, Penguin Books)

Macdonald, Janet *Sir John Moore: The Making of a Controversial Hero* (2016, Pen and Sword Military)

Michener, James A. *Iberia* (1984, Fawcett Crest Books)

Orwell, George *Homage to Catalonia* (1938, Secker and Warburg)

Perez-Reverte, Arturo *The Queen of the South* (2005, Plume)

Pritchett, V. S. *Marching Spain* (1988, Chatto & Windus)

Reader, John *Africa, A Biography of the Continent* (1997, Hamish Hamilton)

Redondo, Dolores *The Invisible Guardian* (2016, Atria Books)

Richardson, Paul *Our Lady of the Sewers* (1998, Abacus)

Steinbeck, John *The Grapes of Wrath* (1939, The Viking Press-James Lloyd)

Twain, Mark *A Tramp Abroad* (1880, American Publishing Company)

Twain, Mark *The Innocents Abroad* (1869, American Publishing Company)

INDEX

Have you enjoyed this book?
If so, why not write a review on your favourite website?

If you're interested in finding out more about our books,
find us on Facebook at **Summersdale Publishers**, on
Twitter/X at **@Summersdale** and on Instagram and TikTok
at **@summersdalebooks** and get in touch.
We'd love to hear from you!

Thanks very much for buying this Summersdale book.

www.summersdale.com